QUEEN MARGARET UNIVERSITY

100 301 988

Queen Margaret University Library

The Business Plan Workbook

D1375685

Withdrawn from
Margaret University Library
QUEEN MARGARET UNIVERSITY LRC

The Business Plan Workbook

*A step-by-step guide to creating and developing
a successful business*

TENTH EDITION

Colin Barrow, Paul Barrow
and
Robert Brown

KoganPage

Publisher's note

Every possible effort has been made to ensure that the information contained in this book is accurate at the time of going to press, and the publishers and authors cannot accept responsibility for any errors or omissions, however caused. No responsibility for loss or damage occasioned to any person acting, or refraining from action, as a result of the material in this publication can be accepted by the editor, the publisher or the authors.

First published in Great Britain and the United States in 2018 by Kogan Page Limited

10th edition published in 2021 by Kogan Page

Apart from any fair dealing for the purposes of research or private study, or criticism or review, as permitted under the Copyright, Designs and Patents Act 1988, this publication may only be reproduced, stored or transmitted, in any form or by any means, with the prior permission in writing of the publishers, or in the case of reprographic reproduction in accordance with the terms and licences issued by the CLA. Enquiries concerning reproduction outside these terms should be sent to the publishers at the undermentioned addresses:

2nd Floor, 45 Gee Street
London
EC1V 3RS
United Kingdom

122 W 27th Street
New York, NY 10001
USA

4737/23 Ansari Road
Daryaganj
New Delhi 110002
India

www.koganpage.com

© Colin Barrow, Paul Barrow and Robert Brown 2018, 2021

The rights of Colin Barrow, Paul Barrow and Robert Brown to be identified as the authors of this work has been asserted by them in accordance with the Copyright, Designs and Patents Act 1988.

ISBNs

Hardback   978 1 78966 739 4
Paperback   978 1 78966 737 0
Ebook   978 1 78966 738 7

British Library Cataloguing-in-Publication Data

A CIP record for this book is available from the British Library.

Library of Congress Cataloging-in-Publication Data

Names: Barrow, Colin, author. | Barrow, Paul, 1948- author. | Brown, Robert, 1937- author.
Title: The business plan workbook : a step-by-step guide to creating and developing a successful business / Colin Barrow, Paul Barrow and Robert Brown.
Description: Tenth edition. | London, United Kingdom; New York, NY : Kogan Page, 2021. | Includes bibliographical references and index.
Identifiers: LCCN 2020048902 (print) | LCCN 2020048903 (ebook) | ISBN 9781789667370 (paperback) | ISBN 9781789667394 (hardback) | ISBN 9781789667387 (ebook)
Subjects: LCSH: Business planning. | Business enterprises–Finance.
Classification: LCC HD30.28 .B3685 2021 (print) | LCC HD30.28 (ebook) | DDC 658.4/01–dc23
LC record available at https://lccn.loc.gov/2020048902
LC ebook record available at https://lccn.loc.gov/2020048903

Typeset by Integra Software Services, Pondicherry
Print production managed by Jellyfish
Printed and bound in Great Britain by CPI Group (UK) Ltd, Croydon CR0 4YY

CONTENTS

PHASE SEVEN
Writing up and presenting your business plan 269

Introduction 271

Assignment 26 Writing up and presenting your business plan 272

Index of key organizations and resources for business planning 287

Index 295

PREFACE

Contrary to a popular misunderstanding, starting and running a business, while certainly risky, is not excessively risky. Though the probability of failure is relatively low, the consequences can be catastrophic. You can literally lose your shirt! The way to mitigate this danger is adopt that most healthy of business habits – planning. The military who came out of the recent pandemic with flying colours have as a core discipline never to undertake any task without first making a plan.

In this workbook we have distilled the knowledge and experience of the faculty at Cranfield School of Management and other world-renowned business schools in teaching the many thousands of students, business executives, entrepreneurs, public sector managers and those charged with running charitable, not-for-profit and social enterprises, who have taken part in enterprise programmes. Entrepreneurs who have prepared business plans on programmes at Cranfield include Lord Bilimoria (Cobra Beer), Nick Jenkins (Moonpig), Sarah Willingham (Let's Save Some Money), Mark Butler (PCL Ceramics Limited, recipient of the 2013 Queen's Award for Enterprise for outstanding performance in International Trade), Deepak Kuntawala (DVK Deepak, named Global Entrepreneur of the Year 2013 at the TiE UK Awards – The Indus Entrepreneurs is the world's largest not for profit dedicated to supporting and fostering entrepreneurship) and Kenneth White (Frosts Ltd, listed as one of the 1,000 companies to Inspire Britain by the London Stock Exchange Group). Big business, too, has played its part in adding to Cranfield's business planning experience. John McFarlane, Chairman at Barclays PLC and Warren East, CEO at Rolls-Royce, are amongst the school's distinguished alumni.

Business planning is at the core of organizational and business strategy and is the essential precursor whether you are starting a new business, expanding an existing one, gaining approval for funding for a project, securing a grant or even entering a competition such as *Dragons' Den*. Over the years we have developed and tested this method of helping people to research and validate their proposals, and then to write up a business plan themselves.

Towards the end of each programme we invite a distinguished panel of senior bankers, venture capital providers and others involved in appraising proposals for external support of various kinds to review and criticize each business plan presentation. Their valued comments have not only spurred our programme participants to greater heights, but have given the faculty at Cranfield a privileged insight into the minds and thought processes of the principal providers of capital for new and growing enterprises.

This workbook brings together the processes and procedures required by the relative novice to write a business plan. Also included throughout are examples from the business plans of entrepreneurs and others who for the most part have gone on to start up successful enterprises.

In addition, we have included criticisms, warnings and the experiences of backers, investors and of recently successful entrepreneurs when they have a direct bearing on writing and presenting a business plan.

We don't pretend to have made writing up business plans an easy task – but we do think we have made it an understandable one that is within the grasp of everyone with the determination to succeed.

Thousands of students have passed through Cranfield's business planning programmes going on to make their mark in business, charities and the public sector in this country and around the world.

HOW TO USE THE WORKBOOK

The workbook contains 26 assignments that, once completed, should ensure that you have all the information you need to write and present a successful business plan. That is, one that helps to accomplish your objective, whether it is to gain a greater understanding of the venture you are proposing to start and its viability, to raise outside money or gain support for your proposals from senior levels of management. Throughout the book the term 'entrepreneur' has been used interchangeably with innovator, manager, champion and similar terms used in a wide range of organizations in both the profit and not-for-profit sectors. The definition of entrepreneur is that of someone who shifts resources from a low to a higher level of value added; this is the defining characteristic of almost everyone who writes a business plan regardless of the nature of their organization, actual or prospective.

The workbook does not set out to be a comprehensive textbook on every business and management subject – finance, marketing, law, etc. Rather, it gives an appreciation as to how these subjects should be used to prepare your business plan. The topics covered under each assignment will often pull together ingredients from different 'academic' disciplines. For example, elements of law and marketing will be assembled in the assignment in which you are asked to describe your service or product and its proprietary position (patents, copyright, design registration, etc).

For some of the assignments you will almost certainly need to research outside the material contained in this workbook. However, 'technical' explanations of such subjects as cash flow, market research questionnaire design and break-even analysis are included.

The assignments are contained in seven phases that, as well as having a practical logic to their sequence, will provide you with manageable 'chunks' either to carry out yourself at different times, or to delegate to partners and professional advisers. While it is useful to make use of as much help as you can get in preparing the groundwork, you should orchestrate the information and write up the business plan yourself. After all, it is your future that is at stake – and every prospective financier will be backing you and your ability to put this plan into action, not your scriptwriter.

The seven phases are:

Phase 1: Strategy and purpose

Here you should describe your organization, innovation or business idea so far as you have already developed it. In particular, explain your aims, objectives and eventual aspirations.

Introduce your management team, yourself included, and show how your skills and experiences relate to this venture.

Describe your product or service, its current state of development or readiness for the market, and whether or not you have any proprietary rights such as a patent, copyright or registered design.

Phase 2: Market research

This involves identifying the data needed both to validate the need for what you are proposing and to decide upon the best start-up or growth strategy. In this phase you will be encouraged to gather market research data from as many sources as possible. Particular emphasis will be laid on researching customer needs, market segments and competitors' strengths and weaknesses. The appropriate research methodology and data sources are also described.

Phase 3: Competitive marketing strategies

This involves planning how you will operate each element of your business, based upon the information collected and analysed in earlier phases. In relation to your chosen product or service, the market segment(s) you plan to serve and the competitive situation, you will decide on such factors as price, promotion, location, and channels of distribution.

Phase 4: Operations

This involves detailing all the activities required to make your strategy happen. It will include such subjects as manufacturing, purchasing, selling, legal matters and insurance. Your business plan must demonstrate that you have taken account of all the principal matters that concern the operations of your venture.

Phase 5: Reviewing financing requirements

Based on the strategy evolved so far, in this phase you will carry out assignments enabling you to forecast the expected results of your venture. Projections will be made showing likely sales volume and value, pro forma profit and loss, cash-flow forecast and balance sheet, and a break-even analysis.

Although these first five phases are shown in sequence here and in the workbook, in practice you would expect to move backwards and forwards from phase to phase, as a result of new information or a modification of your earlier ideas.

Phase 6: Business controls

Here you must demonstrate how you will keep track of your business, both as a whole and for each individual element. As well as a bookkeeping system you will need sales and marketing planning records, customer records, personnel files and production control information.

Phase 7: Writing up and presenting your business plan

The workbook assignments, when completed, are not your business plan. They are intended to help you to assemble the information needed to write up your business plan. The plan will require substantial editing and rewriting; the way in which it is written up will undoubtedly influence the chances of getting a hearing, if you are seeking outside support for your venture.

Finally, you must give some thought as to how you will handle the meeting with your bank, venture capital house, other backers or the boss or organization to whom you have to 'sell' your ideas. Presentation skills and good planning will all help to make for a good 'production', and showbiz counts for a surprising amount when it comes to gaining support for new ideas.

Assignment guidelines

Here are some guidelines to help you and your colleagues complete the business plan assignments:

1   Each assignment will contain:

   a   An introduction or brief description of the content and purpose of the assignment, usually broken down into two or more stages.

   b   Examples of how others preparing business plans have answered or commented on parts of the assignment.

   c   An explanation or amplification of any technical topics that need to be understood immediately.

   At the end there is an assignment worksheet with some specific questions for you to answer concerning your business. On this page you will also find suggestions for further reading on broader aspects of the subject of the assignment.

2   When tackling assignments the following work pattern has proved successful:

   a   Read up on the assignment and draft your own answer to the questions.

   b   Discuss your answers, and any problems concerning the assignment with your prospective business partner(s), colleagues or some other knowledgeable individual such as an adviser, bank manager or accountant. If you are on, or plan to go on, a business training programme, then your course tutor will also be able to help.

   c   Revise your own answers in the light of these discussions – and then let your colleagues, and such other people as are involved, know your latest views on the assignment topic (you may need to go back and forth from steps (b) and (c) several times before you are entirely satisfied).

3   The contents of some assignments will suggest where and how to obtain the information needed to complete the assignment. However, don't expect to be told where to find all of the information about your business in these instructions. You will need to do some research yourself.

4   Example assignment completions taken from other business plans will also be presented to you in each assignment. These are presented only to give you a feel for the subject discussed. Your write-up of the assignment may need to be more or less elaborate, depending on your business.

5   The examples have been taken from actual business plans, but some have been changed in name and content, with some of the information purposely missing. Therefore do not copy a sample, however good it

may sound; use it to help you to understand the purpose of the business plan assignment only.

6   Try to write up as much information as possible after reading each assignment. In this way you will know what remains to be researched (and do not wait until your information flows in perfect English before recording it).

7   Try to strike a balance between qualitative and quantitative statements in writing up your assignments. That is, try to back up as many of your statements as possible with numbers and documented sources of information. However, do not include numbers just because you have them; make sure that they really serve a purpose.

8   *Finally*, before attempting to write up your business plan, make sure the answers to all the assignments are internally consistent – and if you have business partners, make sure you are all in substantive agreement both at each stage and with the final outcome.

Index of key organizations and resources for business planning

These are the principle sources of help and advice for anyone writing a business plan, in alphabetical order. Some of these are referred to throughout the book.

WHY PREPARE A BUSINESS PLAN?

Perhaps the most important step in launching any new venture or expanding an existing one is the construction of a business plan. Such a plan must include your goals for the enterprise, both short and long term; a description of the products or services you will offer and the market opportunities you have anticipated for them; and finally, an explanation of the resources and means you will employ to achieve your goals in the face of likely competition. Time after time, research studies reveal that the absence of a written business plan leads to a higher incidence of failure for new and small businesses, as well as inhibiting growth and development.

Preparing a comprehensive business plan along these lines takes time and effort. In our experience at Cranfield on our programmes, anything between 200 and 400 hours is needed, depending on the nature of your business and what data you have already gathered. Nevertheless, such an effort is essential if you are to crystallize and to focus your ideas, and test your resolve about entering or expanding your business or pursuing a particular course of action. Once completed, your business plan will serve as a blueprint to follow which, like any map, improves the user's chances of reaching his or her destination.

There are a number of other important benefits you can anticipate arising from preparing a business plan:

- This systematic approach to planning enables you to make your mistakes on paper, rather than in the marketplace. One potential entrepreneur made the discovery while gathering data for his business plan that the local competitor he thought was a one-man band was in fact the pilot operation for a proposed national chain of franchised outlets. This had a profound effect on his market entry strategy!

  Another entrepreneur found out that, at the price he proposed charging, he would never recover his overheads or break even. Indeed, 'overheads' and 'break even' were themselves alien terms before he embarked on preparing a business plan. This naive perspective on costs is by no means unusual.

- Once completed, a business plan will make you feel more confident about your ability to set up and operate the venture. It may even compensate for lack of capital and experience, provided of course that you have other factors in your favour, such as a sound idea and a sizeable market opportunity for your product or service.

- Your business plan will show how much money is needed, what it is needed for and when, and for how long it is required.

  As under-capitalization and early cash-flow problems are two important reasons why new business activities fail, it follows that those with a soundly prepared business plan can reduce these risks of failure. They can also experiment with a range of alternative viable strategies and so concentrate on options that make the most economic use of scarce financial resources.

  It would be an exaggeration to say that your business plan is the passport to sources of finance. It will, however, help you to display your entrepreneurial flair and managerial talent to the full and to communicate your ideas to others in a way that will be easier for them to understand – and to appreciate the reasoning behind your ideas. These outside parties could be bankers, potential investors, partners or advisory agencies. Once they know what you are trying to do, they will be better able to help you.

- Preparing a business plan will give you an insight into the planning process. It is this process that is important to the long-term health of a business, and not simply the plan that comes out of it. Businesses are dynamic, as are the commercial and competitive environments in which they operate. No one expects every event as recorded on a business plan to occur as predicted, but the understanding and knowledge created by the process of business planning will prepare the business for any changes that it may face, and so enable it to adjust quickly.

The empirical data also strongly supports the value of business planning. Studies consistently show that organizations with a strong planning ethos constantly outperform those who neglect this discipline.

A review of research articles on this subject has been written by Noah Parsons, *Business Planning Makes You More Successful, and We've Got the Science to Prove It* (2017).

The research concludes that people who prepare a business plan are twice as likely to actual start their business and, once started, grow 30 per cent faster. In addition they are much less likely to fail.

Those would-be entrepreneurs with funds of their own, or, worse still, borrowed from 'innocent' friends and relatives, tend to think that the time spent in preparing a business plan could be more usefully (and enjoyably) spent looking for premises, buying a new car or designing a website. In short, anything that inhibits them from immediate action is viewed as time-wasting.

As most people's perception of their business venture is flawed in some important respect, it follows that jumping in at the deep end is risky – and unnecessarily so. Flaws can often be discovered cheaply and in advance when preparing a business plan; they are always discovered in the market-place, invariably at a much higher and often fatal cost.

There was a myth at the start of the internet boom that the pace of development in the sector was too fast for business planning. The first generation of dot.com businesses and their backers seemed happy to pump money into what they called a 'business' or 'revenue' model. These 'models' were simply brief statements of intent supported by little more than wishful thinking. A few months into the new millennium, a sense of realism came to the internet sector. In any business sector only ventures with well-prepared business plans have any chance of getting off the ground or being supported in later-stage financing rounds.

Strategy and purpose

Introduction

Starting a new venture, whether it is a for-profit business, a social enterprise or public initiative, may seem a daunting task when you first start to gather ideas together and make tentative plans. Many would-be entrepreneurs after putting a toe in the water quickly pull back reckoning that either they don't have the skills, their business concept is not all that compelling or raising the money is going to be challenging, expensive and altogether too risky a proposition.

You may well still be experiencing shock waves from Covid-19 and think this is not a great time to be in business. But coronavirus was preceded by Avian Flu, Cholera, Crimean-Congo haemorrhagic fever, Dengue Fever, Ebola, HIV-Aids, Lassa fever, Marburg virus, Measles Rubela, MERS, SARS, Swine Flu, Nipah disease, Rift Valley fever and Zika, all causing significant disruption to many business organizations (Noy *et al*, 2019). Then of course there were other traumatic economic events – the 1973 oil crisis when the members of the Organization of Arab Petroleum Exporting Countries proclaimed an oil embargo against supporters of Israel, Black Monday (1987), the Dotcom Bubble (2000–02) and the 2008–09 global financial crises to name but a handful causing significant difficulties for businesses. Devastating slumps are nothing new: five, starting with America's first crash in 1792, preceded the Great Depression of 1929 (Lawrence, 2014).

The first useful fact to know is that the rumour of calamities awaiting most new ventures is just that – an unfounded and incorrect piece of oft-repeated misinformation. An exhaustive study by Bruce A Kirchoff of the eight-year destinations of all 814,000 US firms founded in a particular year revealed that just 18 per cent actually failed, meaning that the entrepreneurs were put out of business by their financial backers, lack of demand or competitive pressures (Kirchoff, 1994). True, some 28 per cent of businesses closed their doors voluntarily, their founders having decided for a variety of reasons that either working for themselves or this particular type of business was just not for them. Walsh and Cunningham (2016) in their literature review of the subject of business failure also identified research endorsing Kirchoff's findings.

But the majority of the businesses studied in Kirchoff's mammoth and representative study survived and in many cases prospered. With a degree of preparation, a fair amount of perspiration and a modicum of luck you can get started and may even, as in the Moonpig case study, end up with a substantial, successful and growing enterprise. These first three chapters will help you shape up the framework of your venture. The chapter towards the end of the book – Stress testing your business projections – will show you how to prepare for the inevitable shocks that will come your way.

References

Kirchoff, Bruce A (1994) *Entrepreneurship and Dynamic Capitalism*, Praeger, New York

Lawrence, D (2014) The slumps that shaped modern finance, *The Economist*

Noy, I, Doan, N, Ferrarini, B and Park, D (2019) *Measuring the Economic Risk of Epidemics* (No. 8016), CESifo Group Munich, www.cesifo.org/DocDL/cesifo1_wp8016.pdf (archived at perma.cc/8ENN-965H)

Walsh, G S and Cunningham, J A, (2016) Business failure and entrepreneurship: Emergence, evolution and future research, *Foundations and Trends® in Entrepreneurship*, 12(3), pp 163–285

ASSIGNMENT 1

Coming up with a winning idea for your business plan

In this first assignment you should introduce your 'business' proposition to the future readers of your business plan. Explain something of how you arrived at your business idea, why you think people have a need for your product or service, and what your goals and aspirations for the business are. If your proposition needs financing, you could give some preliminary idea of how much you may need and what you intend to do with those funds. Remember, all these ideas are likely to be significantly modified later on – some more than others – but you need to have some idea at the outset of where you are going if you are to have any chance at all of getting there.

Here are the proven routes to establishing the proposition around which to base your business plan.

Recognizing a gap in the market

The classic way to identify an idea for a business is to see something that people would buy if only they knew about it. The demand is latent, lying beneath the surface, waiting to be recognized and met.

These are some of the ways to go about identifying a market gap:

- Adapting: Can you take an idea that's already working in another part of the country or abroad and bring it to your own market?
- Locating: Do customers have to travel too far to reach their present source of supply? This is a classic route to market for shops, hairdressers and other retail-based businesses, including those that can benefit from online fulfilment.

- Size: If you made things a different size, would that appeal to a new market? Anita Roddick, founder of The Body Shop, found that she could only buy the beauty products she wanted in huge quantities. By breaking down the quantities and sizes of those products and selling them, she unleashed a huge new demand.

- Timing: Are customers happy with current opening hours? If you opened later, earlier or longer, would you tap into a new market?

CASE STUDY

The Northern Dough Company

This Lancashire-based company is the brainchild of husband and wife team Chris and Amy Cheadle. The idea for the business came after they hosted 'make your own' pizza dinner parties. 'We started the business as an alternative for dining out,' says Chris. 'Our friends were invited into the kitchen to create their own favourite recipes. They enjoyed it so much they often went home with a bagful of dough.'

Chris had something of a head start as he came from a family of three generations of bakers in Lancashire. But the business idea wasn't born in an oven. It was only when he looked for an alternative at the supermarket that he saw a gap in the market for a convenient and authentic-tasting product, and the business was born. The idea was tested at a local food market where they sold out everything they had brought in 90 minutes. By 2017 their customers included 250 Waitrose stores as well as Booths Supermarkets, Ocado, Whole Foods and 130 individual farm shops.

Revamping an old idea

A good starting point is to look for products or services that used to work really well but have stopped selling. By finding out why they seem to have died out you can establish whether, and how, that problem can be overcome. Or you can search overseas or in other markets for products and services that have worked well for years in their home markets but have so far failed to penetrate into your area.

Sometimes with little more than a slight adjustment you can give an old idea a whole new lease of life. For example, the Monopoly game, with its emphasis on the universal appeal of London street names, has been launched in France with Parisian rues and in Cornwall using towns rather than streets.

Solving customer problems

Sometimes existing suppliers just aren't meeting customers' needs. Big firms very often don't have the time to pay attention to all their customers properly because doing so just isn't economical. Recognizing that enough people exist with needs and expectations that aren't being met can constitute an opportunity for a new small firm to start up.

Start by recalling the occasions when you've had reason to complain about a product or service. You can extend that by canvassing the experiences of friends, relatives and colleagues. If you spot a recurring complaint, that may be a valuable clue about a problem just waiting to be solved.

Next you can go back over the times when firms you've tried to deal with have put restrictions or barriers in the way of your purchase. If those restrictions seem easy to overcome, and others share your experience, then you may well be on the trail of a new business idea.

Inventions and innovation

Inventions and innovations are all too often almost the opposite of either identifying a gap in the market or solving an unsolved problem. Inventors usually start by looking through the other end of the telescope. They find an interesting problem and solve it. There may or may not be a great need for whatever it is they invent.

The Post-it note is a good example of inventors going out on a limb to satisfy themselves rather than to meet a particular need or even solve a burning problem. The story goes that scientists at 3M, a giant American company, came across an adhesive that failed most of their tests. It had poor adhesion qualities because it could be separated from anything it was stuck to. No obvious market existed, but they persevered and pushed the product on their marketing department, saying that the new product had unique properties in that it stuck 'permanently, but temporarily'. The rest, as they say, is history.

Be sure to check that someone else doesn't already own your innovation, and that you can put a legal fence around it to keep competitors out. Copyrights, patents and the like are dealt with in Assignment 3.

Network marketing

Network marketing, multilevel marketing (MLM) and referral marketing are the names used to describe selling methods designed to replace the retail outlet as a route to market for certain products. Although referral marketing has been around since the early part of the last century, for many people it's still unfamiliar territory. This is one way of starting a profitable, full-time business with little or no investment. It's also a method of starting a second or part-time business to run alongside your existing business or career. Network marketing is one of the fastest-growing business sectors. Industry turnover has grown from £1 billion 10 years ago to £2 billion today. This way into business provides a low-cost option for over 400,000 people in the UK to get into business, earn money and run a business with very little risk.

In most cases network marketing involves selling a product or service that a parent company produces and supplies. You take on the responsibilities of selling the products and introducing other people to the company. You get paid commission on the products/services you sell yourself and a smaller commission on the products/services that the people you've introduced to the company sell. In addition to this, you often get a percentage commission based on the sales of the people that the people you introduced to the company also introduce, and on and on.

Advocates of network marketing maintain that, when given identical products, the one sold face to face (without the cost of maintaining a shop and paying employees and insurance) is less expensive than the same product sold in a store. Additionally, network marketing fans believe that buying a product from someone you know and trust makes more sense than buying from a shop assistant behind a retail counter.

A wide variety of good-quality network marketing companies from all over the world exist for you to choose from. They offer products and services from a wide range of industries including health, telecommunications, household products, technology, e-commerce, adult products and so on. Household names include Amway, Avon, Betterware, Herbalife, Kleeneze and Mary Kay Cosmetics. Choose a product or service that you're interested in because, when it comes to sales, nothing beats enthusiasm and confidence in the product. Check out the network company using trade associations such as the Direct Selling Association.

Franchising

Franchising can be a good first step into planning their own business for those with no experience of running a business. Franchising is a marketing technique used to improve and expand the distribution of a product or service. The franchiser supplies the product or teaches the service to you, the franchisee, who in turn sells it to the public. In return for this, you pay a fee and a continuing royalty, based usually on turnover. The franchiser may also require you to buy materials or ingredients from it, which gives it an additional income stream. The advantage to you is a relatively safe and quick way of getting into business for yourself, but with the support and advice of an experienced organization close at hand.

Franchising isn't a path to great riches, nor is it for the truly independent spirit, because policy and profits still come from on high. The British Franchise Association Diary website gives details of dates and venues of events around the country where you can meet franchisors and find out more about their propositions.

CASE STUDY
Concentric Lettings

Dawn Bennett wasn't exactly new to the property world when in 2013 she took on a Concentric Lettings Franchise. A single mother with a very young child she embarked on her career in the sector when she was employed as an estate agent sales negotiator in 2003. By 2007 despite leaving school with no formal qualifications she had worked her way up through the ranks from lettings negotiator, to senior negotiator and finally as lettings manager. Arguably she had been in the business longer than Concentric which had launched out as a franchise chain only in 2010.

Concentric looked like it might provide Dawn with a suitable launch platform. Relatively new to franchising, Concentric had only started franchising in 2010. But already under the dynamic leadership of Sally Lawson, a seasoned professional in the lettings field, Concentric had a dozen franchisees on board. Sally has been running her own letting agency since 1990 and been through two major property recessions. In the meantime the industry has moved from paper communications, local advertising and incessant face-to-face meetings, to online, emails, Skype and CMS (Content Management Systems).

Dawn bought out Karen Bowe, a neighbouring franchise, and quickly recognized the gap in the market for compliant and expert HMO (Houses in Multiple Occupation) property management services. Her business has grown from strength to strength each year.

Buying out a business

Buying out an existing business is particularly well suited to people who have extensive experience of general business management but lack detailed technical or product knowledge. When you buy an established business, you not only pay for the basic assets of the business, but also the accumulated time and effort that the previous owner spent growing the business to its present state. You can think of this extra asset as goodwill. The better the business, the more the 'goodwill' costs you.

Advantages of buying a business include:

- You acquire some of the experience and expertise you don't have.
- You gain both access to your potential customers and the credibility of a trading history from the outset, which can save months if not years of hard work in building relationships.
- If the business you buy is already profitable, you can pay yourself a living wage from the outset.
- Bank financing may be easier to acquire for an established business than for a riskier start-up business.

Disadvantages of buying a business include:

- You run the risk of acquiring the existing unsolved problems and mistakes of the person who's selling it.
- Identifying the right potential acquisition and negotiating a purchase can take a very long time, and there's no guarantee that you'll succeed at your first attempt.
- The professional fees associated with buying a business can be a significant, though necessary, cost.

Contact these organizations to find out more about buying a business and to see listings of businesses for sale:

- Businesses For Sale has over 68,000 businesses for sale in the UK, as well as listings of firms in Spain, the US, Australia, Canada, India, Ireland, New Zealand and France.
- Christie & Co claims to have the largest database of businesses for sale in Europe. It's the recognized market leader in the hotel, catering, leisure and retail markets and is also expanding into healthcare.
- Daltons has an online database of over 30,000 businesses for sale around the UK and some overseas countries.

WORKSHEET FOR ASSIGNMENT 1: COMING UP WITH A WINNING
IDEA FOR YOUR BUSINESS PLAN

1 Explain briefly your business idea and how you arrived at it.

2 If you are still considering what business to plan to enter review the options
outlined in this chapter in particular:

(a) Can you identify a market gap that you could meet?

(b) Is there a new twist that you could put onto an old business idea?

(c) Do you have an idea for an innovation or novel product?

(d) Is there a franchise or network marketing proposition that you could
plan for?

(e) Have you explored the possibility of buying out a business?

Suggested further reading

Aaker, D (2019) Winning in the sharing economy: Six keys to Airbnb's success,
Journal of Brand Strategy, 7 (**4**), pp 310–17

Hammond, R (2017) *Smart retail: Winning ideas and strategies from the most
successful retailers in the world*, 4th edn, Pearson Business, Harlow, UK

Kakatkar, C, de Groote, J K, Fueller, J and Spann, M (2018) The DNA of Winning
Ideas: A Network Perspective of Success in New Product Development,
Academy of Management Proceedings (Vol 2018, No 1, p 11047), Briarcliff
Manor, NY 10510: Academy of Management

Kim, W C and Mauborgne, R (2000) Knowing a winning business idea when you
see one, *Harvard business review*, 78 (**5**), pp 129–38

ASSIGNMENT 2

Strategy – the big picture

Credit for devising the most succinct and usable way to get a handle on the big picture has to be given to Michael E Porter, a professor at Harvard Business School. Porter determined that two factors above all influenced a business's chances of making superior profits. Firstly there was the attractiveness or otherwise of the industry in which it primarily operated. Secondly, and in terms of an organization's sphere of influence, more importantly, was how the business positioned itself within that industry.

The five forces theory of industry structure

Porter postulated that the five forces that drive competition in an industry have to be understood as part of the process of choosing which strategy to pursue. The forces he identified are:

- *Threat of substitution.* Can customers buy something else instead of your product? For example, Apple, and to a lesser extent Sony, have laptop computers that are distinctive enough to make substitution difficult. Dell on the other hand, faces intense competition from dozens of other suppliers with near-identical products competing mostly on price alone.

- *Threat of new entrants.* If it is easy to enter your market, start-up costs are low, and there are no barriers to entry – such as IP (intellectual property) protection – then the threat is high.

- *Supplier power.* The fewer the suppliers, usually the more powerful they are. Oil is a classic example where fewer than a dozen countries supply the whole market and consequently can set prices.

- *Buyer power.* In the food market, for example, with just a few powerful supermarket buyers being supplied by thousands of much smaller businesses, the supermarkets are often able to dictate terms.

- *Industry competition.* The number and capability of competitors are one determinant of a business's power. Few competitors with relatively less attractive products or services lower the intensity of rivalry in a sector. Often these sectors slip into oligopolistic behaviour, preferring to collude rather than compete.

Generic strategic options

In Porter's view a business can only pursue one of three generic strategies (see Figure 2.2) if it is to deliver superior performance. It can have a cost advantage in that it could make a product or deliver a service for less than others. Or it could be different in a way that matters to consumers, so that its offer would be unique, or at least relatively so. Porter added a further

FIGURE 2.1 Five forces theory of industry analysis (after Porter)

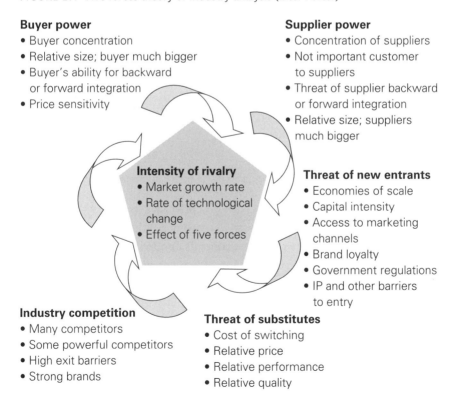

Buyer power
- Buyer concentration
- Relative size; buyer much bigger
- Buyer's ability for backward or forward integration
- Price sensitivity

Supplier power
- Concentration of suppliers
- Not important customer to suppliers
- Threat of supplier backward or forward integration
- Relative size; suppliers much bigger

Intensity of rivalry
- Market growth rate
- Rate of technological change
- Effect of five forces

Threat of new entrants
- Economies of scale
- Capital intensity
- Access to marketing channels
- Brand loyalty
- Government regulations
- IP and other barriers to entry

Industry competition
- Many competitors
- Some powerful competitors
- High exit barriers
- Strong brands

Threat of substitutes
- Cost of switching
- Relative price
- Relative performance
- Relative quality

FIGURE 2.2 Strategic options

Target scope	Advantage	
	Low cost	**Product uniqueness**
Broad (industry wide)	**Cost leadership strategy**	**Differentiation strategy**
Narrow (market segment)	**Focus strategy** (low cost)	**Focus strategy** (differentiation)

twist to his prescription. Businesses could follow either a cost advantage path or a differentiation path industry wide, or they could take a third path – they could concentrate on a narrow specific segment either with cost advantage or differentiation. This he termed 'focus' strategy.

Start-ups need to pick one of these options only; however, an established venture can pursue different types of strategy for different parts of their business or in different markets.

Cost leadership

Low cost should not be confused with low price. A business with low costs may or may not pass those savings on to customers. Alternatively they could use that position alongside tight cost controls and low margins to create an effective barrier to others considering either entering or extending their penetration of that market. Low-cost strategies are most likely to be achievable in large markets, requiring large-scale capital investment, where production or service volumes are high and economies of scale can be achieved from long runs.

Low costs are not a lucky accident; they can be achieved through these main activities.

- *Operating efficiencies.* New processes, methods of working or less costly ways of working. Ryanair and easyJet are examples where analysing every component of the business made it possible to strip out major elements of cost, meals, free baggage and allocated seating, for example, while leaving the essential proposition – we will fly you from A to B – intact.

- *Product redesign.* This involves rethinking a product or service proposition fundamentally to look for more efficient ways to work, or cheaper substitute materials to work with. The motor industry has adopted this approach with 'platform sharing'; that is where major players, including Citroen, Peugeot and Toyota, have rethought their entry car models to share major components, which has become common.

- *Product standardization.* A wide range of product and service offers claiming to extend customer choice invariably leads to higher costs. The challenge is to be sure that proliferation gives real choice and adds value. In 2008 the UK railway network took a long hard look at its dozens of different fare structures and scores of names, often for identical price structures, that had remained largely unchanged since the 1960s and reduced them to three basic product propositions. Adopting this and other common standards across the rail network they estimate will substantially reduce the currently excessive £500,000 transaction cost of selling £5 billion worth of tickets.

- *Economies of scale.* This can be achieved only by being big or bold. The same head office, warehousing network and distribution chain can support Tesco's 3,800 stores against the 1,500 that its nearest rival has. Tesco has a lower cost base by virtue of having more outlets to spread its costs over as well as having more purchasing power.

Differentiation

The key to differentiation is a deep understanding of what customers really want and need, and more importantly, what they are prepared to pay more for. Apple's opening strategy was based around a 'fun' operating system based on icons, rather than the dull text of MS-DOS. This belief was based on their understanding that computer users were mostly young and wanted an intuitive command system, and the 'graphical user interface' delivered just that. Apple has continued its differentiation strategy, but adds design and fashion to ease of control in the ways in which it delivers extra value. Sony and BMW are also examples of differentiators. Both have distinctive and desirable differences in their products and neither they nor Apple offer the lowest price in their respective industries; customers are willing to pay extra for the idiosyncratic and prized differences embedded in their products.

Differentiation doesn't have to be confined to just the marketing arena, nor does it always lead to success if the subject of that differentiation goes out of fashion without much warning. Northern Rock, the failed bank that had to be nationalized to stay in business, thought its strategy of raising most of the money it lent out in mortgages through the money markets was a sure winner. It allowed the bank to grow faster than its competitors who place more reliance on depositors for their funds. As long as interest rates were low and the money market functioned smoothly it worked. But once the differentiators that fuelled its growth were reversed, its business model failed.

Focus

Focused strategy involves concentrating on serving a particular market or a defined geographic region. IKEA, for example, targets young, white-collar workers as its prime customer segment, selling through 235 stores in more than 30 countries. Ingvar Kamprad, an entrepreneur from the Småland province in southern Sweden, who founded the business in the late 1940s, offers home furnishing products of good function and design at prices young people can afford. He achieves this by using simple cost-cutting solutions that do not affect the quality of products.

Businesses often lose their focus over time and periodically have to rediscover their core strategic purpose. Procter & Gamble is an example of a business that had to refocus to cure weak growth. In 2000, the company was losing share in seven of its top nine categories, and had lowered earnings expectations four times in two quarters. This prompted the company to restructure and refocus on its core business; big brands, big customers and big countries. They sold off non-core businesses, establishing five global business units with a closely focused product portfolio.

CASE STUDY
Specsavers

Every once in a while an entrepreneur turns an industry on its head. Dame Mary Perkins is a perfect example. When she launched her business it changed the face of optometry for good. We might be used to visiting showrooms to purchase glasses these days, trying on frames at our leisure until we find the perfect fit, with every item clearly priced, but back in the early 1980s this was not the case. Before Mary launched Specsavers, consumers had very little choice or control when purchasing eyewear. Indeed, before Specsavers came along, when you visited an optician they'd disappear out back to find a few pairs for you to try on. But Mary had a clear vision of how opticians could operate in order to deliver better value, choice and transparency to consumers. Driven by a mission of providing affordable eyecare to all, she built the company around the idea of treating others respectfully. She still describes her billion-pound international company, which she founded with her husband, Doug Perkins, as 'a family-owned business, with family values'.

One of the key lessons Mary learnt early on was the importance of setting yourself apart from the competition. As a new business, there was no point in merely copying a major player – you had to offer customers something different. She identified a number of major problems with the way opticians were doing business at the time, and came up with a proposition that she felt was far more attractive to consumers. First of all, glasses were expensive. Mary believed that she would be able to bring prices down without compromising on quality by negotiating better buying terms and selling larger volumes. For example, instead of buying from wholesalers who added a significant mark-up on their prices, she went to factories directly.

From just two staff working at a table-tennis table, there are now more than 500 based at Specsavers' headquarters in Guernsey and around 26,000 worldwide. The company has more than 1,390 stores across the Channel Islands, the UK, Ireland, the Netherlands, Scandinavia, Spain, Australia and New Zealand. Mary believes that much of her success has been driven by the preservation of the founding culture and ideals, and a focus on giving consumers real value and choice.

Strategic framework

The strategic framework shown in Figure 2.3 should put the whole strategic process clearly in view and help you to formulate a clear course of action.

The foundation of this process is a clear statement of the mission of your venture, your objectives and the geographic limits you have set yourself, at least for the time being. These issues were addressed in the first assignment and until they are satisfactorily resolved, no meaningful strategy can be evolved.

Market research data are then gathered on customers, competitors and the business environment, for example, to confirm that your original perception of your product or service is valid. More than likely this research will lead you to modify your product in line with this more comprehensive appreciation of customer needs. You may also decide to concentrate on certain specific customer groups. Information on competitors' prices, promotional methods and location/distribution channels should then be available to help you to decide how to compete.

No business can operate without paying some regard to the wider economic environment in which it operates. So a business plan must pay attention to factors such as:

- The state of the economy and how growth and recession are likely to affect such areas as sales, for example. During a time of economic recession, start-ups sometimes benefit from increased availability of premises, second-hand equipment etc, and find they develop sales strongly as the economy and markets recover. For example, Cranfield MBA Robert Wright developed ConnectAir at the end of one recession and was able to sell to Air Europe at the height of the Lawson boom – a trick that he subsequently repeated for 10 times that value (£75 million) a decade later!

- Any legislative constraints or opportunities. One Cranfield enterprise programme participant's entire business was founded solely to exploit recent laws requiring builders and developers to eliminate asbestos from existing properties. His business was to advise them how to do so.

- Any changes in technology or social trends that may have an impact on market size or consumer choice. For example, the increasing number of single-parent families may be bad news at one level, but it's an opportunity for builders of starter unit housing. And the increasing trend of wives returning to work is good news for convenience food sales and restaurants.

- Any political pressures, either domestic or pan-European, that are likely to affect your business. An example was New Labour's law against late payment of bills. The government's aim was to help small firms get paid more quickly by large firms. However, experience elsewhere, where such legislation is in force, showed clearly that large firms simply alter their terms of trade. In that way many small firms actually ended up taking longer to collect money owed them, rather than just the unlucky or the inefficient ones.

FIGURE 2.3 Elements of a business strategy

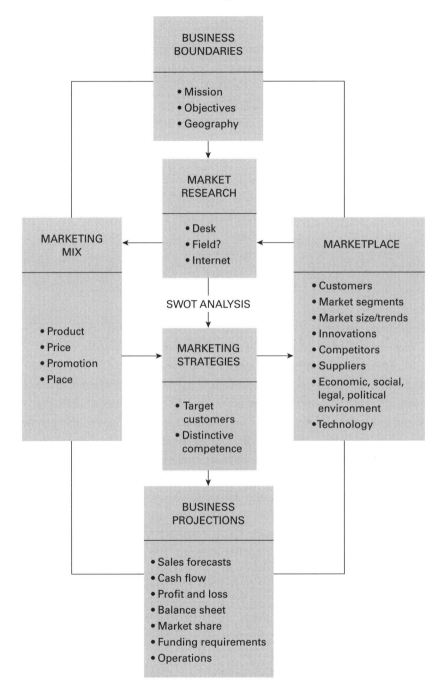

CASE STUDY
Husk – Surviving the coronavirus crisis – strategy not straightjacket

HUSK, a Bristol-based custom-kitchen business, hadn't even filed their first year's accounts when their world changed radically. The accounts due by 26 August covering the period to 30 November 2019 were destined to be a near irrelevance. HUSK, founded by friends Dave Young and Ross Norgate, who were both on the same furniture course, aimed to exploit a gap in the market that they reckoned they had spotted for affordable kitchens that are customizable and durable.

A joint passion for well-crafted minimal design led them develop a range of beautifully simple, custom-made kitchen cabinet fronts and worktops designed to work with IKEA cabinets that can also be adapted to work with alternative cabinet suppliers. With prices for fronts starting from around £1,900 for a small kitchen, the pair were sure they had a winning formula. Their new Cargo showroom, in Bristol's fashionable Wapping Wharf, was set to open to the public on Friday 28 February 2020. Home to a host of independent eateries, shops and more, Cargo is a new retail concept made entirely of converted shipping containers. The pair planned to showcase their newest colour range and panelled oak fronts and have a full range of kitchen front samples available for visitors to the showroom to take away.

That entire strategy was confined to the dustbin when all non-essential retail outlets were ordered to close by the government on the evening of the 23 March 2020. With new orders down by 90 per cent, showrooms shut and teams unable to work together, HUSK had to rapidly adapt to its new circumstances. They rapidly focused on making easy-to-assemble flat pack desks for people working from home or home-schooling their children. A single carpenter was able to produce about eight a day from their workshop in Bristol, while most colleagues were furloughed as the business got through the crisis. HUSK sold 40 desks in eight days and while kitchen cabinet fronts will remain core for the company, its new line of desks has the potential to be a longer-term fixture in their product range.

SWOT (Strengths, Weaknesses, Opportunities and Threats)

The process by which all these data are examined is called the SWOT analysis: your company's strengths and weaknesses are analysed and compared with the perceived environment, opportunities and threats. Its purpose is to allow you to develop a strategy using areas in which you are more able than the competition to meet the needs of particular target customer groups.

Our experience with new starters at Cranfield has emphasized the importance for the small company of the second and third of these generic strategies, sometimes judiciously mixed, particularly bringing into play the four major elements of the marketing mix (product, price, promotion and place) to emphasize your differentiation and focus.

Many new start-ups at the turn of the millennium sought to benefit from the newly available internet technology and vigorously pursued a cost leadership strategy. The low margins often implicit in this strategy left little room for manoeuvre when things went awry. For example, Cranfield MBA Dexter Kirk, with 12 traditional clothing stores, noted: 'My heart is only gladdened by the final reality that has set in on dot.com apparel marketing. Funny, we old lags called it "mail order" and knew that you should allow for 30 per cent returns. When I told Boo.com that at a meeting before Christmas, they thought I was mad. I also warned my daughter who is in dotcom PR that "brown boxes" would be the problem, ie fulfilment is the most unsexy part of the job. Sure enough, one of her B2C clients delivered all their Christmas trees on January 5th!'

Needless to say, neither company survived. Hence the need to emphasize differentiation and focus with better margins in the early learning phase of start-up and business growth.

First-to-market fallacy

'Gaining first mover advantage' are words used like a mantra to justify skipping the industry analysis and strategy formulation stages in preparing a business plan. This myth is one of the most enduring in business theory and practice. Entrepreneurs and established giants are always in a race to be first, believing that it is necessary for success. Research from the 1980s which showed that market pioneers had enduring advantages in distribution, product-line breadth, product quality and, especially, market share, underscored this principle.

Beguiling though the theory of first-mover advantage is, it is probably wrong. Gerard Tellis, of the University of Southern California, and Peter Golder, of New York University's Stern business school, argued in their book, *Will and Vision: How latecomers grow to dominate markets* (2001, McGraw-Hill Inc, US) and subsequent research, that previous studies on the subject were deeply flawed. In the first instance earlier studies were based on surveys of surviving companies and brands, excluding all the pioneers that failed. This helps some companies to look as though they were first to market even when they were not. Procter & Gamble (P&G) boasts that it created America's disposable-nappy (diaper) business. In fact, a company called Chux launched their product a quarter of a century before P&G entered the market in 1961.

Also, the questions used to gather much of the data in earlier research were at best ambiguous, and perhaps dangerously so. For example the term 'one of the pioneers in first developing such products or services' was used as a proxy for 'first to market'. The authors emphasize their point by listing popular misconceptions of who were the real pioneers across the 66 markets they analysed. Online book sales – Amazon (wrong), Books.com (right); Copiers – Xerox (wrong), IBM (right); PCs – IBM/Apple (both wrong). Micro Instrumentation Telemetry Systems (MITS) introduced its PC, the Altair, a US$400 kit, in 1974, followed by Tandy Corporation (Radio Shack) in 1977.

In fact the most compelling evidence from all the research was that nearly half of all firms pursuing a first-to-market strategy were fated to fail, while those following fairly close behind were three times as likely to succeed. Tellis and Golder claim the best strategy is to enter the market 19 years after pioneers, learn from their mistakes, benefit from their product and market development and be more certain about customer preferences.

Vision

A vision is about stretching the organization's reach beyond its grasp. Few now can see how the vision can be achieved, but can see that it would be great if it could be. Microsoft's vision of a computer in every home, formed when few offices had one, is one example of a vision that has nearly been reached. Stated as a company goal back in 1990, it might have raised a wry smile: after all it was only a few decades before then that IBM had estimated the entire world demand for its computers as seven! Their updated vision to 'Create experiences that combine the magic of software with the power of Internet services across a world of devices' is rather less succinct! Apple, Microsoft's arch rival, has the vision to: 'make things that make an impact'. They do this by using the latest technology, investing in packaging and design, making their products easier to use and more elegant than anything else around, and selling them at a premium price. Personal computers, music players, smartphones and tablet computers – and now cloud-based services – have all been treated to the Apple visionary touch with considerable success. By 2011 Apple overtook Microsoft in terms of its stock market value.

Ocado, the online grocer floated on the stock market in 2010, was established with a clear vision: to offer busy people an alternative to going to the supermarket every week. IBM's vision is to package technology for use by businesses. Starting out with punch-card tabulators, IBM adapted over its 100 year+ history to supply magnetic-tape systems, mainframes, PCs and consulting (since it bought the consulting arm of PricewaterhouseCoopers, an accounting firm, in 2002). Building a business around a vision, rather than a specific product or technology, makes it easier to get employees, investors and customers to buy into a long-term commitment to a business, seeing they could have opportunities for progression in an organization that knows where it is going.

Mission

A mission is a direction statement, intended to focus your attention on the essentials that encapsulate your specific competence(s) in relation to the market/customers you plan to serve. First, the mission should be narrow enough to give direction and guidance to everyone in the business. This concentration is the key to business success because it is only by focusing on specific needs that a small business can differentiate itself from its larger competitors. Nothing kills off a business faster than trying to do too many different things too soon. Second, the mission should open up a large enough market to allow the business to grow and realize its potential. You can always add a bit on later. In summary, the mission statement should explain:

- what business you are in and your purpose;
- what you want to achieve over the next one to three years, ie your strategic goal.

Above all, mission statements must be realistic, achievable – and brief.

Nestlé's mission is captured in these words: 'Good Food, Good Life'. Their claim here is to provide consumers with the best tasting, most nutritious choices in a wide range of food and beverage categories and eating occasions, from morning to night.

Amazon's mission – 'We seek to be Earth's most customer-centric company for three primary customer sets: consumer customers, seller customers and developer customers' – though punchy enough, doesn't provide much guidance to the rank and file on what to do every day.

Values

A business faces tough choices every day and the bigger it gets the greater the number of people responsible for setting out what you ultimately stand for – profits alone, or principled profits. Defining your values will make it possible for everyone working for you to know how to behave in any situation. Your values should be seen to run through the business – a common thread touching every decision. Southwest Airlines, the first and arguably the best low-cost airline, has cultivated a reputation for being the 'nice' airline. A past CEO, James Parker, tells a story that sums up their values ('we want people to consistently do the right thing because they want to'): One evening flight landed in Detroit and all the passengers, bar one, a young girl, disembarked. She should have got off at Chicago, an earlier stop, but failed to do so. Despite this being the night before Thanksgiving, the pilot and crew knew they had to get the passenger back to her anxious parents. Without asking for company permission they just took off and returned the girl to her correct destination. They knew what should be done, regardless of the additional cost and inconvenience, and just got on with it.

Objectives

The milestones on the way to realizing the vision and mission are measured by the achievement of business objectives. Your business plan should set out the primary goals in terms of profit, turnover and business value, particularly if you want to attract outside investment. Pizza Express, for example, set out its goal of aiming to nearly double their number of outlets from 318 to 700 by 2020. Majestic Wine announced a similar-sounding goal, aiming to add 12 new stores a year for the coming 10 years.

Make sure that your business plan contains SMART objectives:

- **Specific**: Relate to specific tasks and activities, not general statements about improvements.
- **Measurable**: It should be possible to assess whether or not they have been achieved.
- **Attainable**: It should be possible for the employee to achieve the desired outcome.
- **Realistic**: Within the employee's current or planned-for capability.
- **Timed**: To be achieved by a specific date.

WORKSHEET FOR ASSIGNMENT 2: STRATEGY – THE BIG PICTURE

1 Using Porter's five forces, analyse the factors at work in your industry.

2 If you are expecting to be first to market, what other advantages for your proposition can you expand on in your business plan?

3 Describe the strategic direction being pursued by the business you are/will be competing with, ie focus, differentiation, cost.

4 What strategic option will you be going for and why?

5 Explain how you arrived at your proposition.

6 What makes you believe it will succeed?

7 Write a mission statement linking your product or service to the customer needs it is aimed at.

8 Write vision and values statements.

9 What are your principal objectives:
   – short term?
   – long term?

10 List your tasks and action plans as you see them at present.

Suggested further reading

Grundy, T (2014) *Demistifying Strategic Thinking*, Kogan Page, London

Hague, P (2019) *The Business Models Handbook: Templates, Theory and Case Studies*, Kogan Page, London

Johnson, S and Van de Ven, A H (2017) A framework for entrepreneurial strategy. Strategic entrepreneurship: Creating a new mindset, pp 66–85.

Porter, M E (2004) *Competitive Strategy Techniques for Analyzing Industries and Competitors*, Free Press, New York

Wootton, S (2010) *Strategic Thinking: A nine-step approach to strategy and leadership for managers and marketers*, Kogan Page, London

ASSIGNMENT 3

You and your team

The two essential ingredients for success in any new venture are a good proposition and the right people to turn that idea into a business. Your business plan must therefore not only include a description of your purpose or mission, but give full details of your and your prospective partners' experience and 'suitability' for this venture.

You also need to explain the name of your business, why you chose it, and under what legal form you propose to trade. If your business has been trading for some time, you should give a brief description of achievements to date and a summary of financial results. Full accounts can be included in an appendix to your business plan. Let's look at each in turn.

You and your team

The right stuff

To launch a new venture successfully, you have to be the right sort of person, your business idea must be right for the market and your timing must be spot on. The world of business failures is full of products that are ahead of their time.

The entrepreneur is frequently seen as someone who is always bursting with new ideas, is highly enthusiastic, hyperactive and insatiably curious. But the more you try to create a picture of the typical entrepreneur, the more elusive he or she becomes.

Peter Drucker, the international business guru, captured the problem clearly with this description:

Some are eccentrics, others painfully correct conformists; some are fat and some are lean; some are worriers, some relaxed; some drink quite heavily, others are total abstainers; some are men of great charm and warmth, some have no more personality than a frozen mackerel.

That said, there are certain characteristics that successful newcomers to business do have in common, and you should emphasize these in respect of yourself in the business plan.

Self-confident all-rounders

Entrepreneurs are rarely geniuses. There are nearly always people in their business who have more competence, in one field, than they could ever aspire to. But they have a wide range of ability and a willingness to turn their hands to anything that has to be done to make the venture succeed. They can usually make the product, market it and count the money, but above all they have self-confidence that lets them move comfortably through uncharted waters.

CASE STUDY
Sir Paul Smith

Sir Paul Smith, who left school at 15, launched his clothing business and within a decade had opened three shops in London – one of which was in Covent Garden – and a further one in Tokyo, and turnover was above £2 million pa. Now 'Paul Smith' is an internationally recognized fashion brand.

Explaining his success, Sir Paul states, 'It's not that I'm a particularly brilliant designer or businessman, but I can run a business and I can design. There are so many excellent designers or excellent people but so often the designers can't run the business and businessmen do not have the right product.'

Resilient

Rising from the ashes of former disasters is also a common feature of many successful entrepreneurs.

Henry Ford had been bankrupted twice before founding the Ford Motor Corporation with a loan of US$28,000 in his 40th year.

CASE STUDY
Timothy Waterstone

Timothy Waterstone, founder of one of the fastest-growing bookshop chains in the West, was fired from WH Smith's US operation in the most bloodcurdling circumstances. He took the first plane back to the United Kingdom and spent two months wondering what to do.

Until this time, Waterstone's career path had been smooth and unmeteoric. After Cambridge he did a spell in the family tea-broking business in Cochin, followed by 10 years as a marketing manager for Allied Breweries. Books had always been his obsession, so he went to work for WH Smith. He was quickly sent to New York, where he remained for four years. His wife was in the UK for long periods, so he spent his spare time wandering around Manhattan bookshops. They were brilliant places: lively and consumer-led with huge stock, accessible staff and long opening hours. He felt there was a gap for similar bookselling in the UK, but at the time did nothing about it.

A trip to the dole office acted as a catalyst. It was the most horrific experience of his life. Not waiting for his turn, he rushed out and sat in the car. Instead of trying to get a new job, he formulated the Waterstone's concept. High street banks turned him down. He then went to a finance house and struck lucky. He pledged his house, £6,000 savings, £10,000 borrowed from his father-in-law, and the rest was raised through the government's loan guarantee scheme.

Three months later the first Waterstone's opened, based on a simple store plan an art student sketched out for £25. He filled the shops with the type of books that appeal to book lovers, not best-seller buyers. Midnight hours, Sunday trading (where possible) and bonus schemes for staff led to dazzling sales and the company employed 500 people in 40 branches, with a turnover of £35 million a year. The ultimate achievement was to sell back the company to WH Smith for the modest sum of £50 million. Don't get mad, start your own bookshop!

Innovative skills

Almost by definition, entrepreneurs are innovators who either tackle the unknown, or do old things in new ways. It is this inventive streak that allows them to carve out a new niche, often invisible to others.

CASE STUDY
TomTom

The first quarter of 2017 saw TomTom having over 4,700 employees and 58 offices in 35 countries worldwide. Since 2011 the company has sold over 2.7 million of its new Sports Products, a category fast approaching its success in the navigation arena. With revenue approaching the billion dollars a year mark, the company has come a long way since 1991 when TomTom was founded and began a journey that would change the way people drive forever.

Harold Goddijn and Corinne Vigreux, married for more than two decades, are the co-founders of the satellite navigation device that has come to define the sector. Vigreux studied at a Paris business school, starting out at a French games firm before moving to the UK to Psion, then a FTSE 100 technology company famed for its handheld PDA (Personal Digital Assistant). Goddijn read economics at Amsterdam University and while working for a venture capital firm came across some of Psion's handheld computers and organizers and was impressed. He approached Psion suggesting a joint distribution venture selling the company's products in the Netherlands. Vigreux was sent to the Netherlands to negotiate with Goddijn, the first time the pair had met. They married in 1991 and Vigreux resigned from Psion and moved to Amsterdam.

A brief spell working for a Dutch dairy co-operative saw Vigreux suffering from technology withdrawal symptoms. With Peter-Frans Pauwels and Pieter Geelen, software wizards, she started Palmtop Software, later to become TomTom, designing software such as dictionaries, accounting packages and diet books that could be loaded on to Palm Pilots and Pocket PCs. In late 1998 Goddijn and Vigreux saw a navigation system built for a computer and gradually the idea took shape. Three years and €4 million later the quartet had created the TomTom, launching it at €799. Even at this price it was far cheaper than existing products and superior in that it featured a touch screen, a first for the sector.

The year after launch, the business floated, and 50 per cent of the business was sold to fund growth and acquisition. But 2008 saw the business hit turbulence. The credit crunch, market saturation, a high level of debt and Google starting to offer maps for free represented more serious problems in a single year than many face in a lifetime. The company restructured, reduced debt and now generate half their revenue from selling licences to their maps, constructing in-built systems for the car industry and telematics. TomTom Telematics is now recognized as a leading provider of telematics solutions.

Results oriented

Successful people set themselves goals and get pleasure out of trying to achieve them. Once a goal has been reached, they have to get the next target in view as quickly as possible. This restlessness is very characteristic. Sir James Goldsmith was a classic example, moving the base of his business empire from the United Kingdom to France, then the United States – and finally into pure cash, ahead of a stock market crash.

Professional risk-taker

The high failure rate shows that small businesses are faced with many dangers. An essential characteristic of someone starting a business is a willingness to make decisions and to take risks. This does not mean gambling on hunches. It means carefully calculating the odds and deciding which risks to take and when to take them.

Having total commitment

You will need complete faith in your idea. How else will you convince all the doubters you are bound to meet that it is a worthwhile venture? You will also need single-mindedness, energy and a lot of hard work to get things started; working 18-hour days is not uncommon. This can put a strain on other relationships, particularly within your family, so they too have to become involved and committed if you are to succeed.

CASE STUDY
Innocent

In the summer of 1998 when Richard Reed, Adam Balon and Jon Wright had developed their first smoothie recipes but were still nervous about giving up their jobs, they bought £500 worth of fruit, turned it into smoothies and sold them from a stall at a London music festival. They put up a sign saying 'Do you think we should give up our jobs to make these smoothies?' next to bins saying 'YES' and 'NO', inviting people to put the empty bottle in the appropriate bin. At the end of the weekend the 'YES' bin was full, so they went to work the next day and resigned. The rest, as they say, is history. Virtually a household name, Innocent Drinks has experienced a decade of rapid growth.

But the business stalled in 2008, with sales slipping back and their European expansion soaking up cash at a rapid rate. The founders, with an average age of 28, decided that they needed some heavy-weight advice and talked to Charles Dunstone, Carphone Warehouse founder, and Mervyn Davies, chairman of Standard Chartered. The strong advice was to get an investor with deep pockets and ideally something else to bring to the party to augment the youthful enthusiasm of the founders. They launched their search for an investor the day that Lehman Brothers filed for bankruptcy. In April 2009 the Innocent team accepted Coca-Cola as a minority investor in their business, paying £30 million for a stake of between 10 and 20 per cent. They chose Coca-Cola because as well as providing the funds, the company can help get Innocent products out to more people in more places. They'll also be able to learn a lot from Coca-Cola, who have been in business for over 120 years.

All too often budding entrepreneurs believe themselves to be the right sort of person to set up a business. Unfortunately, the capacity for self-deception is enormous. When a random sample of male adults were asked recently to rank themselves on leadership ability, 70 per cent rated themselves in the top 25 per cent; only 2 per cent felt they were below average as leaders. In an area in which self-deception ought to be difficult, 60 per cent said they were well above average in athletic ability and only 6 per cent said they were below.

A common mistake made in assessing entrepreneurial talent is to assume that success in big business management will automatically guarantee success in a small business.

Checking out your entrepreneurial strengths

You can find out more about your likely strengths and weakness as an entrepreneur by taking one or more of the many online entrepreneurial IQ-type tests. A couple of sources can be found in the Index of Key Organizations and Resources for Business Planning at the end of the book, but an entry in Google will produce a small torrent!

Building the team

Not surprisingly, an investor's ideal proposal includes an experienced and balanced management team, who have all worked together for a number of years. That will ensure management in depth, thus providing cover for everything from illness to expansion, and guaranteeing some stability during the turbulent early years. For this reason management buy-outs are a firm favourite.

At the other end of the scale is the lone inventor whose management skills may be in doubt, and who is anyway fully stretched getting his or her product from the drawing board to the production line. This type of proposal is unlikely to attract much investment capital. It has obvious risks beyond those every company expects to experience in the marketplace. In any case, without a management team in place the business is ill-prepared for the rapid growth required to service an investor's funds.

In practice, most business proposals lie somewhere between these extremes. Your business plan should explain clearly what the ideal composition of key managers should be for your business; who you have identified, or recruited so far; and last but certainly not least, how you will motivate them to remain with you and perform well for at least the first few all-important years.

Certainly investors will look for reassurance in this respect and will expect to see more reference to the steps you will take to encourage loyalty.

Your business name

A good name can, in effect, become a one- or two-word summary of your business strategy. Jeff Bezos originally chose Cadabra as the name for his business – as in abracadabra – summing up the magic of being able to find any book online. After a few phone calls to canvas opinions, he ditched Cadabra as it was too easily confused with 'Cadaver'! He settled on Amazon, figuring that most people thought it to be the largest river in the world, and he wanted to convey the image of having the 'Earth's Biggest Book Store'.

PayPal, Body Shop, Toys R Us and Kwik-Fit are other good examples of names that sum up the essence of their businesses. Google, though a colossally successful venture, struggled in arriving at a meaningful business name. They started with 'BackRub', as their algorithms checked backlinks to estimate the importance of a site, but moved on to use Google, a misspelling of the word 'googol' – the number one followed by 100 zeros. This was chosen to convey the idea of large quantities of information being sifted for useful data. It's unlikely that many people outside the Stanford University campus (where the founders developed their business idea) would have any idea what a googol was or why it would help describe the biggest search engine. But at the time, 'geeks' populated the internet, and the name caught on.

Your business name is almost always the first way people get to hear about your venture and it needs to convey the essence of the business quickly and clearly. Once you have to start explaining what you do, the job of communicating gets harder. As you are going to have to put some effort into creating this name and that of your web presence (domain name) if you plan to have one, it makes good sense to take some steps to protect your investment.

Your company name can be the starting and sustaining point in differentiating you from your competitors, and as such it should be carefully chosen, be protected by trademarks where possible and be written in a distinctive way. It follows therefore that the main consideration in choosing a business name is its commercial usefulness.

When you choose a business name, you are also choosing an identity so it should reflect:

- who you are;
- what you do;
- how you do it.

Given all the marketing investment you will make in your company name, you should check with a trademark agent whether you can protect your chosen name (descriptive words, surnames and place names are not normally allowed except after long use).

First, anyone wanting to use a 'controlled' name will have to get permission. There are some 80 or 90 controlled names, which include words such as 'International', 'Bank' and 'Royal'. This is simply to prevent a business implying that it is something that it is not.

Second, all businesses that intend to trade under names other than those of their owner(s) must state who does own the business and how the owner can be contacted. So if you are a sole trader or partnership and you only use surnames with or without forenames or initials, you are not affected. Companies are also not affected if they simply use their full corporate name.

If any name other than the 'true' name is to be used, then you must disclose the name of the owner(s) and an address in the United Kingdom to which business documents can be sent. This information has to be shown on all business letters, orders for goods and services, invoices and receipts, and statements and demands for business debts. Also, a copy has to be displayed prominently on all business premises. The purpose of the Companies Act requirements is simply to make it easier to 'see' who you are doing business with.

If you are setting up as a limited company you will have to submit your choice of name to the Companies Registration Office along with the other documents required for registration. It will be accepted unless there is another company with that name on the register or the Registrar considers the name to be obscene, offensive or illegal.

Changing your name

It's not the end of the world if you decide after a year or so that your business name is not quite right, as the case study below shows. But you will have largely wasted any earlier marketing effort in building up awareness.

CASE STUDY
Bridgewater

Emma Bridgewater set up her business 18 months after completing an English degree at Bedford College, London. At first she wasn't sure what business to start but her boyfriend at the time, with whom she lived in Brixton, wanted to set up a craft studio to teach students how to slip-cast (an ancient method of making pottery with liquid clay poured into a mould). Emma visited factories in Stoke-on-Trent and discovered a number of people with this skill. 'Their mug shapes were revolting, though. So I drew my own. I found, doing so, that all my frustration evaporated just like that. Suddenly I knew what I wanted to do.'

She equipped herself with sponges and colours so that she could apply her designs to her mugs in the factories. 'At first the people in Stoke thought I was mad and were sceptical but helpful.' However, within a few months she won her first order, worth £600, from the General Trading Company, and in April she joined a lot of 'hysterical stall-holders with lavender bags' at a trade fair in Kensington: Brixton Spongeware was launched.

She has since changed the name: 'I was fed up with jokes about reggae music and sweet potatoes. The name "Bridgewater" is far more appropriate. It sounds like an old, established industry. People often imagine it's a family business that has been going for years. That's exactly the mood I want to create.' Just over two years later she had a file full of orders from top department stores in London and New York. Cheap imitators quickly started copying her designs. Now Bridgewater has an established name and a turnover in the millions.

Deciding the legal form of your business

Before you start trading you will need to consider what legal form your business will take. There are four main forms that a business can take, and the one you choose will depend on a number of factors: commercial needs, financial risk and your tax position. Each of these forms is explained briefly below, together with the procedure to follow on setting them up.

Relative business populations

At the beginning of 2020 there were around 6 million active businesses in the UK, up from 5.5 million in 2016. The UK private sector business population comprised 3.5 million sole proprietorships (59 per cent of the total), 2 million actively trading companies (34 per cent) and 405,000 ordinary partnerships (7 per cent). Most new business start out as sole traders and if successful move on to limited liability to afford owners the protections described earlier in this chapter. In 2009 limited companies made up just short of 26 per cent of the business population, with partnerships accounting for 12 per cent and sole traders 62 per cent. By the end of 2016 those proportions were 30 per cent, 64 per cent and 6 per cent respectively.

Sole trader

The vast majority of new businesses set up each year in the United Kingdom choose to do so as sole traders. This has the merit of being relatively formality-free, and unless you intend to register for VAT, there are few rules about the records you have to keep. There is no requirement for your accounts to be audited, or for financial information on your business to be filed at Companies House.

As a sole trader there is no legal distinction between you and your business – your business is one of your assets, just as your house or car is. It follows from this that if your business should fail, your creditors have a right not only to the assets of the business, but also to your personal assets, subject only to the provisions of the Bankruptcy Acts (these allow you to keep only a few absolutely basic essentials for yourself and family).

It is possible to avoid the worst of these consequences by ensuring that your private assets are the legal property of your spouse, against whom your creditors have no claim. (You must be solvent when the transfer is made, and that transfer must have been made at least two years prior to your business running into trouble.) However, to be effective such a transfer must be absolute and you can have no say in how your spouse chooses to dispose of his or her new-found wealth!

The capital to get the business going must come from you – or from loans. There is no access to equity capital, which has the attraction of being risk-free. In return for these drawbacks you can have the pleasure of being your own boss immediately, subject only to declaring your profits on your tax return. (In practice you would be wise to take professional advice before doing so.)

Partnerships

Partnerships are effectively collections of sole traders, and as such, share the legal problems attached to personal liability. There are very few restrictions to setting up in business with another person (or persons) in partnership, and several definite advantages. By pooling resources you may have more capital; you should be bringing several sets of skills to the business; and if you are ill the business can still carry on.

There are two serious drawbacks that merit particular attention. First, if your partner makes a business mistake, perhaps by signing a disastrous contract, without your knowledge or consent, every member of the partnership must shoulder the consequences. Under these circumstances your personal assets could be taken to pay the creditors even though the mistake was no fault of your own.

Second, if your partner goes bankrupt in his or her personal capacity, for whatever reason, his or her share of the partnership can be seized by creditors. As a private individual you are not liable for your partner's private debts, but having to buy him or her out of the partnership at short notice could put you and the business in financial jeopardy. Even death may not release you from partnership obligations, and in some circumstances your estate can remain liable. Unless you take 'public' leave of your partnership by notifying your business contacts and legally bringing your partnership to an end, you could remain liable.

The legal regulations governing this field are set out in the Partnership Act 1890, which in essence assumes that competent businesspeople should know what they are doing. The Act merely provides a framework of agreement that applies 'in the absence of agreement to the contrary'. It follows from this that many partnerships are entered into without legal formalities – and sometimes without the parties themselves being aware that they have entered a partnership!

The main provisions of the Partnership Act state that:

- All partners contribute capital equally.
- All partners share profits and losses equally.
- No partner shall have interest paid on his/her capital.
- No partner shall be paid a salary.
- All partners have an equal say in the management of the business.

It is unlikely that all these provisions will suit you, so you would be well advised to get a 'partnership agreement' drawn up in writing by a solicitor at the outset of your venture.

One possibility that can reduce the more painful consequences of entering a partnership as a 'sleeping partner' is to have your involvement registered as a limited partnership. It means you (or your partner) can play no active part in running the business, but your risks are limited to the capital that you put in.

Unless you are a member of certain professions (eg law, accountancy) you are restricted to a maximum of 20 partners in any partnership.

Cooperative

A cooperative is an enterprise owned and controlled by the people working in it. Once in danger of becoming extinct, the workers' cooperative is enjoying something of a comeback, and there are over 5,450 operating in the United Kingdom, employing 237,800 people. They are growing at the rate of 20 per cent per annum.

Cooperatives are governed by the Industrial and Provident Societies Act 1965, whose main provisions state:

- Each member of the cooperative has equal control through the principle of 'one person one vote'.
- Membership must be open to anyone who satisfies the stipulated qualifications.
- Profits can be retained in the business or distributed in proportion to members' involvement, eg hours worked.
- Members must benefit primarily from their participation in the business.
- Interest on loan or share capital is limited in some specific way, even if the profits are high enough to allow a greater payment.

It is certainly not a legal structure designed to give entrepreneurs control of their own destiny and maximum profits. However, if this is to be your chosen legal form you can pay from £90 to register with the Chief Registrar of Friendly Societies, and must have at least seven members at the outset. They do not all have to be full-time workers at first. Like a limited company, a registered cooperative has limited liability (see under 'Limited liability companies') for its members and must file annual accounts, but there is no charge for this. Not all cooperatives bother to register, as it is not mandatory, in which case they are treated in law as a partnership with unlimited liability.

Limited liability companies

In the United Kingdom, before the 1895 Companies Act it was necessary to have an Act of Parliament or a Royal Charter in order to set up a company. Now, out of the 4.5 million businesses trading in the UK, over 1.4 million are limited companies. As the name suggests, in this form of business your liability is limited to the amount you state that you will contribute by way of share capital (although you may not actually have to put that money in!).

A limited company has a legal identity of its own, separate from the people who own or run it. This means that, in the event of failure, creditors' claims are restricted to the assets of the company. The shareholders of the business are not liable as individuals for the business debts beyond the paid-up value of their shares. This applies even if the shareholders are working directors, unless of course the company has been trading fraudulently. (In practice, the ability to limit liability is severely restricted these days as most lenders, including the banks, often insist on personal guarantees from the directors.) Other advantages include the freedom to raise capital by selling shares.

Disadvantages include the cost involved in setting up the company and the legal requirement in some cases for the company's accounts to be audited by a chartered or certified accountant. Usually it is only businesses with assets approaching £3 million that have to be audited but if, for example, you have shareholders who own more than 10 per cent of your firm they can ask for the accounts to be audited. You can find out the latest information on auditing small firms either from your accountant or by searching for 'running a limited company' on the GOV.UK website.

A limited company can be formed by two shareholders, one of whom must be a director. A company secretary must also be appointed, who can be a shareholder, director or an outside person such as an accountant or lawyer.

The company can be bought 'off the shelf' from a registration agent, then adapted to suit your own purposes. This will involve changing the name, shareholders and articles of association, and will cost about £250 and take a couple of weeks to arrange. Alternatively, you can form your own company, using your solicitor or accountant. This will cost around £500 and take six to eight weeks.

The behaviour of companies and their directors is governed by the various Companies Acts that have come into effect since 1844, the latest of which came into effect in November 2006.

Past achievements

If your business has already been trading for some time, your business plan should include a summary of past results and achievements. Annual reports, audited accounts, etc, if voluminous, can be included in an appendix, and referred to in this section of your business plan. Otherwise they can be shown in detail. You should emphasize what you have learnt so far that convinces you that your strategies are soundly based.

CASE STUDY
Notonthehighstreet Enterprises Limited

When Holly Tucker and Sophie Cornish decided that a business selling well-designed, high-quality products that cannot easily be found on the high street was a good business idea, choosing a name for their venture was the easy bit.

Notonthehighstreet was distinct and captured the essence of their proposition. The aim was to bring together businesses that lacked the resources to have an effective presence on the high street and put them all under one roof, spreading the cost base accordingly. The 'one roof' as a physical concept was ditched in favour of the internet at the early planning stage.

Their first draft of the business plan called for a £40,000 investment, but within months of starting up that grew to £140,000. After scrabbling around family, loans and bank overdrafts to fund the first year's growth they pitched to Spark Ventures, an early stage venture capital company that includes Brent Hoberman, co-founder of Lastminute.com, in its portfolio.

Spark pumped in a sizeable six-figure sum, taking a minority stake in the business which allowed it to plan to more than double sales in its third year of operations (see Table 3.1).

TABLE 3.1 Sales history of Notonthehighstreet

Year	Sales (£000)
1	100
2	1,000
3	2,500 (forecast)

For a joining fee of £450 suppliers can promote their products on Notonthehighstreet's website for five years. Notonthehighstreet also takes a 20 per cent slice of any sales generated. It offers a tailored audience and a professional web presence that small firms would find hard if not impossible to emulate without spending tens of thousands of pounds. The site has been voted a top 50 website by the *Independent* magazine.

The pair knew from the outset that protecting their intellectual property was essential to both survival and prosperity. Not only have they protected all their IP, they assert those rights unambiguously on their website: "We own, or are the licensee to, all right, title and interest in and to the Service, including all rights under patent, copyright, trade secret or trademark law, and any and all other proprietary rights, including all applications, renewals, extensions and restorations thereof. You will not modify, adapt, translate, prepare derivative works from, decompile, reverse-engineer, disassemble or otherwise attempt to derive source code from the App or any other part of the Service."

It's hardly surprising then that the business hit £6.4 million turnover in year two and in 2010 they reached £14 million. The business hired Jason Weston, formerly of Amazon, as COO and Mark Hodson from PayPal in 2011. The company's latest accounts filed in March 2019 show turnover had reached £139 million.

WORKSHEET FOR ASSIGNMENT 3: YOU AND YOUR TEAM

1 How did you arrive at your new idea?

2 What is your business name and why have you chosen it?

3 What experience and skills do you have that are particularly relevant to this venture?

4 Who else will be working with you and what relevant experience and skills do they have?

5   What professional advisers (accountant, lawyer, patent agent, etc) have you
    used, or do you plan to use?

6   Under what legal form will you trade and why?

7   If your business is already trading, give a brief summary of financial and
    marketing results and achievements to date.

Suggested further reading

Adair, J (2007) *The Art of Creative Thinking: How to be innovative and develop great ideas*, Kogan Page, London

Bridge, R (2009) *How I Made It: 40 successful entrepreneurs reveal how they made millions*, Kogan Page, London

Pullan, P and Archer, J (2013) *Business Analysis and Leadership,* Kogan Page, London

Watkins, A (2015) *4D leadership: Competitive advantage through vertical leadership development*, Kogan Page, London

Market research

Introduction

Assignments 4–6 are intended to help you to bring your customers, competitors and the marketplace more sharply into focus, and to identify areas you have yet to research. The research should be done before the business is started or a new strategy is pursued, so saving the time and cost incurred if expensive mistakes are made. Obviously, the amount of research undertaken has to be related to the sums at risk. If a venture calls for a start-up investment of £/$/€1,000, spending £/$/€5,000 on market research would be a bad investment. However, new and small businesses that do not want to join the catastrophically high first-year failure statistics would be prudent to carry out some elementary market research, whatever level their start-up capital is to be.

As a President of the Harvard Business School said: 'If you think knowledge is expensive, try ignorance.'

The starting point in any market research has to be a definition of the scope of the market you are aiming for. A small general shop may only service the needs of a few dozen streets. A specialist restaurant may have to call on a much larger catchment area to be viable.

You may eventually decide to sell to different markets. For example, a retail business can serve a local area through the shop and a national area by mail order. A small manufacturing business could branch out into exporting.

People all too often flounder in their initial market research by describing their markets too broadly: for example, saying that they are in the motor industry when they really mean they sell second-hand cars in Perth; or saying they are in health foods, when they are selling wholemeal bread from a village shop. While it is important to be aware of trends in the wider market, this must not obscure the need to focus on the precise area that you have to serve.

The purpose of gathering the market research data is to help you decide on the right marketing strategy when it comes to such factors as setting your price, deciding on service and quality levels and choosing where and how much to advertise. Assignments 4 and 5 pose the main questions you need to answer concerning your customers and competitors, and Assignment 6 covers the principal ways in which basic market research can be conducted, and where such data can be found.

ASSIGNMENT 4

Researching customers

Without customers no business can get off the ground, let alone survive. Some people believe that customers arrive after the firm 'opens its doors'. This is nonsense. You need a clear idea in advance of who your customers will be, as they are a vital component of a successful business strategy, not simply the passive recipients of new products or services.

Knowing something about your customers and what you plan to sell to them seems so elementary it is hard to believe that any potential business-person could start a business without doing so. But it is all too common, and one of the reasons many new businesses fail.

Recognizing customer needs

The founder of a successful cosmetics firm, when asked what he did, replied, 'In the factories we make perfume, in the shops we sell dreams.'

Those of us in business usually start out defining our business in physical terms. Customers on the other hand see businesses having as their primary value the ability to satisfy their needs. Even firms that adopt customer satisfaction, or even delight, as their maxim often find it a more complex goal than it at first appears. Take Ella's Kitchen, the case study that follows, for example. Their end customer, babies, were carefully considered when designing their product, though they were not the actual purchasers. They were the parents concerned.

Until you have clearly defined the needs of your market(s) you cannot begin to assemble a product or service to satisfy them.

CASE STUDY
Ella's Kitchen

Paul Lindley had no experience of either the industry his business started up in or indeed of running his own business. Lindley, aged 50, was a UK director of Nickelodeon, the cable children's television channel, and starting up dealing with the UK's big supermarket chains looked like an ambitious project to embark on.

His idea for baby food in squeezy pouches was triggered by the problems in trying to get his own daughter, Ella, to eat food when they were travelling. Until he launched Ella's the majority of baby food was sold in glass jars for the compelling reason than parents wanted to see the food before they bought it. But feeding children from a jar meant that parents had to take control of the feeding process, not something that many young children readily buy into. Lindley's idea was to use pouches like the ones he had seen sold in French supermarkets, aimed at adults and mostly containing mayonnaises and salad dressings. He reckoned that with children's foods served up in this way kids could hold onto the pouches and feed themselves, making feeding on the go in particular a much easier proposition than with a jar and spoon.

There were a number of other major advantages in using pouches over plain glass bottles. In the first place packaging the product in this way is aimed at the actual consumer – babies and toddlers – not the parents buying the food. So rather than being clear, the packaging is brightly coloured, covered in cartoon-style drawings – and named after his daughter. Also food in pouches can be delivered in pasteurized form rather than having to be sterilized at high temperatures. That in turn means the food retains colour, taste, texture and vitamins more than you would otherwise, so is actually a healthier option.

Ella's Kitchen must be meeting customers' needs – turnover in 2018–19 was over £71 million with profits in excess of £10.3 million and their pouches are sold in supermarkets internationally including UK, Norway, Sweden, Finland, Belgium, the Netherlands, Canada and the United States.

Fortunately help is at hand when it comes to getting an inside track on your customers' thought process. The US psychologist Abraham Maslow demonstrated in his research that 'all customers are goal seekers who gratify their needs by purchase and consumption'. He then went a bit further and classified consumer needs into a five-stage pyramid he called the hierarchy of needs:

- *Self-actualization.* This is the summit of Maslow's hierarchy in which people are looking for truth, wisdom, justice and purpose. It's a need that is never fully satisfied, and according to Maslow only a very small percentage of people ever reach the point where they are prepared to pay much money to satisfy such needs. It is left to the like of Bill Gates and Sir Tom Hunter to give away billions to form foundations to dispose of their wealth on worthy causes. The rest of us scrabble around further down the hierarchy.

- *Esteem.* Here people are concerned with such matters as self-respect, achievement, attention, recognition and reputation. The benefits customers are looking for include the feeling that others will think better of them if they have a particular product. Much of brand marketing is aimed at making consumers believe that conspicuously wearing the maker's label or logo so that others can see it will earn them 'respect'. Understanding how this part of Maslow's hierarchy works was vital to the founders of Responsible Travel. Founded in 2001 with backing from Anita Roddick (Body Shop) in his front room in Brighton, and with his partner Harold Goodwin, Justin Francis set out to create the world's first company to offer environmentally responsible travel and holidays. It was one of the first companies to offer carbon offset schemes for travellers, and Responsibletravel.com boast that they turn away more tour companies trying to list on their site than they accept. They appeal to consumers who want to be recognized in their communities as being socially responsible. In 2010 they launched their US business, Responsible Vacation, and now have over 350 specialist tour operators on their books.

- *Social needs.* The need for friends, belonging to associations, clubs or other groups and the need to give and get love are all social needs. After 'lower' needs have been met, these needs that relate to interacting with other people come to the fore. Hotel Chocolat, founded by Angus Thirlwell and Peter Harris in their kitchen, is a good example of a business based on meeting social needs. They market home-delivered luxury chocolates but generate sales by having 'tasting clubs' to check out products each month. The concept of the club is that you invite friends round and using the firm's scoring system, rate and give feedback on the chocolates.

- *Safety*. The second most basic need of consumers is to feel safe and secure. People who feel they are in harm's way either through their general environment or because of the product or service on offer will not be over interested in having their higher needs met. When Charles Rigby set up World Challenge to market challenging expeditions to exotic locations around the world with the aim of taking young people up to around 19 years old out of their comfort zones and teaching them how to overcome adversity, he knew he had a challenge of his own on his hands: how to make an activity simultaneously exciting and apparently dangerous to teenagers, while being safe enough for the parents writing the cheques to feel comfortable. Six full sections on the website are devoted to explaining the safety measures the company takes to ensure that unacceptable risks are eliminated as far as is humanly possible.

- *Physiological needs*. Air, water, sleep and food are all absolutely essential to sustain life. Until these basic needs are satisfied higher needs such as self-esteem will not be considered.

You can read more about Maslow's needs hierarchy and how to take it into account in understanding customers on the NetMBA website.

Segmenting the market

That customers have different needs means that we need to organize our marketing effort so as to address those individually. However, trying to satisfy everyone may mean that we end up satisfying no one fully. The marketing process that helps us deal with this seemingly impossible task is market segmentation. This is the name given to the process whereby customers and potential customers are organized into clusters or groups of 'similar' types. For example, a carpet/upholstery cleaning business has private individuals and business clients running restaurants and guest houses as its clients. These two segments are fundamentally different, with one segment being more focused on cost and the other more concerned that the work is carried out with the least disruption to the business. Also, each of these customer groups is motivated to buy for different reasons, and the selling message has to be modified accordingly.

These are some of the ways by which markets can be segmented:

- *Psychographic segmentation* divides individual consumers into social groups such as 'Yuppies' (young, upwardly mobile professionals), 'Bumps' (borrowed-to-the-hilt, upwardly mobile, professional show-offs) and 'Jollies' (jet-setting oldies with lots of loot). These categories try to show how social behaviour influences buyer behaviour. Forrester Research, an internet research house, claims when it comes to determining whether consumers will or will not go on the internet, how much they will spend and what they will buy, demographic factors such as age, race, and gender don't matter anywhere near as much as the consumers' *attitudes towards technology*. Forrester (nd) uses this concept, together with its research, to produce Technographics® market segments as an aid to understanding consumers' behaviour as digital consumers.

Forrester has used two categories: technology optimists and technology pessimists, and has used these alongside income and what it calls 'primary motivation' – career, family and entertainment – to divide up the whole market. Each segment is given a new name – 'Techno-strivers', 'Digital Hopefuls' and so forth – followed by a chapter explaining how to identify them, how to tell whether they are likely to be right for your product or service and providing some pointers as to what marketing strategies might get favourable responses from each group.

- *Benefit segmentation* recognizes that different people can get different satisfaction from the same product or service. Lastminute.com claims two quite distinctive benefits for its users. First, it aims to offer people bargains that appeal because of price and value. Second, the company has recently been laying more emphasis on the benefit of immediacy. This idea is rather akin to the impulse-buy products placed at checkout tills, which you never thought of buying until you bumped into them on your way out. Whether 10 days on a beach in Goa or a trip to Istanbul are the types of things people 'pop in their baskets' before turning off their computers, time will tell.

- *Geographic segmentation* arises when different locations have different needs. For example, an inner-city location may be a heavy user of motorcycle dispatch services, but a light user of gardening products. However, locations can 'consume' both products if they are properly presented. An inner-city store might sell potatoes in 1 kg bags, recognizing that its customers are likely to be on foot. An out-of-town shopping centre may sell the same product in 20 kg sacks, knowing its customers will have cars.

QUEEN MARGARET UNIVERSITY LRC

- *Industrial segmentation* groups together commercial customers according to a combination of their geographic location, principal business activity, relative size, frequency of product use, buying policies and a range of other factors.

- *Multivariant segmentation* is where more than one variable is used. This can give a more precise picture of a market than using just one factor.

These are some useful rules to help decide whether a market segment is worth trying to sell into:

- *Measurability.* Can you estimate how many customers are in the segment? Are there enough to make it worth offering something 'different'?

- *Accessibility.* Can you communicate with these customers, preferably in a way that reaches them on an individual basis? For example, you could reach the over-50s by advertising in a specialist 'older people's' magazine with reasonable confidence that young people will not read it. So if you were trying to promote Scrabble with tiles 50 per cent larger, you might prefer that young people did not hear about it. If they did, it might give the product an old-fashioned image.

- *Open to profitable development.* The customers must have money to spend on the benefits that you propose to offer.

- *Size.* A segment has to be large enough to be worth your exploiting it, but perhaps not so large as to attract larger competitors.

Segmentation is an important marketing process, as it helps to bring customers more sharply into focus, and it classifies them into manageable groups. It has wide-ranging implications for other marketing decisions. For example, the same product can be priced differently according to the intensity of customers' needs. The first- and second-class post is one example, off-peak rail travel another. It is also a continuous process that needs to be carried out periodically, for example when strategies are being reviewed.

Business to Business (B2B) buyer criteria

There is a popular theory that business buyers are hard-nosed, cold-hearted Scrooges, making entirely rational choices with the sole goal of doing the best they can for their shareholders. If this were really the case an awful lot of promotional gift suppliers would be out of business. Pharmaceutical companies could fire their sales forces, slashing costs by billions. All doctors and pharmacists would have to do is read up the research proof on drugs and prescribe accordingly. That probably wouldn't take any more time than listening to a rep make their pitch.

At the end of the day, people buy from people and that's where Maslow's needs swing back into play. 'No one ever got fired buying IBM' was a much-quoted phrase in buying departments in the days when IBM's main business was selling computers. This simply meant that the buyer could feel secure in making that decision, as IBM's reputation was high. Buying anywhere else, even if the specification was better and the price lower, was personally risky. IBM's sales force could use the buyer's need to feel safe to great advantage in their presentations.

When understanding the needs of business buyers it is important to keep in mind that there are at least three major categories of people who have a role to play in the B2B buying decision and so whose needs have to be considered in any analysis of a business market.

THE USER, OR END CUSTOMER

This is the recipient of any final benefits associated with the product or service, much as with an individual consumer. Functionality will be vital for this group.

THE SPECIFIER

Though specifiers may not use or even see their purchases, they will want to be sure the end users' needs are met in terms of performance, delivery and any other important parameters. Their 'customer' is both the end user and the budget holder of the cost centre concerned. There may even be conflict between the two (or more) 'customer' groups. For example, in the case of, say, hotel toiletries, those responsible for marketing the rooms will want high-quality products to enhance their offer – while the hotel manager will have cost close to the top of their concerns, and the people responsible for actually putting the product in place will be interested mostly in any handling and packaging issues.

THE NON-CONSUMING BUYER

This is the person who actually places the order. They will be basing their decision on a specification drawn up by someone else, but they will also have individual needs. Some of their needs are similar to those of a specifier, except they will have price at – or near – the top of their needs.

CASE STUDY
Flowcrete

In just 18 years, Dawn Gibbins MBE, co-founder of Flowcrete, took the company from a 400 sq ft unit (the size of a double garage) with £2,000 capital to a plc with a turnover of €52 million in the field of floor screeding technology, and clients including household names such as Cadbury, Sainsbury's, Unilever, Marks & Spencer, Barclays and Ford. Part of Flowcrete's success was down to a continuing focus on technical superiority. This attribute was engendered by Dawn's father, a well-respected industrial chemist with an interest in resin technology.

But arguably Dawn's skills contributed as much if not more to the firm's success. 'We want to be champions of change,' Gibbons claims. 'We have restructured a dozen times, focusing on new trends.' Markets and market segmentation are a vital part of any restructuring process – indeed, the best companies restructure around their customers' changing needs.

The first reappraisal came after seven years in business when Flowcrete realized that its market was no longer those firms that laid floors; it now had to become an installer itself. Changes in the market meant that to maintain growth Flowcrete had to appoint proven specialist contractors, train their staff, write specifications and carry out audits to ensure quality. The business now has a global presence.

The largest, most visited shopping centre in the world, the Dubai Mall, used over 540,000 m^2 of Flowcrete's Deckshield carpark decking to refurbish its huge parking facility.

Defining the product in the customers' terms

Once you know what you are selling and to whom, you can match the features of the product (or service) to the benefits customers will get when they purchase. *Features* are what a product has or is, and *benefits* are what the product does for the customer. For example, cameras, SLR or lens shutters, even film, are not the end product that customers want; they are looking for good pictures. Finally, as in Table 4.1, include 'proof' that these benefits can be delivered.

Remember, the customer pays for the benefits and the seller for the features. So the benefits will provide the 'copy' for most of your future advertising and promotional efforts.

TABLE 4.1   Example showing product features, benefits and proof

Features	Benefits	Proof
We use a unique hardening process for our machine	Our tools last longer and that saves you money	– We have a patent on the process
		– Independent tests carried out by the Cambridge Institute of Technology show our product lasts longest
Our shops stay open later than others in the area	You get more choice when to shop	– Come and see
Our computer system is fault tolerant using parallel processing	You have no down time for either defects or system expansion	– Our written specification guarantees this
		– Come and talk to satisfied customers operating in your field

which means that

you can see this is true because

Who will buy first?

Customers do not sit and wait for a new business to open its doors. Word spreads slowly as the message is diffused throughout the various customer groups. Even then it is noticeable that generally it is the more adventurous types who first buy from a new business. Only after these people have given their seal of approval do the 'followers' come along. Research shows that this adoption process, as it is known, moves through five distinct customer characteristics, from 'innovators' to 'laggards', with the overall population being different for each group (see Table 4.2).

Let's suppose you have identified the market for your internet gift service. Initially your market has been constrained to affluent professionals within five miles of your home to keep delivery costs low. So if market research shows that there are 100,000 people that meet the profile of your ideal customer and they have regular access to the internet, the market open for exploitation at the outset may be as low as 2,500, which is the 2.5 per cent of innovators.

TABLE 4.2 The product/service adoption cycle

Innovators	2.5% of the overall market
Early adopters	13.5% of the overall market
Early majority	34.0% of the overall market
Late majority	34.0% of the overall market
Laggards	16.0% of the overall market
Total market	100%

This adoption process, from the 2.5 per cent of innovators who make up a new business's first customers, through to the laggards who won't buy from anyone until they have been in business for 20 years, is most noticeable with truly innovative and relatively costly goods and services, but the general trend is true for all businesses. Until you have sold to the innovators, significant sales cannot be achieved, so an important first task is to identify these customers. The moral is: the more you know about your potential customers at the outset, the better your chances of success.

One further issue to keep in mind when shaping your marketing strategy is that innovators, early adopters and all the other sub-segments don't necessarily use the same media, websites, magazines and newspapers, or respond to the same images and messages. So they need to be marketed to in very different ways.

At the minimum, your business plan should include information on:

- Who your principal customers are or, if you are launching into new areas, who they are likely to be. Determine in as much detail as you think appropriate the income, age, sex, education, interests, occupation and marital status of your potential customers, and name names if at all possible.
- What factors are important in the customer's decision to buy or not to buy your product and/or service, how much they should buy and how frequently?
- Many factors probably have an influence, and it is often not easy to identify all of them. These are some of the common ones that you should consider investigating:
  - (a) Product considerations
    - (i) price
    - (ii) quality
    - (iii) appearance (colour, texture, shape, materials, etc)

(iv)   packaging
(v)   size
(vi)   fragility, ease of handling, transportability
(vii)   servicing, warranty, durability
(viii) operating characteristics (efficiency, economy, adaptability, etc).

(b) Business considerations

(i)   location and facilities
(ii)   reputation
(iii)   method(s) of selling
(iv)   opening hours, delivery times, etc
(v)   credit terms
(vi)   advertising and promotion
(vii)   variety of goods and/or services on offer
(viii) Appearance and/or attitude of company's property and/or employees
(ix)   Capability of employees.

(c) Other considerations

(i)   weather, seasonality, cyclicality
(ii)   changes in the economy – recession, depression, boom.

- Since many of these factors relate to the attitudes and opinions of the potential customers, it is likely that answers to these questions will only be found through interviews with customers. It is also important to note that many factors that affect buying are not easily researched and are even less easy to act upon. For example, the amount of light in a shop or the position of a product on the shelves can influence buying decisions.

  You could perhaps best use the above list to rate what potential customers see as your strengths and weaknesses. Then see if you can use that information to make your offering more appealing to them.

- As well as knowing something of the characteristics of the likely buyers of your product or service, you also need to know how many of them there are, and whether their ranks are swelling or contracting. Overall market size, history and forecasts are important market research data that you need to assemble – particularly data that refer to your chosen market segments, rather than just to the market as a whole.

CASE STUDY
Victoria's Secret

Roy Raymond, an alumnus of Tufts University, took his MBA at Stanford Graduate School of Business. He opened his first Victoria's Secret store in 1977 at the Stanford Shopping Centre with an $80,000 loan, half provided by a bank and the remainder borrowed $40,000 from relatives. It was an immediate success, exceeding $500,000 sales in its first trading year. The first UK store opened in August 2012 in London's New Bond Street.

Victoria's Secret is the number one intimate apparel brand in the USA, with around 1,600 shops worldwide, one of the most visited websites dating back to 1998 and over 400 million copies of their catalogue are distributed annually. The company rode out the post-2008 downturn with relative ease. In 2014 in less-than-great economic conditions sales at Victoria's Secret Stores and Victoria's Secret Beauty and Victoria's Secret Direct grew 10 per cent and 3 per cent respectively. Gross profit climbed 5 per cent to $945.3 million, gross margin pushed up 270 basis points to 39.4 per cent. Operating income nudged up 1 per cent to $308.9 million and the operating margin moved up to a healthy 12.9 per cent, a near best for the sector. Times have proved rather tougher in 2017 with like-for-like sales dipping from the previous year. However they are still the star turn in their parent company, L Brands, Inc., who reported $951.4 million turnover for the five weeks ended 1 April 2017.

So what's the secret of Victoria's success? The business was founded, so the story goes, out of Raymond's embarrassment at trying to buy lingerie for his wife in the less-than-comfortable environment of a public shopping floor in a department store. Without men, Raymond reckoned, the lingerie business was missing out on half its potential customer base. Men were in fact a major untapped market segment. Men, he reckoned, would be more comfortable if the decor of the stores were along the lines of a Victorian drawing room, complete with Oriental rugs and antique armoires housing lingerie displays. The business's name was inspired by the period of the home that Roy and his wife Gaye were living in at the time. Friendly and inviting staff went out of their way to make purchasing lingerie a unembarrassing, (almost) normal event.

In 1982 Raymond sold the Victoria's Secret company together with its six stores and 42-page catalogue, grossing $6 million per year, to Leslie Wexner, founder of The Limited, for $4 million. Wexner who had taken Limited Brands public in 1977, listed as LTD on the NYSE, was on an acquisition spree. He went on to buy Lane Bryant stores, then in 1985, a single Henri Bendel store was purchased for $10 million, 798 Lerner stores for $297 million and finally in 1988, 25 Abercrombie & Fitch stores were added to the portfolio for $46 million. This represented the high water mark for Wexner, who sold out to the venture capital firm Sun Capital Partners Inc. in stages, completing his exit in 2010.

Victoria's Secret was founded on a simple demographic market segmentation criteria: the sex of the buyer, not the user. The company today still segments its market demographically, but in much greater detail. They know the age, gender, income and social class of their target market in every area in which they operate and deliver specific messages, refining their strategy along the way.

A case study on the company, prepared by Theodore Durbin, an MBA Fellow at the Centre for Digital Strategies at the Tuck School of Business at Dartmouth under the supervision of Adjunct Professor Kathleen L Biro, reviewed how Victoria's Secret went about gathering data to help it segment markets. They developed, Durbin noted, 'a sophisticated algorithm called Recency, Frequency, and Monetary Value (RFM), based on the theory that recent shoppers were more responsive to catalogue mailings, as were more frequent shoppers and those with higher recent order sizes. The RFM algorithm used each customer's transaction history to determine which customers should receive the largest number of mailings based on their calculated propensity to buy as evidenced by their scores across each of those variables.'

Durbin's study noted that the company went well beyond RFM, adopting sophisticated mathematical modelling to segment prospects and current customers. There were, Durbin observed,

> models for customer acquisition, retention and extension. Each segment had different profiles and costs, and it was a difficult balancing act to set priorities by segment. For example, although it cost $20 to acquire a new customer and only $10 to reactivate a previous customer, attracting 'new to file' customers was important for the long-term health of the business, despite the increased costs, as customers in any direct business were always 'rolling off the file'. In addition, 10 per cent of the customer file generated 50 per cent of the business, so it was also important to cultivate heavy buyers.

WORKSHEET FOR ASSIGNMENT 4: RESEARCHING CUSTOMERS

1 What is the geographic scope of the market you intend to serve and why have you so chosen?

2 What customer needs will your product or service satisfy?

3 List and describe the main different types of customer for your product/service.

4 Which of these market segments will you concentrate on and why?

5 Match the features of your product/service to the benefits on offer to customers in each of your chosen market segments. Provide proof, where possible.

6 Who are the innovators in each of your market segments?

7 What factors are important in the customer's decision to buy or not to buy your product/service?

8 Is the market you are aiming at currently rising or falling? What is the trend over the past few years?

9 What share of this market are you aiming for initially?

Suggested further reading

Barrow, C (2016) *The 30 Day MBA in Marketing*, Kogan Page, London

Harrison, M, Cupman, J, Truman, O and Hague, P N (2016) *Market Research in Practice*, Kogan Page, London

Market Research Society (2016), *The Market Research and Insight Yearbook*, Kogan Page, London

Reference

Forrester (nd) Consumer Technographics, go.forrester.com/analytics/consumer-data/ (archived at https://perma.cc/T5PP-GD4Q).

ASSIGNMENT 5

Researching competitors

Researching the competition is often a time-consuming and frustrating job, but there are important lessons to be learnt from it. Some of the information that would be of most value to you will not be available. Particularly hard to find is information relating to the size and profitability of your competitors. Businesses, and particularly smaller businesses, are very secretive about their finances. Because of this, you may have to make estimates of the size and profitability of various firms.

Research on competitors

When you begin your research, it is crucial that you make an accurate determination of your competitors. Remember, just because someone sells a similar product or service, that does not necessarily make him or her a competitor. Perhaps he or she makes the same product but sells it in an entirely different market. (By different market, we mean that it could be sold in a different geographical market, or to a different demographic market, etc.) Conversely, just because someone sells a product or service that is different from yours does not mean that he or she is *not* a competitor. Completely dissimilar products are often substitutable for each other.

Once you have identified your competitors, you need to classify them further as to 'primary', 'secondary', 'potential', etc. There are two reasons for doing this. First, you need to limit the number of firms that you will do your research on to a workable number. If you try to research 25 firms in depth, you won't have time to do anything else. If you end up with more than 10 or 12 primary competitors, you should probably do your research on only a sample. Second, you may want to classify competitors into primary and secondary because your marketing strategy may be different for each group.

As mentioned previously, finding out the size and profitability of your competitors may be difficult. You may be able to get some valuable information from the annual accounts that each company has to file at Companies House. However, you should be aware that these are often not filed when required, or they may be incomplete, or contain information of no value.

A second source of information is local business directories, such as *Keynote* and *Kelly's*. In addition to other types of information, these books list the category in which a particular company's sales volume falls. For instance, while they will not tell you the company's exact sales volume, they may tell you whether the company does less than £/$/€500,000–£/$/€1,000,000, etc.

Another way to find out size and profitability totals is to read the publications that cover the business scene. The financial section of your newspaper and trade magazine often contains stories that can be used for research.

If you have been unable to get the necessary information from published sources, try doing some primary research. Contact the company directly and ask them your questions. Usually you will not get the information that you want, but occasionally this approach does work. Next, contact the firm's suppliers, or other individuals who are in a position to know or estimate the information. Sometimes you can get a ballpark figure, if not an exact one, from a wholesaler or other supplier.

Finally, you may be able to make a reasonable estimate from the bits and pieces of information that you were able to collect. This is commonly done with the use of operating ratios. To illustrate, let us assume that you are researching a large restaurant. You are unable to find out its annual sales volume but after striking up a conversation with one of the employees you find out that the restaurant employs 40 full-time people. Because of your knowledge of the restaurant industry, you feel confident in estimating the restaurant's payroll at £/$/€240,000 a year. From a book that lists operating ratios for the restaurant industry (published by the trade association) you find that payroll expenses, as a percentage of sales, average 40 per cent. With these facts you are able to estimate the annual sales volume of the restaurant at £/$/€600,000.

Several points should be noted here. First, operating ratios are published by a variety of trade associations and businesses. For most types of business they are not that difficult to obtain. Second, this approach is not limited to employment ratios. You can make estimates based upon inventory levels, rent or other expenses. Third, learning to use this technique is not difficult. Once you understand the use and logic of ratio analysis, you should be able to make estimates like the above. These estimates are derived by doing the ratio analysis in reverse. Instead of taking figures and working out the ratio, you start with the ratio and work out the figures. Fourth, the use of estimates resulting from this technique should be only a last resort, or used in conjunction with estimates derived in some other way. The reason for this is not that the ratio you found in the books may be 'average' but that the particular business may, for a variety of reasons, be far from average. (See Assignment 23, 'Financial controls', for a description of the key operating and financial ratios.)

Analysing the competition

The following are some of the areas that you should cover in this section of your business plan.

Description of competitors

Identify those businesses that are or will be competing with you. If the number is few, list them by name. If there are many, then describe the group without naming them individually ('47 charter fishing boat operators'). List any expected or potential competitors.

CASE STUDY
Catalant

Rob Biederman, Peter Maglathlin and Patrick Petitti co-founded Hourly Nerds (rebranded as Catalant in 2016), a uniquely different business consulting proposition, in 2013 while finishing off their MBA programme at the Harvard Business School.

Researching their competitors, the three founders identified two important factors. Consultancy clients were buying an invisible end product whose effectiveness was rarely measured and little if any of the actual consulting work was being done by the consultant who sold the service in; that was being done by freshly minted MBAs like themselves. But there was plenty of demand. The limiting factor in demand from top consultancy practices such as Bain, McKinsey and the Boston Consulting Group is the exorbitant fee structure. Only the biggest organizations with the most serious of issues to address are willing and able to fork out for advice from serious consulting firms. Catalant, set up by three Harvard MBAs, aims to disrupt this market place and change the price–demand curve radically. Essentially Catalant runs a 'marriage bureau' matching up MBA students from the top 20 business schools with small business in need of some consulting. Quality is assured as these 'consultants' have all been in effect vetted by the universities through their rigorous admissions standards.

The average pay has been $35 an hour for projects requiring 10 to 15 hours of work. They now claim to have '25,000 of the world's smartest business experts' on their books. Catalant holds the client's money, only paying the student when the project is completed to the small business person's satisfaction.

Their projects include a small Spanish manufacturer whose objective is to enter the US market and who needs pricing information and primary research for construction bricks, glazed bricks, clinker bricks and facing bricks. They are paying $2,500 for this work. A small private equity firm has budgeted $5,000 to fully research and collect data in order to write a business plan. An online ecommerce portal for attracting digital content from elite contributors and selling the same to elite niche target audience has set $20,000 aside for this project.

The company has raised $750,000 in a first round of seed capital finance, over half from a business owner who is on record as saying that getting an MBA is 'an absolute waste of time'.

Size of competitors

Determine the assets and sales volume of the major competitors. Will you be competing against firms whose size is similar to yours or will you be competing against giant corporations? If assets and sales volume cannot be determined, try to find other indications of size, such as number of employees, number of branches, etc.

Profitability of competitors

Try to determine how profitable the business is for those companies already in the field. Which firms are making money? Losing money? How much?

Operating methods

For each of the major competitors, try to determine the relevant operating methods. For example, what pricing strategy does each firm use? Other issues, besides price, that you may consider are:

- quality of product and/or service;
- hours of operation;

- ability of personnel;
- servicing, warranties and packaging;
- methods of selling: distribution channels;
- credit terms: volume discounts;
- location: advertising and promotion;
- reputation of company and/or principals;
- inventory levels.

Many of the above items will not be relevant to all businesses. Location will not be relevant, perhaps, to a telephone-answering service. On the other hand, there are many items that are not listed above that may be very relevant to your business. In the motor trade, trade-in value and styling may be as relevant as the price. So it is very important for you to determine the relevant characteristics on which you will do your research.

Summary of analysis of competitors

After you have completed your research it is useful to summarize your findings in tabular form, such as shown in Table 5.1. Keep in mind that the characteristics listed are for illustration only. You must decide the relevant characteristics that will go into your own table.

When the table is complete, analyse the information contained in it to reach your conclusions. Is there a correlation between the methods of operation and other characteristics, and the size and/or profitability of the competitors? A thoughtful analysis is essential because there may be many patterns shown. For instance, you may find that all the profitable companies are large, and all the unprofitable companies are small. That would be an easy pattern to spot (and an important one, as well) because it involves only two factors, profitability and size. However, it is more common that success and failure correlate with a number of factors that are not always so easy to discern, even when your findings are summarized on one page.

Looking for patterns is not the only type of analysis that is needed. You may find that a company is very successful, even though its characteristics are completely different from those of the other profitable firms. What factors apparently contribute to its success? Or you may find that a company is failing despite the fact that its operational characteristics are similar to those of the profitable firms. Can you identify the reason?

Once you have reached conclusions about the competition, relate them to your business. What is the competitive situation in the market? Is everyone making money and expanding, or is it a dog-eat-dog situation? Are your competitors likely to be much larger than you? If so, what effect will this have? Are there some operating methods that appear critical to success in this market? If so, will you be able to operate in the necessary fashion? Are there operating methods or characteristics not being widely used in the market which you think have merit? If so, why are they not found at present? Is it because they have been overlooked, or because they have problems that you have not foreseen?

The above are some of the questions you will want to address. You will probably have many others. The important thing, though, is for you to decide the general outlook for your business. At this point in your research, does it appear that you will be able to compete successfully in this market? Do you now feel that you know what it will take in order to compete successfully? If you can answer these two questions to your satisfaction, you have probably done an adequate job of research, like the Brighton Furniture Co Ltd researcher looking into bulk furniture sales, whose results are shown in the example below.

EXAMPLE
Brighton Furniture Co Ltd

Despite the fact that there are over 100 furniture dealers in Brighton, the bulk of the new flats and town house developments get their furniture packages from only six firms. In my market research I found that from 80 to 99 per cent (depending on who you talk to) of the 'packages' were sold by those six firms. The firms are identified by name in Table 5.1.

Product characteristics

To get information on the products sold by each of the firms, I talked to eight developers who had selected one or more of the six firms to provide a furniture package for their units; I also talked to 23 individuals who had purchased a package for their premises from one of the six firms. In general, the purchasers felt that their furniture was performing about as they had expected. The one exception was that buyers of the Apartment Furniture Co products all felt that the quality was not as good as they had been led to believe.

TABLE 5.1 Example showing company characteristics

Competitors' names	Sales (£)	Profits (£)	Year started	Credit terms	Salespeople/Reps	Manufacturer
Condo Supplies Co	750,000	125,000	1993	50% deposit	Salespeople	No
Georgian Furniture	300,000	60,000	1997	50% deposit	Salespeople	No
AAA Furniture Inc	1,250,000	75,000	2000	COD	Salespeople	Yes
Rattan Imports Inc	500,000	125,000	1999	COD	Salespeople	No
Bamboo Things Ltd	600,000	150,000	1998	50% deposit	Salespeople	No
Apartment Furniture Co	400,000	10,000	1999	COD	Salespeople	Yes

A summary of other characteristics for each company is presented in Table 5.1. Based upon these findings, I have divided the six into three groups, and labelled them as follows:

- *High quality, high price.* The only firm in this category is Rattan Imports, which sells only rattan furniture. As one would expect, its sales are to the more expensive developments.

- *Moderate price, high quality.* Again, only one firm, Georgian Furniture, is in this category. The bulk of its sales were made in developments where one-bedroom units cost from £75,000 to £100,000, although it did get the contract for one more expensive building.

- *Low price, varying quality.* Four of the six firms appear to be competing in the lower end of the package-deal market. Three of the four sell 'casual' furniture, and the fourth sells bamboo furniture. Overall, there is not much difference in warranty and delivery service, but there is some variation in price (from a low of £4,200 to a high of £5,100) and upkeep (Apartment Furniture Co and Bamboo Things Ltd products appear to require less maintenance than the other two). There is, however, a wide disparity between the firms in trade-in value.

  Bamboo Things furniture holds its value much better than the other firms' products, being almost 2.5 times better than the products of AAA and Apartment Furniture.

Company characteristics

By talking to four of the six firms (the other two refused) and by researching various published sources, I was able to prepare Table 5.1. Some characteristics that bear mentioning are:

- All six firms use in-house salespeople rather than manufacturers' representatives.

- There does not seem to be any particular correlation between performance and the number of years in business.

- Although the sales of the two firms that concentrate on the higher-price furniture are relatively small, their profits as a percentage of sales are very high.

- The two firms that manufacture their own furniture have the lowest profits as a percentage of sales.

Analysis of competition

Based upon the data gathered, the following analysis of the competition seems reasonable:

- The high-price, high-quality segment of market seems the most profitable. There is only one competitor; the firm has been in existence only a few years and sales are already over £500,000 a year; profit/sales is running at 25 per cent; and the firm is not quite as aggressive as it could be since it requires full payment on delivery.

- The moderate-price, high-quality segment of the market also seems to have good potential since there is only one firm presently in the market. On the negative side, this firm has been operating a year longer than Rattan Imports and seems to be more aggressive than Rattan (as shown by its lower profit/sales ratio and its more liberal credit policy), yet its total sales ratio may be low because of some inefficiencies on the company's part.

- The lower-price segment of the market seems to be very competitive. Of particular concern is the fact that two of the firms manufacture their own furniture. AAA Furniture is the leader in terms of both price and sales, and yet its profits and those of the other manufacturer, Apartment Furniture, seem very low.

   It seems likely that both these companies are willing to accept low profits because they are making the bulk of their money from manufacturing. This fact is important because it means that they could even afford to sell at a cheaper price and make money, whereas I have to make a profit on the retail sales.

   The fact that Condo Supplies is able to remain profitable in the face of this competition is due to the company's years in business, and the reputation for quality and service that it has cultivated with the big developers. A new firm, such as mine, would be at the mercy of the manufacturers since I do not have the reputation of Condo Supplies, nor a unique product such as Bamboo Things Ltd.

Based on this, I conclude that I have neither the unique line nor the reputation to compete successfully in the lower-priced end of the market. However, I feel that I can upgrade sufficiently to enter the moderate-price, high-quality or the high-price, high-quality segment. Of the two, the high-price segment seems most likely since Rattan Imports is not as aggressive as Georgian Furniture; also, the high-price segment seems to be larger and faster growing than the moderate-price segment.

The purpose of your competitive analysis is twofold:

- to determine where your competitor is weak and how he or she might retaliate to your activity;
- to help you define what should be your product's point of difference, based on your understanding of the key factors for success in your industry sector.

Deciding on advantage

The outcome of your research into customers and competitors is a clear idea of the market niche you are going to sell into first, and what will be different or better about your product or service. For a business planning to offer a local gardening service, the outcome of its research should allow it to make the following kind of analysis.

We have two local competitors:

- Thompson's with six employees has been around for 10 years and has a small number of larger domestic clients but mostly does work for schools and business premises. It charges £20 an hour, for a minimum of 4 hours a week, and doesn't take away garden refuse from homes. It covers the whole county.
- Brown is a one-man band that has been operating for three years but he offers a limited service – he doesn't do hedge trimming, tree pruning or take away garden refuse, and charges out at £12 an hour, with no minimum. He claims to cover a radius of 20 miles, but doesn't seem to want to go more than 5 miles.

My initial strategy will be to concentrate on larger domestic clients within 5 miles who need hedges trimmed and trees pruned and would appreciate having their garden refuse removed for them. I will set out to make these clients feel important in a way that Thompson's does not, as they appear to only take on domestic customers as a 'favour'. I will charge out at £15 an hour with a minimum of 2 hours a week per client, and will target a limited number of quality areas with high-value houses. My goal will be to get at least two clients in an area, and stick to areas that are easily accessible from my home.

The easiest way to find out what your competitors are doing right or wrong is to try them out. Even if you don't actually buy or even need what they sell, there is nothing in the rules that says you can't enquire. Suppose for example you intend to set up a bookkeeping service. First search out local small businesses, using if necessary one of the sources described above. Then 'enquire' about their services with a list of questions, some of which you may find answers to in their leaflet or on their website.

WORKSHEET FOR ASSIGNMENT 5: RESEARCHING COMPETITORS

1 List and briefly describe the businesses with which you will be competing directly.

2 Analyse their size, profitability and operating methods, as far as you can.

3 What are their relative strengths and weaknesses compared both with each other and with your business?

4 What, in the light of this competitive analysis, do you believe to be the critical factors for success in your business sector?

5 What is unique about your proposition that makes it stand out from the competition?

Suggested further reading

Brace, I (2018) *Questionnaire Design: How to plan, structure and write survey material for effective market research*, 4th edn, Kogan Page, London

Hague, P, Hague, N and Morgan, C-A (2013) *Market Research in Practice*, Kogan Page, London

Morley, M (2014) *Understanding Markets and Strategy*, Kogan Page, London

ASSIGNMENT 6

A plan for market research

It is unlikely that you will already have the answers to all the important questions concerning your marketplace. The purpose of the market research element of the workbook is to ensure you have sufficient information on customers, competitors and markets so that your market entry or expansion strategy is at least on the target, if not the bullseye itself. In other words, enough people want to buy what you want to sell at a price that will give you a viable business. If you miss the target completely, you may not have the resources for a second shot.

One of the sad aspects of new business starts is that often the one-in-three failure rate for businesses in the first three years of life involves someone investing a lump-sum payment received from a previous redundancy, through taking early retirement or from an inheritance. It is one of the paradoxes of small businesses that whereas you cannot start without investing some time and money, it may be safer to have more time than money. Those with their own money frequently have less pressure from banks or financial investors to research their ideas thoroughly first, simply because they do not have to go to see the bank manager in the early stages to obtain support before starting. Those with time but inadequate resources always have to seek advice before starting, and inevitably this will include researching the market as widely as possible before commencing. You do not have to open a shop to prove there are no customers for your goods or services; frequently some modest DIY market research beforehand can give clear guidance as to whether your venture will succeed or not.

The purpose of practical DIY market research for entrepreneurs investigating or seeking to start a new business is, therefore, twofold:

- To build *credibility* for the business idea; the entrepreneur must demonstrate first to his or her own satisfaction, and later to outside financiers, a thorough understanding of the marketplace for the new product or service. This will be vital if resources are to be attracted to build the new venture.

- To develop a *realistic* market entry strategy for the new business, based on a clear understanding of genuine customer needs and ensuring that product quality, price, promotional methods and the distribution chain are mutually supportive and clearly focused on target customers.

Otherwise, 'fools rush in, where angels fear to tread'; or, as they say in the army, 'time spent in reconnaissance is rarely time wasted'. The same is certainly true in starting a business, where you will need to research in particular:

- *Your customers*: who will buy your goods and services? What particular customer needs will your business meet? How many of them are there?
- *Your competitors*: which established companies are already meeting the needs of your potential customers? What are their strengths and weaknesses?
- *Your product or service*: how should it be tailored to meet customer needs?
- *What price* should you charge to be perceived as giving value for money?
- *What promotional material* is needed to reach customers; which newspapers, journals do they read and which websites and blogs are they likely to visit?
- *Where should you locate* to reach your customers most easily, at minimum cost?

Research, above all else, is not just essential in starting a business, but once it is launched, must become an integral part in the ongoing life of the company. Customers and competitors change; products have life cycles. Once started, however, ongoing market research becomes easier, as you will have existing customers (and staff) to question. It is important that you monitor regularly their views on your business (as the sign in a barber shop stated: 'We need your head to run our business') and develop simple techniques for this purpose (eg touch screens, questionnaires for customers beside the till, suggestion boxes with rewards for employees).

The seven steps to effective market research

Researching the market need not be a complex process, nor need it be very expensive. The amount of effort and expenditure needs to be related in some way to the costs and risks associated with the business. If all that is involved with your business is simply getting a handful of customers for products and services that cost little to put together, then you may spend less effort on market research than you would for, say, launching a completely new product or service into an unproven market that requires a large sum of money to be spent up front.

However much or little market research you plan to carry out, the process needs to be conducted systematically. These are the seven stages you need to go through to make sure you have properly sized up your business sector.

Step 1: Formulate the problem

Before embarking on your market research you should first set clear and precise objectives, rather than just setting out to find interesting general information about the market. The starting point for a business idea may be to sell clothes, but that is too large and diverse a market to get a handle on. So, that market needs to be divided into, say, clothes for men, women and children, then further divided into clothes for working, leisure, sport and social occasions. This process is known as segmenting the market.

So, for example, if you are planning to open a shop selling to young fashion-conscious women, among others, your research objective could be: to find out how many women aged 18 to 28, with an income of over £25,000 a year, live or work within two miles of your chosen shop position. That would give you some idea whether the market could support a venture such as this.

Step 2: Determine the information needs

Knowing the size of the market, in the example given above, may require several different pieces of information. For example, you would need to know the size of the resident population, which might be fairly easy to find out, but you might also want to know something about people who come into the catchment area to work, for leisure purposes, on holiday or for any other major purpose. There might, for example, be a hospital, library, railway station or school nearby that also pulls potential customers to that particular area.

Step 3: Where you can get the information

This will involve either desk research in libraries or on the internet, or field research, which you can do yourself or get help in doing. Some of the most important of these areas were covered earlier in this chapter.

Field research – that is, getting out and asking questions yourself – is the most fruitful way of gathering information for a home-based business.

Step 4: Decide the budget

Market research will not be free even if you do it yourself. At the very least there will be your time. There may well be the cost of journals, phone calls, letters and field visits to plan for. At the top of the scale could be the costs of employing a professional market research firm.

Starting at this end of the scale, a business-to-business survey comprising 200 interviews with executives responsible for office equipment purchasing decisions cost one company £/$/€12,000. Twenty in-depth interviews with consumers who are regular users of certain banking services cost £/$/€8,000. Using the internet for web surveys is another possibility, but that can impose too much of your agenda onto the recipients and turn them away from you.

Check out companies such as Free Online Surveys and Zoomerang which provide software that lets you carry out online surveys and analyse the data quickly. Many such organizations offer free trials.

Whatever the cost of research, you need to assess its value to you when you are setting your budget. If getting it wrong would cost £/$/€100,000, then £/$/€5,000 spent on market research might be a good investment.

Step 5: Select the research technique

If you cannot find the data you require from desk research, you will need to go out and find the data yourself. The options for such research are described in the next section, under 'Field research'.

Step 6: Construct the research sample population

It is rarely possible or even desirable to include every possible customer or competitor in your research. So you have to decide how big a sample you need to give you a reliable indication how the whole population will behave.

Step 7: Process and analyse the data

The raw market research data needs to be analysed and turned into information to guide your decisions on price, promotion and location, and the shape, design and scope of the product or service itself.

First steps

There are two main types of research in starting a business:

- *Secondary, or desk research*, or the study of published information;
- *Primary, or field research*, involving fieldwork in collecting specific information for the market.

Both activities are vital for the starter business.

Desk research

There is increasingly a great deal of secondary data available in published form, and accessible either online or via business sections of public libraries throughout the United Kingdom to enable new home-business starters to quantify the size of market sectors they are entering and to determine trends in those markets.

USING THE INTERNET

The internet is a rich source of market data, much of it free and immediately available. But you can't always be certain that the information is reliable or free of bias, as it can be difficult if not impossible to always work out who exactly is providing it. That being said, you can get some valuable pointers to whether or not what you plan to sell has a market, how big that market is and who else trades in that space. The following sources should be your starting point:

- Blogs are sites where people, informed and ignorant, converse about a particular topic. The information on blogs is more straw in the wind than fact.

- Google Scholar provides a simple way to search for serious academic literature and research. It shows where you can get access to the literature and often to a free source.

- Google News has links to any newspaper article anywhere in the world covering a particular topic. Asking for information on baby clothes will reveal recent articles on how much the average family spends on baby clothes, the launch of a thrift store specializing in secondhand baby clothes and the launch of an organic baby clothes catalogue.

- Google Trends provides a snapshot on what the world is most interested in at any one moment. For example if you are thinking of starting a bookkeeping service, entering that into the search pane produces a snazzy graph showing how interest measured by the number of searches is growing (or contracting) since January 2004 when Google stared collecting the data.

- Trade Association Forum provides a directory of trade associations on whose websites are links to industry-relevant online research sources. For example you will find the Baby Products Association listed, at whose website you can find details of the 238 companies operating in the sector with their contact details.

Field research

If you are contemplating opening a classical music shop in Exeter focused on the young, while desk research might reveal that out of a total population of 250,000 there are 25 per cent of under-30-year-olds, it will not state what percentage are interested in classical music or how much they might spend on classical CDs. Field research (questionnaires in the street) provided the answer of 1 per cent and £2 a week spend, suggesting a potential market of only £65,000 a year (250,000 × 25 per cent × 1 per cent × £2 × 52). The entrepreneurs decided to investigate Birmingham and London instead! But at least the cost had only been two damp afternoons spent in Exeter, rather than the horrors of having to dispose of the lease of an unsuccessful shop.

Fieldwork is big business in the United Kingdom, where market research companies pull in around £1 billion a year from survey work. Most fieldwork carried out consists of interviews, with the interviewer putting questions to a respondent. We are all becoming accustomed to it, whether being interviewed while travelling on a train, or resisting the attempts of enthusiastic salespeople posing as market researchers on doorsteps ('sugging', as this is known, is illegal, though you might be forgiven for believing otherwise). The more popular forms of interview are currently:

- personal (face-to-face) interview: 55 per cent (especially for the consumer markets);

- telephone and email: 32 per cent (especially for surveying companies);

- post: 6 per cent (especially for industrial markets);

- test and discussion group: 7 per cent.

Personal interviews and postal surveys are clearly less expensive than getting together panels of interested parties or using expensive telephone time. Telephone interviewing requires a very positive attitude, courtesy and an ability to not talk too quickly and listen while sticking to a rigid questionnaire. Low response rates on postal services (less than 10 per cent is normal) can be improved by including accompanying letters explaining the questionnaire's purpose and why respondents should reply, by offering rewards for completed questionnaires (a small gift), by sending reminder letters and, of course, by providing prepaid reply envelopes. Personally addressed email questionnaires have secured higher response rates – as high as 10–15 per cent – as recipients have a greater tendency to read and respond to email received in their private email boxes. However, unsolicited emails ('spam') can cause vehement reactions. The key to success is the same as with postal surveys – the mailing should feature an explanatory letter and incentives for the recipient to 'open' the questionnaire.

All methods of approach require considered questions. In drawing up the questionnaire attention must be paid first to these issues:

- Define your research objectives; what exactly is it that you need vitally to know (eg how often do people buy, how much)?
- Who are the customers to sample for this information (eg for DIY products, an Ideal Home Exhibition crowd might be best)?
- How are you going to undertake the research (eg face to face in the street)?

When you are sure of the above, and only then, you are ready to design the questionnaire. There are six simple rules to guide this process:

- Keep the number of questions to a minimum.
- Keep the questions simple! Answers should be either 'Yes/No/Don't know' or offer at least four alternatives.
- Avoid ambiguity – make sure the respondent really understands the question (avoid 'generally', 'usually', 'regularly').
- Seek factual answers, avoid opinions.
- Make sure at the beginning you have a cut-out question to eliminate unsuitable respondents (eg those who never use the product/service).
- At the end, make sure you have an identifying question to show the cross-section of respondents.

The introduction to a face-to-face interview is important; make sure you are prepared, either carrying an identifying card (eg student card, Association of Market Researchers watchdog card) or have a rehearsed introduction (eg 'Good morning, I'm from Manchester University [show card] and we are conducting a survey and would be grateful for your help'). You may also need visuals of the product you are investigating (samples, photographs), to ensure the respondent understands. Make sure these are neat and accessible. Finally, try out the questionnaire and your technique on your friends, prior to using them in the street. You will be surprised at how questions that seem simple to you are incomprehensible at first to respondents!

The size of the survey undertaken is also important. You frequently hear of political opinion polls taken on samples of 1,500–2,000 voters. This is because the accuracy of your survey clearly increases with the size of sample, as Table 6.1 shows.

So if on a sample size of 600, your survey showed that 40 per cent of women in the town drove cars, the true proportion would probably lie between 36 and 44 per cent. For small businesses, we usually recommend a minimum sample of 250 completed replies.

Remember above all, however, that questioning is by no means the only or most important form of fieldwork. Sir Terence Conran, when questioned on a radio programme, implied that he undertook no market research fieldwork (ie formal interviews) at all. Later in the programme he confessed, nonetheless, to spending nearly 'half of his time visiting competitors, inspecting new and rival products, etc'. Visiting exhibitions and buying and examining competitors' products (as the Japanese have so

TABLE 6.1

Size of random sample	95 per cent of surveys are right within … percentage points
250	6.2
500	4.4
750	3.6
1,000	3.1
2,000	2.2
6,000	1.2

painfully done, in disassembling piece-by-piece competitor cars, deciding in the process where cost-effective improvements could be made) are clearly important fieldwork processes. Ian Brace's 2018 book on questionnaire design covers this subject comprehensively (see Suggested further reading).

Interpreting data using statistics can be difficult for the uninitiated. The Index of key organizations and resources for business planning at the end of the book has help with statistics.

TESTING THE MARKET

The ultimate form of market research is to find some real customers to buy and use your product or service before you spend too much time and money in setting up. The ideal way to do this is to sell into a limited area or small section of your market. In that way if things don't quite work out as you expect you won't have upset too many people.

This may involve buying in as small a quantity of the product as you need to fulfil the order so that you can fully test your ideas. Once you have found a small number of people who are happy with your product, price, delivery/execution and have paid up, then you can proceed with a bit more confidence than if all your ideas are just on paper.

Pick potential customers whose demand is likely to be small and easy to meet. For example if you are going to run a bookkeeping business, select 5 to 10 small businesses from an area reasonably close to home and make your pitch. The same approach would work with a gardening, babysitting or any other service-related venture. It is a little more difficult with products, but you could buy a small quantity of similar items in from a competitor or make up a trial batch yourself.

Selling from stalls on a Saturday, or taking part in an exhibition, gives an opportunity to question interested customers and can be the most valuable fieldwork of all. All methods are equally valid, and the results of each should be carefully recorded for subsequent use in presentation and business plans.

Once the primary market research (desk and field research) and market testing (stalls and exhibitions) are complete, pilot testing of the business should be undertaken in one location or customer segment, prior to setting targets and subsequently measuring the impact of a full regional launch.

Doing online questionnaires

Get online user feedback

To get the best out of an online presence you should use your site to learn more about your customers; this will help you to tailor your offerings to their needs. You need to get information about your customers and store it in a way that allows you to use it when they visit your site again. Below are some of the ways in which you can get this user feedback.

COOKIES

These are small files deposited on the hard disk of anyone visiting your site. If you have cookies set up on your site, your server will be able to read visitors' cookie files on their hard drives. The information contained in them can be related back to any information on your customer database. A cookie might contain a customer's name, the type of computer they use, their password for accessing your site and any other routine information that would otherwise have to be re-entered every time they returned to your site.

EXECUTABLE PROGRAMS

Inviting customers to install an 'executable program' is another means of getting online feedback. This will allow you to get a lot more information about the user, but is seen as intrusive by most people. In all probability, fewer than one in five users will let you install such a program, but in some circumstances it may work well.

PERSONALIZATION

You could go a stage further and offer an intelligent internet tool such as My Web, which reacts to customers' shopping habits and suggests different sites related to subjects or products in which they are interested. You can then monitor customers' reactions to these suggestions and use the information to refine your own offerings in a highly sophisticated manner.

QUESTIONNAIRES

Web questionnaires can help by getting very detailed user feedback. They are similar to paper-based questionnaires, but with a few major advantages. As there are no paper or postage costs, you can 'mail' as many users as you like as often as you like. Questionnaire distribution and feedback can be very quick. Also, rudimentary analysis of feedback can be done automatically by inserting links between the questionnaire and some spreadsheets.

EXAMPLE
Julian Talbot-Brady

Julian Talbot-Brady, Cranfield MBA and qualified architect, investigated launching 'EU-architect.com', an internet-based start-up company targeted at the United Kingdom's 30,000 registered architects. The aim was to provide a 'one-stop', all-in-one service to meet the needs of busy architects by providing easily accessible online sources for all their information needs. He designed a questionnaire to be emailed directly to the top 100 architectural practices in the UK, as well as to the leading 500 construction product suppliers. He chose to use Zoomerang.com, which at the time provided a free 30-day trial. Despite an accompanying letter (offering possible equity sharing), the resulting response rate of only 12 per cent made him realize that the potential for his service was much smaller than he had anticipated, leading him to accept a post with an industry supplier to develop a similar site for its own products.

Remember, if you are storing personal data about your customers on your site, they have a right to know what is going to happen to those data. In Europe and elsewhere, there are laws on data protection with which you will have to comply.

Understanding the data

The most common way statistics are considered is around a single figure that claims in some way to be representative of a population at large. This is usually referred to as an average. There are three principal ways of measuring an average and these are the most often confused and frequently misrepresented set of numbers in any business plan.

To analyse any information gathered from market research you first need a 'data set' such as that in the table below.

THE MEAN (OR AVERAGE)

This is the most common measure to express information and is used as a rough and ready check for many types of data. In the example above, adding up the prices: 105 and dividing by the number of competitors: 5, you arrive at a mean, or average, selling price of 21.

TABLE 6.2   Competitor selling prices

Competitors	Selling price £/$/€
1	30
2	40
3	10
4	15
5	10

THE MEDIAN

The median is the value occurring at the centre of a data set. Recasting the figures in the table above puts company 4's selling price of 15 in that position, with two higher and two lower prices. The median comes into its own in situations where the outlying values in a data set are extreme, as they are in our example, where in fact most of our competitors sell for well below 21. In this case the median would be a better measure of the central tendency. You should always use the median when the distribution is skewed. You can use either the mean or the median when the population is symmetrical as they will give very similar results.

THE MODE

The mode is the observation in a data set appearing the most; in this example it is 10. So if we were surveying a sample of customers across the whole market we would expect more of them to say they were paying 10 for their products, though as we know the average price is 21.

RANGE

As well as measuring how values cluster around a central value, to make full use of the data set we need to establish how much those values could vary. The range helps here and is calculated as the maximum figure minus the minimum figure. In the example being used here, that is: 40 – 10 = 30. This figure gives us an idea of how dispersed the data is and so how meaningful the average figure alone might be.

WORKSHEET FOR ASSIGNMENT 6: A PLAN FOR MARKET RESEARCH

1 What information do you currently have on customers, competitors, markets, etc?

2 What information do you still need to find, and why specifically do you need it?

3 What desk research will you have to carry out to answer this question?

4 What field research will you have to carry out?

5 How much time and money will be needed to carry out this market research?

6 Who will be responsible for each element of the research?

7 When will all the key market research information be available?

Suggested further reading

Brace, I (2018) *Questionnaire Design: How to plan, structure and write survey material for effective market research*, 4th edn, Kogan Page, London

Higham, W (2009) *The Next Big Thing: Spotting and forecasting consumer trends*, Kogan Page, London

Kaden, R (2007) *Guerrilla Marketing Research*, Kogan Page, London

Lawes, R (2020) *Using Semiotics in Marketing: How to achieve consumer insight for brand growth and profits*, Kogan Page, London

Marsh, S (2018) *User research: A practical guide to designing better products and services*, Kogan Page, London

Struhl, S (2017) *Artificial Intelligence Marketing and Predicting Consumer Choice*, Kogan Page, London

Competitive marketing strategies

Introduction

Marketing is defined as the process that ensures the right products and services get to the right markets at the right time, and at the right price. The challenge in that sentence lies in the use of the word 'right'. The deal has to work for the customer, because if they don't want what you have to offer the game is over before you begin. You have to offer value and satisfaction, otherwise people will either choose an apparently superior competitor or, if they do buy from you and are dissatisfied, they won't buy again. With online review websites such as Trustpilot and TripAdvisor there is now no hiding place for shoddy trading practices. Worse still, they may bad-mouth you to a lot of other people. For you the marketer, being right means that there have to be enough people wanting your product or service to make the venture profitable; and ideally those numbers should be getting bigger rather than smaller. So inevitably marketing is something of a voyage of discovery for both supplier and consumer, from which both parties learn something and hopefully improve.

The boundaries of marketing stretch from inside the mind of the customer, perhaps uncovering emotions they were themselves barely aware of, out to the logistic support systems that get the product or service into customer's hands. Each part of the value chain from company to consumer has the potential to add value or kill the deal. For example, at the heart of the Amazon business proposition are a superlatively efficient warehousing and delivery system and a simple zero-cost way for customers to return products they don't want and get immediate refunds. These factors are every bit as important as elements of Amazon's marketing strategy as are its product range, website structure, Google placement or its competitive pricing.

Marketing is also a circuitous activity. As you explore the topics below, you will see that you need the answers to some questions before you can move on, and indeed once you have some answers you may have to go back a step to review an earlier stage.

The marketing mix describes the tools available to win business in your chosen market. The term 'marketing mix' has a pedigree going back to the late 1940s when marketing managers referred to mixing ingredients to create strategies. The concept was formalized by E Jerome McCarthy, a marketing professor at Michigan State University, in 1960. The mix of ingredients with which marketing strategy can be developed and implemented was originally the 4 Ps – price, product (or/and service), promotion and place. That has been extended with a focus on the more subtle and less tangible elements that comprise the marketing arena. It is now generally accepted that 7 Ps have to be considered, with the final three being: the people we use to communicate and deliver our product, the process customers have to go through to get the product and the suitability of the physical environment from which a business operates.

Just as with cooking, taking the same or similar ingredients in different proportions can result in very different 'products'. A change in the way these elements are put together can produce an offering tailored to meet the needs of a specific market segment.

ASSIGNMENT 7

Products and/or services

Here you should describe what products or services you propose to market, what stage of development they are at and why they are competitive with existing sources of supply. Part of the information in this section is for the benefit of outside readers who may not be familiar with your business. It should also be useful to you since the research and analysis required will encourage you to examine your offering compared with your competitors'.

Explore these topics in this section of your business plan.

Description of products and/or services

Explain what it is you are selling. Be specific and avoid unnecessary jargon. The reader should end up with more than just a vague idea about your products and/or services. Obviously, some products and services will require much more explanation than others. If you have invented a new process for analysing blood, you will need to provide the reader with many details. On the other hand, if you are selling your services as a bookkeeper, you may need to do little more than list the services you will provide. A danger of this section is in assuming that the reader can easily understand your products without you providing sufficient detail and description.

CASE STUDY
Eat 17

Eat 17, founded by Siobhan O'Donnell with her partner Chris O'Connor, his brother Dan and their stepbrother James Brundle in Walthamstow, north-west London may look at first glance like a run of the mill convenience store, but once inside it rapidly becomes evident that the product on offer is very different. First off Chris is a trained chef and he brings the expertise that ensures their products are fresh and appealing for the whole of the working day. As well as offering independent, artisan and local produce made by small suppliers they have a bakery and pizza restaurant on site, and create their own range of ready-meals. Each week they try a score or so of new products adding those that sell to their core product range. This strategy keeps repeat customer visits high and pulls in new ones bored with the more conventional ranges on offer in neighbouring supermarkets. Their latest creation, a bacon-based condiment, which they called 'Bacon Jam', flies of the shelves, alongside more conventional products provided through their partnering arrangement with the convenience brand Spar. The jam is taking the business in a slightly different direction as it has become a product in its own right, now stocked in 3,000 outlets nationwide including Selfridges, Waitrose and Tesco. It has even expanded to a range of five different flavours.

Sales in 2016, their ninth year in business, delivered a healthy £5,724,432 in annual turnover. They have recently bought a former snooker hall on Chatsworth Road in Lower Clapton taking their investment in the Eat 17 venture to £5.5 million by April 2019. Brundle reckons their product offer is the shape of things to come. Retailers need a different product proposition that relies more on being a destination that people are excited to visit than a chore that simply has to be done to get essential groceries.

In addition to listing and describing your products and/or services, you should note any applications or uses of your products that are not readily apparent to the reader. For instance, a photocopier can also produce overhead transparencies, as well as its more mundane output. When you make your list, show the proportion of turnover you expect each product or service to contribute to the whole, as illustrated in Table 7.1.

TABLE 7.1   Example showing products/services and their applications

Product/service	Description	% of sales
		100%

Readiness for market

Are your products and/or services available for sale now? If not, what needs to be done to develop them? If you are selling a product, does it require more design work or research and development? Have you actually produced one or more completed products?

CASE STUDY
Strida bicycle

When Mark Saunders, Cranfield enterprise programme participant, put his proposal for the Strida, a revolutionary folding bicycle, before the venture capital panel, the only projections he could include with any degree of certainty were costs.

The business proposal he sought backing for was to take his brainchild from the drawing board to a properly costed production prototype. For this he needed time (about two years), living expenses for that period, the use of a workshop and a modest amount of materials.

Saunders's business plan detailed how he would develop the product over this period, and as a result the concept was backed by James Marshall, one-time manager of golfer Greg Norman. Marshall put together the manufacturing and marketing elements of the business plan, and within 18 months the Strida was in full-scale production and on sale through stores such as Harrods, Next Essentials, John Lewis and many others. Worldwide distribution covers some forty countries, alphabetically listed from Australia to Vietnam. The carbon version of the STRiDA 5.0 won the award of Taiwan Excellence in 2015.

If you are selling a service, do you presently have the skills and technical capability to provide it? If not, what needs to be done?

If additional inputs are required before your products or services are ready to be sold, state both the tasks to be done and time required, as shown in Table 7.2.

TABLE 7.2   Example showing products/services and additional inputs to be made

Product/service	State of development	Tasks to be done	Completion date

Proprietary position

Do your products or services have any special competitive advantage? If so, explain the advantages and state how long this proprietary position is likely to last. You should state any other factors that give you a competitive advantage, even though the advantage is not protected by contractual agreements of the law. Examples could include a special skill or talent not easily obtainable by others. (If you have none of these, and many businesses do not, do not just make something up!)

Getting inventions to market can be an expensive and time-consuming business, as James Dyson is only too eager to confirm. It took five years and 5,127 prototypes before the world's first bagless vacuum cleaner arrived on the scene. It's hardly surprising then that the Dyson story includes a legendary but victorious 18-month battle with Hoover, based in the UK, over patent infringement (Dyson, 2001).

If, like Dyson, you have a unique business idea, you should investigate the four categories of protection: *patenting*, which protects 'how something works'; *trademark registration*, which protects 'what something is called'; *design registration*, which protects 'how something looks'; and *copyright*, which protects 'work on paper, film and CD'. Some products may be covered by two or more categories, eg the mechanism of a clock may be patented while its appearance may be design-registered.

Each category requires a different set of procedures, offers a different level of protection and extends for a different period of time. They all have one thing in common, though: in the event of any infringement your only redress is through the courts, and going to law can be wasteful of time and money, whether you win or lose.

CASE STUDY
Facebook

When Mark Zuckerberg, then aged 20, started Facebook from his college dorm back in 2004 with two fellow students he could hardly have been aware of how the business would pan out. Facebook is a social networking website on which users have to put their real names and email addresses in order to register, then they can contact current and past friends and colleagues to swap photos, news and gossip. Within three years the company was on track to make US$100 million sales, partly on the back of a big order from Microsoft which appears to have its sights on Facebook as either a partner or an acquisition target.

Zuckerberg, wearing jeans, Adidas sandals and a fleece, looks a bit like a latter-day Steve Jobs, Apple's founder. He also shares something else in common with Jobs. He had a gigantic intellectual property legal dispute on his hands. Until it was settled in May 2011 he had to deal with a lawsuit brought by three fellow Harvard students who claimed, in effect, that he stole the Facebook concept from them. However, IP disputes continue to dog Facebook and many other internet giants. In January 2017 Zuckerberg was back in court defending a case against one of his recent acquisitions, Oculus VR, where his €2 billion bet on the virtual reality headset market was under threat from a rival games company.

Patents protect 'how something works'

A patent can be regarded as a contract between an inventor and the state. The state agrees with the inventor that if he or she is prepared to publish details of the invention in a set form and if it appears that he or she has made a real advance, the state will then grant the inventor a 'monopoly' on the invention for 20 years: 'protection in return for disclosure'. The inventor uses the monopoly period to manufacture and sell his or her innovation; competitors can read the published specifications and glean ideas for their research, or they can approach the inventor and offer to help to develop the idea under licence.

What inventions can you patent? The basic rules are that an invention must be new, must involve an *inventive* step and must be capable of *industrial exploitation*. You cannot patent scientific/mathematical theories or mental processes, computer programs or ideas that might encourage offensive, immoral or anti-social behaviour. New medicines are patentable but not medical methods of treatment. Neither can you have just rediscovered a long-forgotten idea (knowingly or unknowingly).

If you want to apply for a patent, it is essential not to disclose your idea in non-confidential circumstances. If you do, your invention is already 'published' in the eyes of the law, and this could well invalidate your application.

There are two distinct stages in the patenting process:

- from filing an application up to publication of the patent;
- from publication to grant of the patent.

Two fees are payable for the first part of the process and a further fee for the second part. The whole process takes some two and a half years. Forms and details of how to patent are available free from the Patent Office.

It is possible – and cheaper – to make your own patent application, but this is not really recommended. Drafting a specification to give you as wide a monopoly as you think you can get away with is the essence of patenting and this is the skill of professional patent agents. They also know the tricks of the trade for each stage of the patenting procedure. A list of patent agents is available from the Chartered Institute of Patent Agents.

What can you do with your idea? If you have dreamt up an inspired invention but don't have the resources, skill, time or inclination to produce it yourself, you can take one of three courses once the idea is patented:

- *Outright sale.* You can sell the rights and title of your patent to an individual or company. The payment you ask should be based on a sound evaluation of the market.

- *Sale and royalty.* You can enter into an agreement whereby you assign the title and rights to produce to another party for cash but under which you get a royalty on each unit sold.

- *Licensing.* You keep the rights and title but sell a licence for manufacturing and marketing the product to someone else. The contract between you and the licensee should contain a performance clause requiring the licensee to sell a minimum number of units each year or the licence will be revoked.

Whichever option you select, you need a good patent agent/lawyer on your side.

Trademarks protect 'what something is called'

A trademark is the symbol by which the goods or services of a particular manufacturer or trader can be identified. It can be a word, a signature, a monogram, a picture, a logo or a combination of these.

To qualify for registration the trademark must be distinctive, must not be deceptive and must not be capable of confusion with marks already registered. Excluded are misleading marks, national flags, royal crests and insignia of the armed forces. A trademark can only apply to tangible goods, not services (although pressure is mounting for this to be changed).

The Trade Marks Act of 1938 and the Copyright, Designs and Patents Act of 1988 and subsequent amendments offer protection of great commercial value since, unlike other forms of protection, your sole rights to use the trademark continue indefinitely.

To register a trademark you or your agent should first conduct preliminary searches at the trademarks branch of the Patent Office to check there are no conflicting marks already in existence. You then apply for registration on the official trademark form and pay a fee (currently £200 for one class of goods or services, then £50 for each additional class). Registration is initially for 10 years. After this, it can be renewed for periods of 10 years at a time, with no upper time limit.

It is not mandatory to register a trademark. If an unregistered trademark has been used for some time and could be construed as closely associated with a product by customers, it will have acquired a 'reputation', which will give it some protection legally, but registration makes it much simpler for the owners to have recourse against any person who infringes the mark.

Design registration protects 'how something looks'

You can register the shape, design or decorative features of a commercial product if it is new, original, never published before or – if already known – never before applied to the product you have in mind. Protection is intended to apply to industrial articles to be produced in quantities of more than 50. Design registration applies only to features that appeal to the eye – not to the way the article functions.

To register a design, you should apply to the Design Registry and send a specimen or photograph of the design plus a registration fee (currently £90). The specimen or photograph is examined to see whether it is new or original and complies with other requirements of the Registered Designs Act 1949 and the Copyright, Designs and Patents Act 1988 and subsequent amendments to the Act. If it does, a certification of registration is issued which gives you, the proprietor, the sole right to manufacture, sell or use in business articles of that design.

Protection lasts for a maximum of 25 years. You can handle the design registration yourself, but, again, it might be preferable to let a specialist do it for you. There is no register of design agents but most patent agents are well versed in design law.

CASE STUDY
Wagamama

This small London-based restaurant chain, which has prospered by selling Japanese noodles to city 'trendies', sees the need to protect its idea as the main plank of its business strategy. Alan Yau, who founded the business, came to the UK as an 11-year-old economic immigrant from Hong Kong. He joined his father running a

Chinese takeaway in King's Lynn, Norfolk. Within 10 years he was running two Chinese restaurants of his own, one of which is close to the British Museum. From the outset he had plans to run a large international chain of restaurants.

Yau's food style is healthy, distinctive and contemporary. The name 'Wagamama' conjures up someone who is a bit of a spoilt brat in Japanese, and the word lodged in Yau's mind. His informal communal dining room, opened under the Wagamama banner, received favourable reviews and the queues, which have become an essential part of the Wagamama experience, started forming. Realizing he had an idea with global potential, Yau took the unusual step of registering his trademark worldwide. It cost £60,000, but within two years that investment began to pay off. A large listed company opened an Indian version of Wagamama. The concepts looked similar enough to have led ordinary people to think the two businesses were related. As Yau felt he could lose out, he decided to sue. The case was heard quickly, and within three months Yau had won and his business idea was safe – at least for the five years his trademark protection runs.

Since he started up, Yau has opened more than 167 restaurants in the UK, Europe, the Pacific Rim, the Middle East and the United States. By April 2019 with new openings in Ayia Napa, Gibraltar, Rotterdam, Istanbul, Jeddah, Auckland and Dundonald (Belfast), turnover was in excess of £326 million and growing at 16 per cent a year.

Copyright protects 'work on paper, film and CD'

Copyright is a complex field and since it is unlikely to be relevant to most business start-ups we only touch on it lightly here. Basically, the Copyright, Designs and Patents Act 1988 gives protection against the unlicensed copying of original artistic and creative works – articles, books, paintings, films, plays, songs, music, engineering drawings. To claim copyright the item in question should carry this symbol: © (author's name) (date). At a diplomatic conference in Geneva in December 1996, new international copyright and performances and phonograms treaties, which govern the protection of databases, were agreed on and came into force in January 1998.

You can take the further step of recording the date on which the work was completed for a moderate fee with the Registrar at Stationers' Hall. This, though, is an unusual precaution to take and probably only necessary if you anticipate an infringement.

Copyright protection in the UK lasts for 70 years after the death of the person who holds the copyright, or 50 years after publication if this is the later. Copyright is infringed only if more than a 'substantial' part of your work is reproduced (ie issued for sale to the public) without your permission, but since there is no formal registration of copyright the question of whether or not your work is protected usually has to be decided in a court of law.

Protecting internet assets

Now that you have gone to so much trouble to develop a business model incorporating your mission, vision, objectives and culture so that you are all set for meteoric growth, it would be an awful pity if someone were to come along and steal it.

Even when times are hard, this is probably not an area to include in any cost-cutting exercise. In the internet world, where all the value is placed in the anticipation of profits from day one, intellectual property may be all that's really worth saving.

The advent of softer terms, such as 'sharing' music, rather than stealing it, doesn't alter the fact that all the usual intellectual property laws apply to the internet, it is just harder to enforce them. You can find out more about protecting internet assets in the output of the Digital Curation Centre (DCC) where the practical issues in setting up digital rights management systems (DRM) are examined.

Further information on protecting your products

The UK Intellectual Property Office has all the information needed to patent, trademark, copyright or register a design.

For information on international intellectual property see these organizations: European Patent Office, US Patent and Trade Mark Office and the World Intellectual Property Association.

The Chartered Institute of Patents and Attorneys and the Chartered Institute of Trade Mark Attorneys, despite their specialized-sounding names, can help with every aspect of intellectual property, including finding you a local adviser.

The British Library links to free databases for patent searching to see whether someone else has registered your innovation. The library is willing to offer limited advice to enquirers.

Their IP Centre supports small business owners, entrepreneurs and inventors. Their team is on hand all day, six days a week, to help you take the right steps to start up, protect and grow your business.

Comparison with competitive products and services

Identify those products and/or services that you think will be competing with yours. They may be similar products/services or they may be quite different, but could be substituted for yours. An example of the latter is a business that sells copying machines, which competes not only against other copying machines, but also against carbon paper and copy shops.

Once you have identified the major competing products, compare yours with them. List the advantages and disadvantages of yours compared with the competition. Later on, when you do your market research, you will probably want to address this question again and revise this section.

After making the comparison, draw your conclusions. If your products/services will compete effectively, explain why. If not, explain what you plan to do to make them compete.

Remember also that some products differentiate themselves from competitors by their service or warranty terms. For example, KIA claims to be the only car manufacturer to offer a fully transferrable seven-year, 100,000-mile warranty.

Additionally, all retailers in the distribution network are offered extended payment terms, finance for display stock and inventory as well as dealer support for advertising.

Similarly, most management consultants in the 'service' sector ensure that their 'products', their final reports, are faultless and immaculately presented, as are the premises and facilities of the best restaurants and fast food chains.

Guarantees and warranties

Will you be providing either of these with your product or service? Describe the scope of the warranty or guarantee, what it may cost, the benefits you expect from providing it, and how it will work in practice.

Possible future developments

If your product or service lends itself to other opportunities, with relatively minor alteration, which can be achieved quickly and will enhance your business, briefly describe these ideas.

Some product turn-offs

Is one product enough?

One-product businesses are the natural output of the inventor, but they are extremely vulnerable to competition, changes in fashion and to technological obsolescence. Having only one product can also limit the growth potential of the enterprise. A question mark must inevitably hang over such ventures until they can broaden out their product base into, preferably, a 'family' of related products or services.

CASE STUDY
Osprey

It was Mike Pfotenhauer's 'love of building products, making things for myself and my friends' that got him into building daypacks and backpacks for customers in Santa Cruz. He was fresh out of university and enjoyed setting his own hours, building gear and 'listening to stories about how that gear had travelled to some peaks or around the world'. Osprey, Pfotenhauer's company, is focused on making one product, backpacks, but making that product as good as it can be. At the heart of the business is a passion for the outdoors and they are guided by three key objectives: 'Enable others to have rich outdoor experiences; protect the environment for all to enjoy; and to live and breathe the outdoors ourselves.'

Founded in 1974, Osprey has grown since its founder sat at a single sewing machine, with a head full of ideas, to being stocked by hundreds of retailers across the globe. Gary Burnand, Osprey's marketing director since the spring of 2019, claims that by specializing in backpacks alone they don't get distracted, and stick to the knitting where their reputation is unrivalled. Its 'All Mighty Guarantee' states 'Should you find any defect in the way your pack has been built, we will repair or replace it without any charge, within its reasonable lifetime.' It backs up its repair promise with repair centres and distributors in Australia, Canada, China, all over Europe, Hong Kong, Taiwan, Indonesia, Israel, Japan, South Korea, Mexico, New Zealand, the Philippines, Singapore, South Africa, Malaysia, Thailand, Brazil, Uruguay, Argentina, Bolivia, Chile, Colombia, Ecuador and Peru.

Having built its reputation on a single product and making that as good as it can be, Osprey has extended its product range to cover specific activities. It makes hundreds of different packs targeted at diverse segments of the outdoor market: travel, hiking, backpacking, lifestyle, running, biking, climbing, snowsports and diving. They also have a modest range of accessories including packing cubes, raincovers, pack liners, washbags and wallets. Osprey's big focus in 2020 is to work with outdoor and environmentally focused charities to protect the environment and reduce waste. For example, they support 'Gift Your Gear', a charity that provides backpacks and other outdoor gear otherwise destined for landfill to youth organizations that need them most.

Single-sale products

Medsoft was a business founded to sell a PC and a tailor-made software package to hospital doctors. Unfortunately, the management had no idea of the cost and effort required to sell each unit. Worse still, there were no repeat sales. It was not that customers did not like the products: they did, but each user needed only one product. This meant that all the money and time spent on building up a 'loyal' customer were largely wasted.

In another type of venture, for example selling company cars, you could reasonably expect a satisfied customer to come back every two or three years. In the restaurant business the repeat purchase cycle might be every two to three months.

Non-essential products

Entrepreneurs tend to be attracted to fad, fashion and luxury items because of the short response time associated with their promotion and sale. Companies producing for these markets frequently run into financial difficulties arising out of sudden market shifts. Market security is more readily gained by having products that are viewed as 'essential'.

Too simple a product

Simplicity, usually a desirable feature, can be a drawback. If a business idea is so basic that little management or marketing expertise is required for success, this is likely to make the cost of entry low and the value added minimal. This makes it easy for every Tom, Dick or Harry to duplicate the product idea, and impossible for the original company to defend its market, except by lowering the price.

The video rental business was a classic example of the 'too simple product' phenomenon. Too many people jumped on the bandwagon as virtually anyone with a couple of thousand pounds could set themselves up. Rental prices fell from pounds to pence in a year or so, and hundreds of businesses folded.

CASE STUDY
BlaBlaCar

On 16 September 2015 BlaBlaCar, the French ride hailing start-up, announced that it had raised $200 million, primarily from US investors, which in turn places a value on the company of $1.6 billion. The business was started up by Frédéric Mazzella, son of a brace of professors, one of maths and one of philosophy. Coming from the Vendée region on France's Atlantic coast some 500 km from Paris, where he had made his home since leaving university, he had his eureka moment as a result of the frustrations of making that journey. On 24 December 2003 Mazzella was trying to get from Paris to his family home for Christmas. As the trains were full his sister had to come to pick him up so they could drive down together. 'The highway goes the same way as the trains and I could see the trains were full with no seats left and the cars were empty. I was like: Oh my God, there were seats to go to the Vendée but not on trains, in cars.'

Founded in 2006, BlaBlaCar aims to connect people who want to split the cost of long distance journeys, a simple enough concept and one that was basically following in the footsteps of other on-demand services like Uber, the ride booking company, and Airbnb, the vacation rental website. Success was a slow-burn process with Mazella trying out six business models and endured listening to 'endless people telling me I was wasting my time' before hitting on the right one. In 2006, Nicolas Brusson, Francis Nappez and Mazzella wrote up a business plan while at INSEAD, a business school near Paris, for a company to be called 'covoiturage.fr'. Ride sharing followed the Airbnb model of owners getting more mileage from their assets, in this case literally. Mazzella's proposition is that it costs €5,000–6,000 a year to run a car in France and 96 per cent of the time the cars are parked and not moving ... and three out of four cars that are moving have only one person on board. Ergo France's 38 million cars provide a €200 million a year optimization opportunity.

The name was changed from covoiturage.fr to BlaBlaCar as it seemed more likely to resonate around the world. Its expansion beyond its European roots into a growing number of emerging markets like Turkey, India and Russia supports that supposition. The company now has an impressive headquarters in north central Paris near to Google France. The company's 360 employees have an average age of 29 and adopting a unique 'fun and serious' attitude, the crowd at BlaBlaCar take their job seriously, yet at the same time know how to bring the fun. The BlaBlaCar bistro is home to the Friday morning 'breakfast' during which staff brainstorm and the next generation of winning strategies are fostered.

One product must: quality

One of the biggest problems for a new company is creating in the customer's mind an image of product quality. Once there was an almost faddish belief in 'dynamic obsolescence', implying that low quality would mean frequent and additional replacement sales. The inroads that the Japanese car makers have made on Western car manufacturers through improving quality, reliability and value for money have clearly demonstrated the fallacy of this proposition.

You cannot sell a product you do not believe in and as James Knock, founder president of a beer company, explained, 'In cold calling the only thing standing between you and the customers' scorn is the integrity of your product.'

The Cranfield entrepreneurs that we have seen prosper have all learnt to fight the cost, quality and service trade-off: 'We are only interested in making the best quality and freshest pasta around,' explained Farshad Rouhani in describing how Pasta Masters had grown to become the leading supplier of fresh pasta to retailers and restaurants in London. Equally, David Sinclair and his team at Bagel Express were at work at 4 am each day to ensure that only freshly baked bagels were on sale each morning. To show the freshness of the product, the bagels were baked each day in open kitchens in front of the customers.

Quality is not just what you do, but also how you do it; each contact point between the customer and company is vital, be it on the telephone, at the counter, at the till. The customer who complains is probably your best friend. Julian Richer, the founder of Richer Sounds, maintains one of his key tasks is to maximize his customers' opportunities to complain. By that he certainly doesn't mean giving them cause to be dissatisfied; just the chance to give feedback. Everything from having a bell at the door of each shop to ring if you have enjoyed your shopping experience, to a personally assigned response card in each packaged product is a step aimed at maintaining a direct link with the customer. Getting your customers to help you maintain your quality and standards is perhaps one of the keys to business success. And it isn't easy. It is believed that 96 per cent of complaints don't happen. In other words the customer can't or can't be bothered to complain. The quality obsession is clear; if you do not catch it, you will not survive, and unless you get regular feedback from your customers you will never know.

WORKSHEET FOR ASSIGNMENT 7: PRODUCTS AND/OR SERVICES

1 Describe your product or service, as if explaining it to a novice.

2 Is it currently available for sale? If not, what needs to be done, how much will that work cost and how long will it take?

3 Do you have, or plan to have, any legal protection such as patents? If so, explain what you have done so far to establish your rights.

4 How is your product or service different from those already on the market?

5 Will you be providing any warranties, guarantees or after-sales service?

6 Are there any possibilities of developing new products or services complementary to the one(s) described above?

Suggested further reading

Debruyne, M and Tackx, K (2019) *Customer innovation: Delivering a customer-led strategy for sustainable growth*, Kogan Page, London

Jolly, A (ed) (2013) *The Innovation Handbook: How to profit from your ideas, intellectual property and market knowledge*, Kogan Page, London

Leboff, G (2020), *Myths of Marketing: Banish the misconceptions and become a great marketer*, Kogan Page, London

McDonald, K (2013) *Innovation: How innovators think, act and change our world*, Kogan Page, London

Narang, R and Devaiah, D (2014) *Orbit-Shifting Innovation: The dynamics of ideas that create history*, Kogan Page, London

Westwood, J (2019), *How to Write a Marketing Plan: Define your strategy, plan effectively and reach your marketing goals*, 6th edn, Kogan Page, London

Reference

Dyson (2001) Dyson Appliances Limited v Hoover Limited (No. 2) 11 January 2001, CMS, 22 January, www.cms-lawnow.com/ealerts/2001/01/dyson-appliances-limited-v-hoover-limited-no-2?sc_lang=en (archived at https://perma.cc/CT8D-WM49)

ASSIGNMENT 8

Pricing

The most frequent mistake made when setting a selling price for the first time is to pitch it too low. This mistake can occur either through failing to understand all the costs associated with making and marketing your product, or through yielding to the temptation to undercut the competition at the outset. Both these errors usually lead to fatal results, so in preparing your business plan you should guard against them.

These are the important issues to consider when setting your selling price.

Costs

Make sure you have established all the costs you are likely to incur in making or marketing your product. Don't just rely on a 'guess' or 'common sense' – get several firm quotations, preferably in writing, for every major bought-in item. Don't fall into the trap of believing that if you will initially be working from home, you will have no additional costs. Your phone bill will rise (or you will fail!), the heating will be on all day and you'll need somewhere to file all your paperwork. Your car, too, will see more use and so incur more costs.

Also make sure you analyse the effect of changes in turnover on your costs. This can be done by breaking down your costs into direct and indirect (see Assignment 20 for an explanation of break-even analysis, as this area is sometimes referred to).

Consumer perceptions

Another consideration when setting your prices is the perception of the value of your product or service to the customer. His or her opinion of value may have little or no relation to the cost. They may be ignorant of the price charged by the competition, especially if the product or service is a new one. In fact, many consumers perceive price as a reliable guide to the quality they can expect to receive. The more you pay, the more you get. With this in mind, had Dyson launched his revolutionary vacuum cleaner, with its claims of superior performance, at a price below that of its peers, then some potential customers might have questioned those claims. In its literature Dyson cites as the inspiration for the new vacuum cleaner the inferior performance of existing products in the same price band. A product at six times the Dyson price is the one whose performance Dyson seeks to emulate. The message conveyed is that, although the price is at the high end of general run-of-the-mill products, the performance is disproportionately greater. The runaway success of Dyson's vacuum cleaner would tend to endorse this argument.

Competition

The misconception that new and small firms can undercut established competitors is usually based on ignorance of the true costs of a product or service, such as in the example given above; a misunderstanding of the meaning and characteristics of overheads; and a failure to appreciate that 'unit' costs fall in proportion to experience. This last point is easy to appreciate if you compare the time needed to perform a task for the first time with that when you are much more experienced (eg changing a fuse, replacing a Hoover bag, etc).

The overheads argument usually runs like this: 'They (the competition) are big, have a plush office in Mayfair, and lots of overpaid marketing executives, spending the company's money on expense account lunches, and I don't. Ergo I must be able to undercut them.' The errors with this type of argument are, first, that the Mayfair office may be an investment in image creation and second, the marketing executives may be paid more than the entrepreneur, but if they don't deliver a constant stream of new products and new strategies they'll be replaced with people who can.

Clearly, you have to take account of what your competitors charge, but remember price is the easiest element of the marketing mix for an established company to vary. They could follow you down the price curve, forcing you into bankruptcy, far more easily than you could capture their customers with a lower price.

Elasticity of demand

Economic theory suggests that, all others things being equal, the lower the price, the greater the demand. Unfortunately (or perhaps not!), the demand for all goods and services is not uniformly elastic – that is, the rate of change of price versus demand is not similarly elastic. Some products are actually price inelastic. For example, Apple's iPhone and Bentley Motors would be unlikely to increase sales if they knocked 5 per cent off the price – indeed, by losing 'snob' value they might even sell fewer. So, if they dropped their price they would simply lower profits. However, people will quite happily cross town to save 2p in the £1 on a litre of petrol.

So setting your price calls for some appreciation of the relative elasticity of the goods and services you are selling.

Company policy

The overall image that you try to portray in the marketplace will also influence the prices you charge. However, within that policy there will be the option of high pricing to skim the market and lower pricing to penetrate. Skim pricing is often adopted with new products with little or no competition and is aimed at affluent 'innovators'. These people will pay more to be the trend setters for a new product. Once the innovators have been creamed off the market, the price can be dropped to penetrate to 'lower' layers of demand.

The danger with this strategy is that high prices attract the interest of new competitors, who see a good profit waiting to be made.

Opening up with a low price can allow you to capture a high market share initially, and it may discourage competitors. This was the strategy adopted by Dragon Lock, Cranfield enterprise programme participants (the executive puzzle makers), when it launched its new product. Its product was easy to copy and impossible to patent, so it chose a low price as a strategy to discourage competitors and to swallow up the market quickly.

Business conditions

Obviously, the overall conditions in the marketplace will have a bearing on your pricing policy. In certain conditions, where products are virtually being rationed, the overall level of prices for some products could be expected to rise disproportionately. For example, in the early stages of the 2020 coronavirus crisis hand sanitisers were reported as being sold at £15 for 250 ml, toilet rolls for £1 per roll and Calpol at £10. Loaves of bread that normally sold for £1.25 more than doubled in price to £3.

Seasonal factors can also contribute to changes in the general level of prices. A turkey, for example, costs a lot less on the afternoon of Christmas Eve than it does at the start of Christmas week.

Channels of distribution

Your selling price will have to accommodate the mark-ups prevailing in your industry. For example, in the furniture business a shop may expect to set a selling price of double that charged by its supplier. This margin is intended to cover its costs and hopefully make a profit. So if your market research indicates that customers will pay £/$/€100 for a product bought from a shop, you, as the manufacturer selling to a shop, would only be able to charge £/$/€50.

Capacity

Your capacity to 'produce' your product or service, bearing in mind market conditions, will also influence the price you set. Typically, a new venture has limited capacity at the start. A valid entry strategy could be to price so high as to just fill your capacity, rather than so low as to swamp you. A housewife who started a home ironing service learnt this lesson on pricing policy to her cost. She priced her service at £5 per hour's ironing, in line with competition, but as she only had 20 hours a week to sell she rapidly ran out of time. It took six months to get her price up to £10 an hour and her demand down to 20 hours a week. Then she was able to recruit some assistance and had a high enough margin to pay some outworkers and make a margin herself.

Margins and markets

Pricing is perhaps the toughest decision to make. It is part science, taking into consideration all the costs. It is also part art, in assessing what the market will bear, a figure influenced by factors such as the state of the economy and the competitive environment. In any event, you should endeavour to ensure that you achieve a gross profit margin of at least 40 per cent (sales price less the direct materials and labour used to make the article, the resulting margin expressed as a percentage of the sales price). If you do not achieve such margins, you will have little overhead resource available to you to promote and build an effective, differentiated image for your company.

Your competitive analysis will give you some idea as to what the market will bear. We suggest you complete a comparison with your competitors (Table 8.1) to give you confidence that you can match or improve upon your competitors' prices. At the very least you will have arguments to justify your higher prices to your customers and, importantly, your future employees.

TABLE 8.1   Product comparison with competitors

(Score each product factor from −5 to +5 to justify your price versus the competition)

Rating score	Much worse	Worse	Same or nearly so	Better	Much better
Product attributes	−5	−4 −3 −2	−1 0 +1	+2 +3 +4	+5
Design					
Performance					
Packaging					
Presentation					
Appearance					
After-sales service					
Availability/ distribution					
Delivery methods/time					
Colour/flavour					

(continued)

TABLE 8.1 (Continued)

Rating score	Much worse	Worse	Same or nearly so	Better	Much better
Odour/touch					
Image/street cred.					
Specification					
Payment terms					
Other					
Total					

Price is, after all, the element of the marketing mix that is likely to have the greatest impact on your profitability. It is often more profitable for a new company to sell fewer items at a higher price while you are getting your organization and product offerings sorted out; the key is to concentrate on obtaining good margins, often with a range of prices and quality (eg Tesco has its 'Finest' range offered at premium prices alongside similar categories of standard products at lower prices). And if you have to increase prices? Try to combine the increase with some new feature (eg new design, colour scheme) or service improvement (eg the Post Office reintroducing Sunday collections at the same time as a 1p increase in price).

Real-time pricing

The stock market works by gathering information on supply and demand. If more people want to buy a share than sell it, the price goes up until supply and demand are matched. If the information is perfect (that is, every buyer and seller knows what is going on), the price is optimized. For most businesses this is not a practical proposition. Their customers expect the same price every time for the same product or service – they have no accurate idea what the demand is at any given moment.

However, for the internet company, computer networks have made it possible to see how much consumer demand exists for a given product at any time. Anyone with a point-of-sale till could do the same, but the reports might come in weeks later. This means online companies could change their prices hundreds of times each day, tailoring them to certain circumstances or certain markets, and so improve profits dramatically. easyJet.com, a budget airline operating out of Luton, does just this. It prices to fill its planes, and you could pay anything from £30 to £200 for the same trip, depending on the demand for that flight. Ryanair (Stansted) and Eurotunnel (Waterloo) have similar price ranges based on the simplest rule of discounted low fares for early reservations and full fares for desperate late callers!

CASE STUDY
Secret Escapes

Some business sectors, in particular double glazing, travel and hotels are famous, or perhaps it would be more accurate to say infamous, for misleading pricing. Endless sales on the high street have made consumers justifiably cynical about price-led promotion. Secret Escapes, founded in 2010 relies on selling discounted luxury hotel stays as the heart of its business model. The company's skill lies in convincing customers that the 70 per cent discount touted is real. They achieve this by using television advertising, a believable media, to get across their message that 'even the best hotels don't want empty beds'. They hand pick the best hotels in their sector in the UK, Germany, Sweden, Poland and the USA, the markets in which they operate, and offer deals that are exclusive to Secret Escapes for the period they are on offer making sure their proposition is significantly cheaper than anyone else in the market.

Founders Alex Saint (42) and Tom Valentine (33) come from related industries. Saint, a Geography graduate of Nottingham University, began his career at Unilever, before launching Dealchecker.co.uk, an aggregator travel deals website. Valentine has always been in online market places, starting out with eBay before coming across from online fashion brand Koodos. Getting visibility on television isn't cheap; their first month's campaign cost £250,000. It was £14 million worth of fundraising from Octopus Ventures, Atlas Venture and Index Ventures, the private equity firm who backed online clothing retailer Asos and LoveFilm, the online movie rental business acquired by Amazon, that made heavy-hitting TV commercials a practical strategy.

Although the founders now only own 30 per cent of the shares of Secret Escape, they have a business that can confidently spend over £10 million annually on promoting its pricing proposition. The company's latest accounts (December 2018) show annual revenue of £121.2 million, up from £30.9 million in 2016 and £11.6 million three years before that. They have over 23 million people on their mailing list.

WORKSHEET FOR ASSIGNMENT 8: PRICING

1   List all the costs you are likely to incur in making or marketing your product.

2   Refer forward to Assignment 20 and then calculate the fixed and variable costs associated with your product.

3   Using the costs as calculated above and your profit objective, calculate the optimal price you should charge.

4   What price do your competitors charge?

5   Compared with your product/service how much better/worse are those of your competitors?

6   Are any of your possible market segments less price-sensitive than others?

7   Does your answer to question 6 lead you to believe that there is an opportunity to sell at different prices in each market segment – and so enhancing profits?

Suggested further reading

Hill, P (2013) *Pricing for Profit: How to develop a powerful pricing strategy for your business*, Kogan Page, London

Hinterhuber, A and Liozu, S M (2019) *Pricing Strategy Implementation: Translating pricing strategy Into results*, Routledge, London

Mackenzie, R (2008) *Why Popcorn Costs so Much at the Movies: And other pricing puzzles*, Springer-Verlag, New York

ASSIGNMENT 9

Advertising and promotion

In this section of your business plan, you should discuss your planned advertising and promotion programme. A major decision is to choose a method of advertising that will reach most of your customers for the least cost.

Promotion/advertising checklist

Advertising is to some extent an intangible activity, although the bills for it are certainly not. It is, as Lord Bell, formerly of Saatchi & Saatchi, has described it, 'essentially an expensive way for one person to talk to another!' We assume by now you know the target customers you wish to reach. The answers to these five questions should underpin the advertising and promotional aspects of your business plan:

- What do you want to happen?
- How much is that worth?
- What message will make it happen?
- What media should be used?
- How will results be checked?

What are your advertising objectives?

There is no point in informing, educating or pre-selling unless it leads to the opportunity in a significant number of instances for a sale to result. So what do potential customers have to do to enable you to make these sales? Do you want them to visit your showroom or website, to phone you, to write to your office, to return a card or to send an order in the post? Do you expect them to have an immediate need to which you want them to respond now, or is it that you want them to remember you when they have a need for whatever it is you are selling?

The more you are able to identify a specific response in terms of web hits, orders, visits, phone calls or requests for literature, the better your promotional effort will be tailored to achieve your objective, and the more clearly you will be able to assess the effectiveness of your promotion and its cost versus its yield.

The more some particular promotional expenditure cannot be identified with a specific objective but is, for example, to 'improve your image' or 'to keep your name in front of the public', then the more likely it is to be an ineffective way of spending your money.

How much is it worth to achieve your objective?

Once you know what you want a particular promotional activity to achieve, it becomes a little easier to provide for it in your business plan. In practice, four methods are most commonly used, and they each have their merits, with the exception of the first.

The '*what can we afford?*' approach has its roots in the total misconception of promotional activity, which implies that advertising is an extravagance. When times are good, surplus cash is spent on advertising and when times are bad this budget is the first to be cut back. In fact, all the evidence points to the success of businesses that increase promotional spending during a recession, usually at the expense of their meaner competitors.

The '*percentage of sales*' method very often comes from the experience of the entrepreneur or his or her colleagues, or from historical budgets. So if a business spent 10 per cent of sales last year, it will plan to spend 10 per cent in the next, particularly if things went well. This method at least has some logic and provides a good starting point for preparing the overall budget.

'*Let's match the competitors*' becomes a particularly important criterion when they step up their promotional activity. Usually this will result in your either losing sales or feeling threatened. In either case you will want to retaliate, and increasing or varying your promotion is an obvious choice.

The '*cost/benefit*' approach comes into its own when you have clear and specific promotional goals and an experience base to build on. If you have spare capacity in your factory or want to sell more out of your shop, you can work out what the 'benefit' of those extra sales is worth.

Suppose a £1,000 advertisement is expected to generate 100 enquiries for our product. If our experience tells us that on average 10 per cent of enquiries result in orders, and our profit margin is £200 per product, then we can expect an extra £2,000 profit. That 'benefit' is much greater than the £1,000 cost of the advertisement, so it seems a worthwhile investment.

In practice, you should use all of these last three methods to decide how much to spend on promoting your products.

What message will help to achieve the objectives?

To answer this question you must look at your business and its products/ services from the customer's standpoint and be able to answer the hypothetical question 'Why should I buy your product?' It is better to consider the answer in two stages.

1 'Why should I buy your *product* or *service*?' The answer is provided naturally by the analysis of factors that affect choice. The analysis of buying motives or satisfactions is an essential foundation of promotional strategy.

2 'Why should I buy *your* product or service?' The only logical and satisfactory answer is: 'Because it is different.' The difference can arise in two ways:

   – We – the sellers – are different. Establish your particular niche.

   – It – the product or service – is different. Each product or service should have a unique selling point, based on fact.

Your promotional message must be built around these factors and must consist of facts about the company and about the product.

The stress here is on the word 'facts', and while there may be many types of facts surrounding you and your products, your customers are only interested in two: the facts that influence their buying decisions, and the ways in which your business and its products stand out from the competition.

These facts must be translated into benefits. There is an assumption sometimes that everyone buys for obvious, logical reasons only, when we all know of innumerable examples showing this is not so. Does a woman only buy a new dress when the old one is worn out? Do bosses have desks that are bigger than their subordinates' because they have more papers to put on them?

Having decided on the objective and identified the message, now choose the most effective method of delivering your message.

What media should you use?

Your market research should produce a clear understanding of who your potential customer group are which in turn will provide pointers as to how to reach them. But even when you know who you want to reach with your advertising message its not always plain sailing. The *Fishing Times*, for example, will be effective at reaching people who fish but less so at reaching their partners who might be persuaded to buy them fishing tackle for Christmas or birthdays. Also the *Fishing Times* will be jam-packed with competitors. It might just conceivably be worth considering a web ad on a page giving tide tables to avoid going head to head with competitors, or getting into a gift catalogue to grab that market's attention.

Another factor to consider in making your choice of media is the 'ascending scale of power of influence', as marketers call it. This is a method to rank media in the order in which they are most likely to favourably influence your customers. At the top of the scale is the personal recommendation of someone whose opinion is trusted and who is known to be unbiased. An example here is the endorsement of an industry expert who is not on the payroll, such as an existing user of the goods or services, who is in the same line of business as the prospective customer. While highly effective, this method is hard to achieve and can be expensive and time-consuming. Further down the scale is an approach by you in your role as a sales person. While you may be seen to be knowledgeable you clearly stand to gain if a sale is made, so you can hardly be unbiased. Sales calls, however they are made, are an expensive way to reach customers, especially if their orders are likely to be small and infrequent.

Further down still comes advertising in the general media: websites, press, radio, television and so forth. However, while these methods may be lower down the scale, they can reach much more of the market, and if done well can be effective.

How will the results be checked?

A glance at the advertising analysis in Table 9.1 will show how to tackle the problem. It shows the advertising results for a small business course run in

London. At first glance the Sunday paper produced the most enquiries. Although it cost the most, £3,400, the cost per enquiry was only slightly more than for the other media used. But the objective of this advertising was not simply to create interest; it was intended to sell places on the course. In fact, only 10 of the 75 enquiries were converted into orders – an advertising cost of £340 per head. On this basis the Sunday paper was between 2.5 and 3.5 times more expensive than any other medium.

Judy Lever, co-founder of Blooming Marvellous, the upmarket maternity-wear company, believes strongly not only in evaluating the results of advertising, but in monitoring a particular media capacity to reach her customers:

> We start off with one-sixteenth of a page ads in the specialist press, then once the medium has proved itself we progress gradually to half a page, which experience shows to be our optimum size. On average there are 700,000 pregnancies a year, but the circulation of specialist magazines is only around the 300,000 mark. We have yet to discover a way of reaching all our potential customers at the right time – in other words, early on in their pregnancies.

Measuring advertising effectiveness on the internet

Seeing the value from internet advertising can be a difficult proposition. The first difficulty is seeing exactly what you are getting for your money. With

TABLE 9.1 Measuring advertising effectiveness

Media used	Cost per advert £	Number of enquiries	Cost per enquiry £	Number of customers	Advertising cost per customer £
Sunday paper	3,400	75	45	10	340
Daily paper	2,340	55	43	17	138
Posters	1,250	30	42	10	125
Local weekly paper	400	10	40	4	100

press advertising you get a certain amount of space, on television and radio you get airtime. But on the internet there are at least three new ways to measure viewer value, aside from the largely discredited 'hits', used only because there was no other technique available. (Hits measured every activity on the web page, so every graphic on a page as well as the page itself counts as a hit.)

- *Unique visitors*: This is more or less what it says – new visitors to a website. What they do once there and how long they stay is not taken into account, so it's a bit like tracking the number of people passing a billboard. Could be useful, but perhaps they just stumbled across the site by accident. Also if users clear their cookies and clean up their hard drive there is no way to identify new and old visitors.
- *Time spent*: Clearly if a visitor stays on a website for a few minutes they are more likely to be interested or at least informed about your products and services than if they were there for a second or two.
- *Page views*: Much as in hardcopy world, a page on the web can now be recognized and the number of viewers counted.

Nielsen, a market-leading audience and market research measurement company, believes that 'time spent' is the best way to measure advertising effectiveness, other of course than actual sales if you can trace them back to their source. The order of the world-wide top websites is changed radically using this measure. For example in January 2008 Google ranked second for 'unique visitors' and 'page views', but only third for time spent.

Advertising and promotion options

In practice most new ventures have little to spend on advertising and there are an awful lot of options. For example if consumers already know what they want to buy and are just looking for a supplier then, according to statistics, the overwhelming majority will search online. Only 3 per cent will turn to a friend. But if you are trying to persuade consumers to think about buying a product or service at a particular time, a leaflet or flyer may be a better option. Once again it's back to your objectives in advertising. The more explicit they are, the easier it will be to chose your medium.

The power of print

Over £1.5 billion is spent each year on mailing UK households. It is considered to be the third most effective promotional tool after social media and emails. Consumers reading paper print are twice as likely to remember content as those reading online only. The printed word is probably still the way in which most organizations communicate with their publics. The rules for writing apply to advertising copy too. The content needs to be:

- Clear, using straightforward English, with short words, up to three syllables and short sentences, no more than 25–30 words. The text should be simply laid out and easy to read.
- Concise, using as few words as possible and be free of jargon or obscure technical terms.
- Correct, as spelling mistakes or incorrect information will destroy confidence in you and your product or service.
- Complete, providing all the information needed for the reader to do all that is required to meet *your* advertising objective.

Business cards and stationery

Everything you send out needs to be accompanied by something with all your contact details and a message or slogan explaining what you do. That includes invoices, bills, price lists and technical specifications. This may be all that anyone ever sees of you and your business. If it is effective they will remember you by it, and better still, they will remember to pass the information on to anyone else they know who could be a customer.

Direct mail (leaflets, flyers, brochures and letters)

These are the most practical ways for a new business to communicate with its potential customers. These forms of communication have the merits of being relatively inexpensive, simple and quick to put into operation, can be concentrated into any geographic area, and can be mailed or distributed by hand. Finally, it is easy to monitor results.

CASE STUDY
Goldsmith's (Northern) Ltd

Mark Goldsmith and Simon Hersch started their catering wholesaling business from halls of residence while still students at Manchester University. Taking advantage of a catering strike, they began supplying the student union with portioned cakes sourced from Robert's Fridge Factory, a small London-based manufacturer known to them. Buoyed on by their initial success, they produced a single-sheet leaflet entitled 'Earning more bread is a piece of cake', with a smart Goldsmith's Ltd logo, and itemizing on the reverse side the various small food items they could provide. This was distributed to small snack outlets in the vicinity of the university, and became their primary marketing tool and calling card. Goldsmith's (Northern) Ltd continued to provide Simon and his 40 employees with an interesting and rewarding lifestyle until it was time to cash in and sell the business for a serious seven-figure sum.

These organizations can provide information that will help you with leaflets, brochures and all other forms of direct mail:

- Data HQ lists databases for Consumer and Business. Their lists cover 36 million consumers, by some 90 topics.
- Fast Print has a useful guide to leaflet design and writing.
- Listbroker.com supplies lists of all types, including consumer and business-to-business, mostly in the United Kingdom but some overseas. All list details, including prices, are available on the site. The database is updated daily and offers consumer and business-to-business lists with over 1.6 billion names for rental.

Newspapers, magazines and classified ads

You can get readership and circulation numbers and the reader profile from the Press Gazette under the Audience Data tabs. The National Readership Survey Audience Data produces average readership data on around 260 UK titles and a host of other data, much of which is free and available online to non-subscribers.

However, national newspapers, except for the classified ads sections, are likely to be outside the budget of most new businesses. If that is the case don't despair as local papers have a substantial readership (around 40 million adults a week) and they cost significantly less to advertise in and have a much more focused readership. Hold The Front Page has links to the 200 or so local daily and weekly papers, from the *Aberdeen Evening Express* to the *York Herald*.

Posters, billboards and signs

If you know where your audience are likely to pass you could put a poster or billboard somewhere in their line of sight. This could be something as simple and inexpensive as an A4 sheet in the local newsagent window, bus shelter or supermarket message board, or a more costly and elaborate structure as are seen by the roadside.

Most businesses have a sign outside their door telling passers by what they do. If the premises has a high footfall with lots of people passing, this can get a lot of visibility for very little money. Obviously you don't have a free hand to put up any size or colour of sign you like; it needs to be in keeping with the local environment. Your local council's planning department will be able to advise you on the rules and regulations prevailing in your area.

You could also consider advertising on taxis and buses, where costs are well within a small firm's budget. For information, advice and facts and figures on all outdoor advertising matters visit the Outsmart, the umbrella organization for posters and billboards and all out of home (OOH) media.

Using other media

Increasingly, media such as television and radio, once the prerogative of big business, have filtered down the price band as they have further segmented their own markets with the introduction of digital technology.

LOCAL RADIO, TELEVISION AND CINEMA

These media are priced out on a cost per listener/viewer basis, and you will need to be certain that the audience profile matches that of the market segment you are aiming at. As these media, unlike the written word, are not retained after the event, you will also need to support these media with something like local press advertising or an entry in a directory that you can signpost people too. 'See our entry in Yellow Pages/our advertisement in this week's *Cornishman*' are messages that radio, television and cinema audiences can retain and act on.

Radiocentre is the industry body for commercial radio, working on behalf of over 300 licensed radio stations across the UK and can give further information on these media and contact details for professional firms operating in the sector. Rajar (Radio Joint Audience Research Ltd) publishes radio audience statistics quarterly.

Attending trade shows and exhibitions

Exhibitions are a way to get your product or business idea in front of potential customers face to face. That gives you first-hand knowledge of what people really want as well as providing a means of gathering market research data on competitors.

UK Trade & Investment is the UK government organization responsible for all trade promotion and development work. It provides a comprehensive listing of all the consumer, public, industrial and trade exhibitions to be held in major venues around the UK for two or more years ahead. You can search the list by exhibition type, by exhibition date, by exhibition organizer or by exhibition venue. There is also a complete list of main subject categories and subject headings, the main UK exhibition venues, and exhibition organizers. The data is updated regularly twice a month.

Creating favourable publicity

This is about presenting yourself and your business in a favourable light to your various 'publics' – at little or no cost. It is also a more influential method of communication than general advertising – people believe editorials.

Writing a press release

To be successful, a press release needs to get attention immediately and be quick and easy to digest. Studying and copying the style of the particular paper, magazine or website you want your press release to appear in can make publication more likely.

- *Layout.* The press release should be typed on a single sheet of A4. Use double spacing and wide margins to make the text both more readable and easy to edit. Head it boldly 'Press Release' or 'News Release' and date it.

- *Headline.* This must persuade the editor to read on. If it doesn't attract interest, it will be quickly 'spiked'. Editors are looking for topicality, originality, personality and, sometimes, humour.

- *Introductory paragraph.* This should be interesting and succinct, and should summarize the whole story; it could be in the form of a quote and it might be the only piece published. Don't include sales-oriented blurb as this will 'offend' the journalist's sense of integrity.

- *Subsequent paragraphs.* These should expand and colour the details in the opening paragraph. Most stories can be told in a maximum of three or four paragraphs. Editors are always looking for fillers, so short releases have the best chance of getting published.

- *Contact.* List at the end of the release your name, mobile and other telephone numbers and email address as the contact for further information.

- *Style.* Use simple language, short sentences and avoid technical jargon (except for very specialized technical magazines).

- *Photographs.* Email a standard photograph of yourself, your product or anything else relevant to the story being pitched.

- *Follow-up.* Sometimes a follow-up phone call or email to see whether editors intend to use the release can be useful, but you must use your judgement on how often to do so.

Find out the name of the editor or relevant writer/reporter and address the envelope to him or her personally. Remember that the target audience for your press release is the professional editor; it is he or she who decides what to print. So, the press release is not a 'sales message' but a factual account designed to attract the editor's attention.

WORKSHEET FOR ASSIGNMENT 9: ADVERTISING AND PROMOTION

1 Prepare a leaflet describing your product/service to your main customers. (Don't worry if you don't plan to use a leaflet – the exercise will serve to ensure you have put your offer in terms that recognize customers' needs, rather than simply being a technical specification.)

2 Write a press release announcing the launch of your venture. List the media to whom you will send the release.

3 Prepare an advertising and promotional plan for the upcoming year, explaining:

   (a) what you want to happen as a result of your advertising;

   (b) how much it's worth to you to make that happen;

   (c) what message(s) you will use to achieve these results;

   (d) what media you will use and why;

   (e) how the results of your advertising will be monitored;

   (f) how much you will spend.

4 If you have already done some advertising or promotional work, describe what you have done and the results you have achieved. Has your work on this assignment given you any pointers for future action?

Suggested further reading

Cluley, R (2017) *Essentials of Advertising*, Kogan Page, London

Dowson, R and Bassett, D (2018) *Event Planning and Management: Principles, planning and practice*, Kogan Page, London

Hughes, T, Gray, A and Whicher, H (2018) *Smarketing: How to achieve competitive advantage through blended sales and marketing*, Kogan Page, London

Mullin, R (2014) *Promotional Marketing: How to create, implement and integrate campaigns that really work*, Kogan Page, London

ASSIGNMENT 10

Place and distribution

'Place' is the fourth 'P' in the marketing mix. In this aspect of your business plan you should describe exactly how you will get your products to your customers. If you are a retailer, restaurateur or garage proprietor, for example, then your customers will come to you. Here, your physical location will most probably be the key to success. For businesses in the manufacturing field it is more likely that you will go out to 'find' customers. In this case it will be your channels of distribution that are the vital link.

Even if you are already in business and plan to stay in the same location, it would do no harm to take this opportunity to review that decision. If you are looking for additional funds to expand your business, your location will undoubtedly be an area prospective financiers will want to explore.

Location

From your market research data you should be able to come up with a list of criteria that are important to your choice of location. Here are some of the factors you need to weigh up when deciding where to locate:

- Is there a market for the particular type of business you plan? If you're selling a product or service aimed at a particular age or socioeconomic group, analyse the demographic characteristics of the area. Are there sufficient numbers of people in the relevant age and income groups? Are the numbers declining or increasing?
- If you need skilled or specialist labour, is it readily available?
- Are the necessary back-up services available?
- How readily available are raw materials, components and other supplies?

- How does the cost of premises, rates and utilities compare with other areas?
- How accessible is the site by road, rail, air?
- Are there any changes in the pipeline that might adversely affect trade, eg a new motorway bypassing the town, changes in transport services, closure of a large factory?
- Are there competing businesses in the immediate neighbourhood? Will these have a beneficial or detrimental effect?
- Is the location conducive to the creation of a favourable market image? For instance, a high-fashion designer may lack credibility trading from an area famous for its heavy industry and notorious for its dirt and pollution.
- Is the area generally regarded as low or high growth? Is the area probusiness?
- Can you and your key employees get to the area easily and quickly?

You may even have spotted a 'role model' – a successful competitor, perhaps in another town, who appears to have got his or her location spot on.

Using these criteria you can quickly screen out most unsuitable areas. Other locations may have to be visited several times, at different hours of the day and week, before screening them out.

CASE STUDY
Phoenix Training

Phoenix was started by Bill Osmond and was joined three and a half years later by Tim Holmes. Initially they located at premises at Leather Market, close to London Bridge, making a virtue out of being in the shadow of the Shard. Phoenix paid over the odds for their location but strategically speaking they started in exactly the right spot. SMEs, one of their client sweet spots, comprised the largest segment of the local business population in that part of London. However, they were close enough to be attractive to large City corporations.

   Currently, Phoenix is firmly established with a portfolio of blue chip clients including wealth managers Rathbone, Samsung and Superdrug. However, Phoenix found over time that a decreasing proportion of their clients used their costly central London training centre, preferring to use either their own premises or another facility closer to their own premises. While still remaining in London, the company no longer feels the need to be absolutely at its heart.

When writing up this element of your business plan keep these points in mind:

- Almost every benefit has a cost associated with it. This is particularly true of location. Make sure that you carefully evaluate the cost of each prospective location against the expected benefits. A saving of a couple of hundred pounds a month in rent may result in thousands of pounds of lost sales. On the other hand, don't choose a high-rent location unless you are convinced that it will result in higher profits. Higher costs do not necessarily mean greater benefits.

- Choose the location with the business in mind. Don't start with the location as a 'given'. You may think it makes sense to put a bookshop in an unused portion of a friend's music shop since the marginal cost of the space is zero. The problem with this approach is that you force the business into a location that may or may not be adequate. If the business is 'given' (ie already decided upon), then the location should not also be given. You should choose the best location (ie the one that yields the most profit) for the business. 'Free' locations can end up being very expensive if the business is not an appropriate one.

- When you write your business plan as a financing tool, you often may not have the specific business location selected prior to completion of the business plan. This is fine, since there is no point in wasting time deciding on a location until you know you will have the money to start the business. Besides, even if you do select a location before obtaining the money, it is very possible that the location will already be gone by the time you get through the loan application process and have the business firm enough to sign a lease or purchase agreement. Another consideration is that you may wear out your welcome with an estate agent if you make a habit of withdrawing from deals at the last minute, due to lack of funds.

It will suffice if you are able to explain exactly what type of location you will be acquiring. Knowing this, you will be able to make a good attempt at cost and sales estimates, even though the specific location has yet to be determined.

Outsourcing

The most important choice at the outset of planning how much space you will need when starting a business is to decide what you will do in-house and what you will buy. The process of getting others to do work for you rather than simply supplying you with materials for you to work on is called 'outsourcing'. There is little in terms of business functions that can't be outsourced. It would be prudent to consider outsourcing, at least initially, any activity that requires a substantial amount of capital.

You can read up on the sorts of activities a small home-based business can outsource, how to chose outsourcing partners and how to draw up a supply agreement with outsource suppliers at the Deloitte website.

CASE STUDY
Outsourcing

No manufacturing. No salesmen. No research and development. Jill Brown grew her business from a standing start to a turnover of £2 million a year in just five years as much by deciding what not to do as by what it actually does. The business she founded, Brown Electronics, supplies switches for computer equipment, the kind of gadget that, for example, allows half a dozen personal computers to use one printer between them.

She says: 'I didn't want to get into manufacturing myself. I save myself the headaches. Why should I start manufacturing as long as I've got my bottom line right? Turnover is vanity, profit is sanity. I have worked for other people who wanted to grow big just for the kudos.' Instead, Jill contracts out to other people's factories. She feels she still has control over quality, since any item that is not up to standard can be sent back. She also has the ultimate threat of taking away trade, which would leave the manufacturers she uses with a large void to fill. 'We would do so if quality was not good enough. Many manufacturers have under-utilized capacity.'

Jill uses freelance salesmen on a commission basis. She explains: 'I didn't want a huge sales force. Most sales managers sit in their cars at the side of the road filling in swindle sheets. Research and development are another area where expenses would be terrific. We have freelance design teams working on specific products. We give them a brief and they quote a price. The cost still works out at twice what you expected, but at least you have a measure of control. I could not afford to employ R&D staff full time and I would not need them full time. My system minimizes the risks and gives us a quality we could not afford as a small business.' Indirectly, Jill provides work for about 380 people, while still being able to operate out a space not much larger than a two-bedroom flat.

Premises

In your business plan you will need to address these issues with respect to premises.

Can the premises you want be used for your intended business?

The main categories of 'use' are retail, office, light industrial, general industrial and special categories. If your business falls into a different category from that of a previous occupant you may have to apply to the local authority for a 'change of use'.

An unhappy illustration of this came from a West Country builder who bought a food shop with living accommodation above. His intention was to sell paint and decorative products below and house his family above. Within three months of launching his venture he was advised that as his shop stock was highly flammable, the house would need fire-retardant floors, ceilings and doors – at a cost of £20,000, even doing the work himself. The business was effectively killed off before it started.

There are many regulations concerning the use of business premises. You should contact the Health & Safety Executive to ensure that whatever you plan to do is allowed.

Will you be making any structural alterations?

If so, planning permission may be needed and building regulations must be complied with. Any structural alterations, increase in traffic, noise, smells or anything such as operating unreasonable hours or any disturbance that could affect nearby homes or other businesses may need permission.

You can find out whether approval is likely informally from your local council before applying. You can also get details of most of the organizations involved in the planning, as well as guides to the planning system.

Securing permissions to alter property or its uses takes time and will incur costs that should be allowed for in your cash-flow projections.

Are the premises the appropriate size?

It is always difficult to calculate just how much space you will require, since your initial preoccupation is probably just to survive. Generally, you won't want to use valuable cash to acquire unnecessarily large premises. However, if you make it past the starting post you will inevitably grow, and if you haven't room to expand, you'll have to begin looking for premises all over again. This can be expensive, not to say disruptive.

To calculate your space requirements, prepare a layout that indicates the ideal position for the equipment you will need, allowing adequate circulation space. Shops require counters, display stands, refrigeration units, etc. In a factory, machinery may need careful positioning and you may also have to consider in great detail the safe positioning of electricity cables, waste pipes, air extractors, etc.

The simplest way to work out space requirements is to make cut-out scale models of the various items and lay these on scaled drawings of different-sized premises – 400 square feet, 1,000 square feet, etc.

By a process of trial and error you should arrive at an arrangement that is flexible, easy to operate, pleasant to look at, accessible for maintenance, and comfortable for both staff and customers. Alternatively you can use space planning software such as Instant Planner, Autodesk or plan3D, all of which have free or very low cost tools for testing out your space layout.

Only now can you calculate the likely cost of premises to include in your business plan.

Will the premises conform with existing fire, health and safety regulations?

The Health and Safety at Work Act (1974), the Factories Act (1961), the Offices, Shops and Railway Premises Act (1963) and the Fire Precautions Act (1971) set out the conditions under which most workers, including the self-employed and members of the public at large, can be present. (The Health & Safety Commission have an online advice form on their website.)

Will you be working from home?

If you plan to work from home, have you checked that you are not prohibited from doing so by the house deeds, or whether your type of activity is likely to irritate the neighbours? This route into business is much in favour with sources of debt finance, as it is seen to lower the risks during the vulnerable start-up period. Venture capitalists, on the other hand, would probably see it as a sign of 'thinking too small' and steer clear of the proposition. Nevertheless, working from home can make sound sense.

CASE STUDY
Road Runner Despatch

For example, Peter Robertson, aged 20, who founded Road Runner Despatch, started out running his business as a very domestic affair operated from his home in Brightlingsea, Essex. His mother answered the telephone and frequently his father used the family car to make collections. Within two years he was employing 10 full-time motorcycle riders. Only at this stage did Robertson put together a plan, which involved raising £100,000 capital, to open an office on a central site, complete with a state-of-the-art radio-telephone system.

Will you lease or buy?

Purchasing premises outright frequently makes sense for an established, viable business as a means of increasing its asset base. But for a start-up, interest and repayments on the borrowings will usually be more than the rental payments. But leasing itself can be a trap; eg a lease rental of £5,000 a year may seem preferable to a freehold purchase of say £50,000. But remember, as the law currently stands, if you sign and give a personal guarantee on a new 21-year lease (which you will be asked to do), you will remain personally responsible for payments over the whole life of the lease. Landlords are as reluctant to allow change in guarantors as they are to accept small business covenants. You could then be committing yourself, in these circumstances, to a minimum £105,000 outlay! Some financiers feel that your business idea should be capable of making more profit than the return you could expect from property. On this basis you should put the capital to be raised into 'useful' assets such as plant, equipment, stocks, etc.

However, some believe that if you intend to spend any money on converting or improving the premises, doing so to leased property is simply improving the landlord's investment and wasting your (their) money. You may even be charged extra rent for the improvements, unless you ensure that tenant improvements are excluded from the rent reviews.

In any event, your backers will want to see a lease long enough to get your business firmly established and secure enough to allow you to stay on if it is essential to the survival of your business. Starting up a restaurant in short-lease premises might actually be a sensible way to test your business at minimum risk as a means to simply test the market. The ideal situation, which can sometimes be obtained when landlords are in difficulties, is to negotiate a short lease (say one or two years) with an option to renew on expiry. All leases in Singapore and Malaysia are for two years, with options to renew at prevailing rates, which might seem much more helpful to encourage new business start-ups. It may be best for you to brief a surveyor to help you in your search and negotiation (their charge is normally 1 per cent, with payment only by result).

If appropriate, you could consider locating in a sympathetic and supportive environment

For example, universities and colleges often have a science park on campus, with premises and starter units for high-tech ventures. Enterprise agencies often have offices, workshops and small industrial units attached. In these situations you may have access to a telex, fax, computer, accounting service and business advice, on a pay-as-you-use basis. This would probably be viewed as a plus point by any prospective financial backer. United Kingdom Science Park Association (UKSPA) has directories of incubators or innovation centres, as these new business friendly starter units are known.

What opening/works hours do you plan to keep, and why?

Many new retailers survive by working very long hours; be careful with many of the new shopping 'malls', where hours of opening are strictly controlled, thereby preventing you from 'being different' by having unusual operating hours.

Check on insurance

Any personal insurance policy you have will not cover business activity so you must inform your insurer what you plan to do. You can find out more about business insurance cover and where to find an insurance company from the Association of British Insurers.

Channels of distribution

If your customers don't come to you, then you have the following options in getting your product or service to them. Your business plan should explain which you have chosen and why.

- *Retail stores*. This general name covers the great range of outlets from the corner shop to Harrods. Some offer speciality goods such as hi-fi equipment, where the customer expects professional help from the staff. Others, such as Marks & Spencer and Tesco, are mostly self-service, with customers making up their own mind on choice of product.
- *Wholesalers*. The pattern of wholesale distribution has changed out of all recognition over the past two decades. It is still an extremely important channel where physical distribution, stock holding, finance and breaking bulk are still profitable functions.
- *Cash and carry*. This slightly confusing route has replaced the traditional wholesaler as a source of supply for smaller retailers. In return for your paying cash and picking up the goods yourself, the 'wholesaler' shares part of its profit margin with you. The attraction for the wholesaler is improved cash flow, and for the retailer it is a bigger margin and a wide product range. Hypermarkets and discount stores also fit somewhere between the manufacturer and the marketplace.
- *Mail order*. This specialized technique provides a direct channel to the customer, and is an increasingly popular route for new small businesses.

CASE STUDY
Rohan

Paul Howcroft, who built his clothing 'casuals with toughness and durability' business, Rohan, from modest beginnings when he had just £60 in the bank, to a £7 million business in less than a decade, puts much of his success down to changing distribution channels. For the first two years most of his sales were to retail shops, which either wouldn't take enough produce or didn't pay up when they did. He set up his mail-order branch, using his box of enquiries and letters built up over the years as a mailing list. Today Rohan has 56 stores and an annual turnover of £30 million. He moved a year's sales in two months, getting all the cash in up front.

Other direct from 'producer to customer' channels include:

- *Internet.* Revenue generation via the internet is big business and getting bigger. In some sectors – advertising, books, music and video – it has become the dominant route to market. See 'Building a website' in Assignment 12 for the nuts and bolts of operating online.

CASE STUDY
Liberty Control Networks

A Cornish company won a £150,000 order from South Africa for high-tech equipment just over 12 months after it was established. Liberty means freedom but not for thousands of criminals in an African prison soon to be secured by a locking system supplied by Liberty Control Networks. David and Sharon Parker established their firm at St Austell, in mid-Cornwall, and gained the big order in South Africa via their website. A prison management team thousands of miles away was 'surfing the net' to find someone who could supply a state-of-the-art jail locking system. Liberty Control Networks was one of four companies to respond to the challenge, with the Parkers providing the best solution.

Mr Parker said:

As with any new company, long hours are expected, and at about 11.30 pm one Friday evening in January, I finished work by checking my emails before going to bed. I found this enquiry from South Africa. They were asking for 500 of this, 100 of that and so on. Needless to say, I didn't go to bed but put together our proposal.

Burning the midnight oil produced a bumper dividend, resulting in the first of what hopefully will be a series of orders, each in excess of £150,000.

- *Door-to-door selling.* Traditionally used by vacuum cleaner distributors and encyclopedia companies, this is now used by insurance companies, cavity-wall insulation firms, double-glazing firms and others. Many use hard-sell techniques, giving door-to-door selling a bad name. However, Avon Cosmetics has managed to sell successfully door to door without attracting the stigma of unethical selling practices.
- *Party plan selling.* This is a variation on door-to-door selling that is on the increase, with new party plan ideas arriving from the United States. Agents enrolled by the company invite their friends to a get-together

where the products are demonstrated and orders are invited. The agent gets a commission. Party plan has worked very well for Avon and other firms that sell this way.

On a more modest scale, one man turned his hobby of making pine bookcases and spice racks into a profitable business by getting his wife to invite neighbours for coffee mornings where his wares were prominently displayed.

- *Telephone selling.* This too can be a way of moving goods in one single step, from 'maker' to consumer. Few products can be sold easily in this way; however, repeat business is often secured via the phone.

Selecting distribution channels

These are the factors you should consider when choosing channels of distribution for your particular business:

- *Does it meet your customers' needs?* You have to find out how your customers expect their product or service to be delivered to them and why they need that particular route.

- *Will the product itself survive?* Fresh vegetables, for example, need to be moved quickly from where they are grown to where they are consumed.

- *Can you sell enough this way?* 'Enough' is how much you *want* to sell.

CASE STUDY
TWS

TWS, a window systems manufacturer, wanted to increase its sales. A customer survey was commissioned which revealed that 80 per cent of TWS customers did not have forklift trucks, resulting in manual offloading of deliveries by employees at its customers' premises. The TWS solution was to order delivery vehicles, complete with their own forklift, facilitating unloading at customer premises in 15 minutes instead of two hours, giving faster turnaround time and requiring no customer assistance. This, in turn, did not waste the valuable time of customer employees and encouraged extra orders from existing TWS customers as well as opening up new customer possibilities.

CASE STUDY
Atrium

Atrium, a £5 million-annual-turnover company whose executives attended Cranfield's Business Growth Programme, uses an actively managed website to have periodic sales. The company sells modern furniture, mostly via architects who have been retained to build or refurbish business premises. Atrium has products on display in its London showroom, and from time to time these have to be sold off to make way for new designs. But having hundreds of people milling around looking for bargains in a sale is not quite the atmosphere that is conducive to an architect and his or her client reviewing plans for a new project.

So, 'sale' products are displayed and sold on Atrium's website saleroom. 'Enough' products are sold with no disruption to the normal showroom activity.

- *Is it compatible with your image?* If you are selling a luxury product, then door-to-door selling may spoil the impression you are trying to create in the rest of your marketing effort.

- *How do your competitors distribute?* If they have been around for a while and are obviously successful, it is well worth looking at how your competitors distribute and using that knowledge to your advantage.

- *Will the channel be cost-effective?* A small manufacturer may not find it cost-effective to sell to retailers west of Bristol because the direct 'drop' size – that is, the load per order – is too small to be worthwhile.

- *Will the mark-up be enough?* If your product cannot bear at least a 100 per cent mark-up, then it is unlikely that you will be able to sell it through department stores. Your distribution channel has to be able to make a profit from selling your product too.

- *Push–pull.* Moving a product through a distribution channel calls for two sorts of selling activity. 'Push' is the name given to selling your product in, for example, a shop. 'Pull' is the effort that you carry out on the shop's behalf to help it to sell your product out of that shop. That pull may be caused by your national advertising, a merchandising activity or the uniqueness of your product. You need to know how much push and pull are needed for the channel you are considering. If you are not geared up to help retailers to sell your product, and they need that help, then this could be a poor channel.

- *Physical distribution.* The way in which you have to move your product to your end customer is also an important factor to weigh up when choosing a channel. As well as such factors as the cost of carriage, you will also have to decide about packaging materials. As a rough rule of thumb, the more stages in the distribution channel, the more robust and expensive your packaging will have to be.

- *Cash flow.* Not all channels of distribution settle their bills promptly. Mail order customers, for example, will pay in advance, but retailers can take up to 90 days or more. You need to take account of this settlement period in your cash-flow forecast.

WORKSHEET FOR ASSIGNMENT 10: PLACE AND DISTRIBUTION

1   What type and size of premises are required for your business?

2   Describe the location.

3   Why do you need this type of premises and location? What competitive advantage does it give you?

4   If freehold, what is/are the:

   − value?

   − mortgage outstanding?

   − monthly repayments?

   − mortgage with whom?

5   If leasehold:

   − What is the unexpired period of lease?

   − Is there an option to renew?

   − What is the present rent payment?

   − What is the date of rent payment?

   − What is the date of the next rent review?

6   What rates are payable on your business premises?

7   What are the insurance details:

   − sum insured?

   − premium?

8   Are these premises adequate for your future needs? If not, what plans do you have?

9   If you have not found your premises yet, what plans do you have to find them?

10   What channels of distribution are used in your field; which do you plan to use and why?

11   What operating risks – fire, health and safety, etc – need to be considered?

Suggested further reading

Baker, P, Croucher, P and Rushton, A (2017) *The Handbook of Logistics and Distribution Management: Understanding the supply chain*, Kogan Page, London

Bruel, O (2016) *Strategic Sourcing Management: Structural and operational decision-making*, Kogan Page, London

Dent, J and White, M (2018) *Sales and Marketing Channels: How to build and manage distribution strategy*, Kogan Page, London

Gee, R, Sloan, D and Symes, G (2019) *The Retail Start-Up Book: Successfully plan, launch and grow a business*, Kogan Page, London

O'Brien, J (2017) *The Buyer's Toolkit*, Kogan Page, London

McKinnon, A, Browne, M, Whiteing, A and Piecyk, M (2015) *Green Logistics: Improving the environmental sustainability of logistics*, Kogan Page, London

ASSIGNMENT 11

People, process and physical environment

According to management guru Peter Drucker 'there is only one valid definition of a business purpose; to create a customer'. This has led to the belief that three elements other than the 4 Ps are as important – and hence the name 7 Ps. These additional Ps are:

- People – friendly helpful staff are better than rude untrained ones.
- Process – how the product or service is delivered matters. So complicated ordering systems, confusing websites and unhelpful returns policies can work against a business.
- Physical Evidence – the physical environment needs to be attractive and appropriate, particularly for retail businesses. So for McDonald's a play area is a plus, but would perhaps be inappropriate for a bank.

The original marketing mix had just 4 Ps – product, price, place and promotion. However, this mix has since been extended to 7 Ps, with people, process and physical evidence added to accommodate the increasing emphasis on customers focus in business. The originators of the extra three had in mind the unique problems in marketing intangible services. But as almost every 'product' has a major service element, the 7 Ps have been adopted into the mainstream marketing mix analysis.

Understanding the role of people in marketing

Marketing managers often believe that the most important aspects of marketing lie in areas such as creating sensational advertising campaigns, launching innovative and well-designed products or creating brand identity.

Not to denigrate these factors in any way, but the single most prevalent reason for a marketing strategy failing lies in its implementation and, by extension, the people who carry out marketing tasks. Often known as the fifth P of the marketing mix, the selection of people to implement strategy and the way in which they are organized that contributes the most to your business's success. Stated like that it sounds a fairly simple task. Just work your way through those headings and you should be able to get the desired results. Unfortunately, people – both individually and collectively – are rarely malleable and are infinitely variable in their likely responses to situations, making their behaviour hard to predict.

The famous German military strategist Moltke came up with a useful statement: 'No campaign plan survives first contact with the enemy', which applies here (if the word 'enemy' is replaced by 'organization'). However, by understanding and applying the following basic principles and concepts in the areas of leadership, motivation and team-building, you, the MBA student, can improve an organization's chances of achieving its objectives. In chapter 6 we cover all aspects of leadership and team building.

CASE STUDY
B&Q

Sometimes something as basic as getting your employees to more properly reflect your customer base can change your business proposition as dramatically as a shift in price, promotion, product or place. In 1989, B&Q, the largest home improvement and garden centre retailer in the UK and Europe and the third-largest in the world, made a major change to the profile of its workforce. In response to customer comments that they wanted to be served by someone who had lived in their own home and knew something about home improvements, B&Q set each of its 330 UK stores the objective of employing a workforce that reflects the make-up of the local community, with an emphasis on employing people over 50. This initiative delivered 18 per cent higher profits, with one-sixth of the previous level of staff turnover. Not only are the shareholders happy, B&Q – owned by Kingfisher whose other main retail brands include Castorama, Brico Dépôt, Screwfix and Koçtaş – the employees are too. The company is one of only eight organizations in the world to have won Gallup's Great Workplace Award three years in a row, scoring 4.24 out of five, a near 'world-class' achievement.

Physical evidence

The physical environment needs to be attractive and appropriate, particularly for retail businesses. So when Tiffany's flagship London store opened in 2018 they built in features that encouraged creative interaction and play, including an in-store Tiffany fragrance vending machine. Services as we know are largely intangible when you think about marketing them. However, customers tend to rely on physical cues to help them evaluate the product before they buy it.

To make a service tangible to the customer, marketers develop what is called physical evidence to replace these physical cues in a service. The role of the marketer is to design and implement such tangible evidence, varying it as appropriate in the marketing mix process.

For example ambience can be used to help customers experience the service on offer. In a club, loud music and flashing lighting will be the order of the day, while in a spa candles and the smell of scent can be used to deliver a calm therapeutic environment. The marketer task is to make ambience support and enhance the service being sold.

Process

How you deliver your product or service (the process) is another element in the marketing mix that you can be varied or improved so as to give your business a competitive edge. Complicated ordering systems, confusing websites and unhelpful returns policies can work against your business. So for example customers going on a package holiday will have first-hand experience of all the elements of process that make up a streamlined process to ensure a satisfactory trip – they'll expect to be able to book the holiday on a website, get their e-tickets issued by email, check in and retrieve their baggage without lengthy queues, experience smooth transit from the airport to the hotel and receive a swift resolution to any handling problems.

Process is now such a critical element in the marketing mix that it has attracted a whole new business discipline, business process re-engineering (BPR). This re-engineering process involves a fundamental rethinking and radical redesign of business processes to achieve dramatic improvements in critical measures of performance such as cost, quality, service and speed.

CASE STUDY
Ingredient Solutions Limited

Getting the marketing mix right is as important as getting its food raw materials to exacting standards for Ingredients Solutions Limited. The leading producer of innovative cheese ingredients for the food industry, Ingredient Solutions first opened its doors for business in 2000, when founder and managing director Ian Galletly moved to Ireland from the UK, where he had been working in the industry for 14 years. By 2020 the company has achieved annual turnover approaching €50 million by successfully satisfying the increasingly diverse tastes of today's ever more discerning consumer. It certainly helps being located in Boherbue, County Cork, the heart of the cheese producing region of Ireland.

Galletly has an interesting approach to keeping all his employees fully up to speed on what really matters. A full-length window wall exposes the factory to the team responsible for administration and maintaining customer relationships. Everyone can see if the highest standards of hygiene are being maintained – nothing kills off a business in this sector like a food scare. Even the biggest, most established business can be brought down in this area. The window onto the factory floor also lets Ingredient Solution's support team actually see what orders and new product trials are going through the factory in real time, lending authority and confidence to their communication with customers.

Ingredient Solutions' customer service department, technical support and NPD team work with customers and suppliers alike in order to make profitable products from great ideas. In fact, the company is committed to achieving and exceeding the needs of its customers by meeting the demands of today's fast-changing cheese marketplace.

Ingredient Solutions has also recently won major contracts in the UK, thanks to its ability to not only meet but exceed customers' requirements when compared to their existing suppliers. The company expects to continue to attract new work by providing this excellent quality of product and service.

WORKSHEET FOR ASSIGNMENT 11: PEOPLE, PROCESS
AND PHYSICAL ENVIRONMENT

1 Are all people who come in contact with customers the right people for that type of work and have they been properly trained?

2 Are customers being given the right level of after-sales support and advice?

3 Do customers know where their order is in the production – despatch – delivery process?

4 Can customers reach you by phone, email or your website and get their questions answered quickly and efficiently?

5 Can you demonstrate in some way that is visible to your customers and employees that you are meeting the appropriate quality standards?

Suggested further reading

Chartered Institute of Marketing. *Marketing and the 7Ps,* www.cim.co.uk/files/7ps.
    pdf (archived at perma.cc/78M6-272P)

Tutor2U, Extended Marketing Mix (7P's), www.tutor2u.net/business/reference/
    the-extended-marketing-mix-7ps (archived at perma.cc/25Y2-CRKY)

ASSIGNMENT 12

Competing online

Few if any businesses can hope to survive – let alone compete – without an online presence. However, for many new businesses their marketing effort starts and stops with getting a website.

According to the Office for National Statistics internet sales as a percentage of total retail sales was 22 per cent in February 2020, up from 2.5 per cent in November 2006. The coronavirus pandemic of 2020 took the ratio to upwards of 25 per cent. Research shows that many retailers already report that around two thirds of website browsing takes place on smartphones and tablets, and a rapidly growing number of consumers conclude their purchase in this way.

The range of products sold online is extending considerably, and with it the way business does business is changing. For example, car buyers used to make five or more visits to a dealer while making up their minds, but now, according to research by the University of Buckingham, 86 per cent do most of their tyre-kicking online, making barely one showroom visit before making their choice. So showrooms have been supplanted by websites and social media work on platforms like Facebook and Twitter.

Of course the internet business world and the 'real' world overlap and, in some cases, overtake. Jessops, for example, died on the UK high street in January 2013, closing 187 stores, only to be born again on 28 March that year with a slimmed-down estate of 30 shops and a major presence on the internet, under a new owner, Peter Jones of *Dragons' Den* fame. Many of the old economy entrants to the e-economy have kept the 'mortar' as well as acquiring 'clicks'. Trust stems from customers being able to physically see what the company stands for. Tesco, the UK-based international retailer, uses specially developed software to offer an intelligent internet tool that reacts to customers' shopping habits, suggesting different sites related to subjects or products they're interested in. In this way, Tesco hopes to build a similar level of trust to that achieved in its stores, but over the internet. The firm uses its local stores for 'pick and pack' and delivers locally using smaller vehicles.

Making your online presence effective, then, is vitally important. This chapter gives you a good grounding in what you need to know to harness the power of the internet.

CASE STUDY
Minerva Tutors

Founded in 2014 by Hugh Viney, London-based Minerva works with over 60 tutors to help children aged 5–18 with their exams and education, both through tutoring classes and home-schooling. Viney, former Head Boy and Top Academic Scholar at Stowe School, read Classics at UCL and began tutoring soon after graduating. Frustrated by his own experiences of the industry, he has as his company's mission 'to improve standards and professionalism for parents and tutors alike'.

Described by the Good Schools Guide as 'the Innocent Drinks of the tutor world', the business has proved a success. Their latest accounts filed in June 2019 show that they have been profitable from the outset, accumulating close on a £250,000 profit in their short life.

In February 2020, when the coronavirus pandemic dealt a hammer blow to the business world in general, businesses such as Minerva, which centred on close contact tutoring in-person, had to reinvent themselves or die. Viney switched to tutoring entirely online, staying in touch with his tutors via Google Hangouts and keeping students engaged using online whiteboards. Fortunately, the operations side of Minerva was already online. Their own tech platform, Temple, is designed so that parents can log in and monitor pupil progress via detailed, individual lesson reports.

Registering a domain name

Having an internet presence means that you need a domain name, the name by which your business is known on the internet which lets people find you by entering your name into their browser address box, such as example.com. Ideally, you want a domain name that captures the essence of your business neatly so that you come up readily on search engines, and one that's as close as possible to your business name (see Assignment 3 where we cover naming your business).

Domain names come in all shapes and sizes. Those such as '.com', exude an international/US flavour, and '.co.uk' implies a UK orientation. Charities usually opt for '.org', or '.org.uk', and '.net' or '.net.uk' are used by network service providers. Businesses often use '.biz', but it doesn't really matter what domain you use: what you want is to be seen. Some domains are restricted. For example '.ac.uk' is used by higher education institutes in the UK and '.gov.uk' is used by UK government departments.

If your business name is registered as a trademark (see Assignment 7) you may (as current case law develops) be able to prevent another business from using it as a domain name on the internet.

After you've decided on a selection of domain names your internet service provider (ISP), the organization that you use to link your computer to the internet, can submit a domain name application on your behalf. Alternatively, you can use:

- Nominet UK, the registry for British internet domain names, where you find a list of members who can help you register (though you can do so yourself if you're web aware).

- A world directory of internet domain registries if you want to operate internationally, for example, by using a '.com' suffix or a country-specific domain.

- A company that sells domain names, such as Own This Domain and 123 Domain Names, which provide an online domain-name registration service, usually with a search facility so you can see whether your selected name has already been registered. Electric Names has a detailed domain name registration on its websites as well as offering a same-day registration service for prices between £10 and £25 per annum.

- Free domain that you obtain along with free web space by registering with an internet community. These organizations offer you web pages within their community space as well as a free domain name, but most communities only offer free domain names that have their own community domain tagged on the end and this addition can make your domain name rather long and hard to remember, and unprofessional.

CASE STUDY
Moonpig

Nick Jenkins saw that reliance on word-of-mouth promotion is also a desirable attribute in a company's name. He wanted a domain name that was easy to remember and fun enough that customers would want to tell their friends about it. He was looking for a two-syllable domain but couldn't find the right combination available and didn't want to buy one from somebody else. Moonpig – Nick's school nickname – worked. At the time, if you entered it into Google nothing came up, and there was the added advantage that it lent itself well to a logo – it's easy enough to remember a pig in a space helmet.

Building a website

You might be forgiven for thinking that a website is just for those selling on the internet; that, however, is just one of the many uses a website can be put to.

In fact, as the list below confirms, a well-thought-out website is the heart of the operations function in almost any venture of any size:

Recruitment. Once established, you can advertise for staff on your own website. In that way you can be sure applicants will know something of your business, and you could cut out most of the costs of recruitment.

Market research. By running surveys you can find out more about your customers' needs, check out whether new products or services would appeal to them, and monitor complaints to prevent them becoming problems.

Save communication costs. Businesses get dozens of phone calls and letters asking essentially the same questions. By having an FAQ (frequently asked questions) section on your website you can head off most of those and save time and money.

Designing your website

Good website design is essential: short loading time (use graphics, not photographs), short, sweet, legible text and an attractive layout. Research indicates that within three clicks, visitors must be captivated or they will leave. Clear signposting is necessary, including a menu on every page so that visitors can return to the homepage or move to other sections in just one click.

These are the dos and don'ts in website design.

Do:

- *think about design*: create a consistent visual theme grouping elements together so that your reader can easily follow the information you are presenting;
- *prepare your content*: it should be focused on the needs of your target audience, and be credible, original, current and varied;
- *plan your site navigation*: your pages need to be organized intuitively so they are easy to navigate;
- *consider usability and accessibility*: use graphics sparingly as not everyone has super access speeds;

- *optimize your HTML*, especially on your home page, to minimize file size and download time by removing excess spaces, comments, tags and commentary;
- *optimize for searching*: build in key words and tags and markers so your site will be found easily.

Don't:

- *have long pages*: content beyond the first one and a half to two page lengths is typically ignored;
- *have pointless animation*: many of these are distracting, poorly designed in terms of colour and fonts, and add unnecessarily to file size, slowing down your reader's search;
- *use the wrong colours*, since colour choice is crucial; black text on a white background is the easiest to read while other colours such as reds and greens are harder to read (check out VisiBone's website for a simulation of the web designer's colour palette of browser-safe colours);
- *have stale information anywhere*, especially on your homepage: nothing turns readers off so much as seeing information that relates to events long gone (recipes for Christmas pudding at Easter, for example);
- *waste your readers' time*: making readers register on your site may be useful to you, but unless you have some compelling value to offer, don't – or if you absolutely must, keep registration details to a couple of lines of information.

Check out Bad Website Ideas to see how to avoid the biggest howlers, and in consequence how to get your website design right.

Doing it yourself

You probably already have a basic website writing tool with your business software. You will also find hundreds of packages from £10 to around £500 that with varying amounts of support will help you create your own website. Website Builder Expert reviews the latest out-of-the-box websites and has tools, resources and articles to help a complete novice get started; or if they get stuck to find a web designer to take over.

Getting outside help

There are thousands of consultants who claim to be able to create a website for you. Prices start from £150, where an off-the-peg website package will be tweaked slightly to meet your needs, to around £5,000 to get something closer to tailor-made for you.

The Web Design Directory list hundreds of consultants, some one-man bands, others somewhat larger. You can look at their websites to see whether you like what they do. It also has some useful pointers on choosing a designer.

If you are working within a set budget you could consider auctioning off your web design project. With sites such as Freelancer you state how much you are prepared to pay, with a description of the project, and freelancers around the world bid under your price, with the lowest bidder winning. Also check out Fiverr, People Per Hour and Upwork.

Getting seen – search engines

Nine out of 10 visitors reach internet sites via a search engine or equivalent, so you need to fill the first page with 'key terms' that search engines can latch onto. This process is known as SEO (search engine optimization), where your website is 'optimized' so that it improves its position in search engine rankings.

Getting listed

If you want to be sure of getting listed appropriately in a search engine, first make a list of the words that you think a searcher is most likely to use when looking for your products or services. For example, a repair garage in Penzance could include keywords such as car, repair, cheap, quick, reliable, insurance, crash and Penzance in the home page to pull in searchers looking for a competitive price and a quick repair. As a rule of thumb, for every 300 words you need a keyword or phrase to appear between 10 and 15 times. Search engines thrive on content, so the more relevant content, the better. You can use products such as that provided by Good Keywords which has a free Windows program to help you find words and phrases relevant to your business and provides statistics on how frequently those are used. Keywords have a paid-for product (priced at £35) which has several additional filters and tools to help you refine your keyword lists.

Search engine algorithms also like important, authoritative and prestigious terms. So while you may not be able to boast 'by Royal Appointment', if you can get your press releases quoted in the *Financial Times*, your comments included in postings on popular blogs or your membership of professional institutes and associations into your homepage, your chances of being 'spidered' will rise accordingly.

Next on the list of strategies is to get your website linked to other sites with related but not competing information. So if you are selling garden pots, websites selling plants, gardening tools, fencing or compost are likely to have people hitting them who are of value to you. Being linked to dozens of other sites improves your chances of being spotted by a search engine. You can offer the sites in question a link to your site as a quid pro quo, and you could both benefit from the relationship.

Using a submissions service

You can build words into your website to help search engines find you. You can also go to a professional. Submission services such as Submit Express, Rank4u and Wordtracker have optimization processes that aim to move you into the top 10 ranking in key search engines. 'Aim' is the important word here. These services don't guarantee anything, so the proof of the pudding is in the eating. If it works, you can always go back for a second helping.

Payment methods vary. For example, Rank4u has a no-placement, no-fee deal where you pay only after it's achieved the positioning you want. This service isn't on offer to every business all the time, so you need to check it out yourself. 123 Ranking has optimization packages aimed at small and new businesses from £344 per annum. Search Engine Guide has a guide to all aspects of search engine marketing.

Paying for placement

If you don't want to wait for search engines to find your website, you can pay to have your web pages included in a search engine's directory. That won't guarantee you a position; so, for example, if your page comes up at 9,870 in Google's list then the chance of a customer slogging his way to your page is zero. The only way to be sure you appear early in the first page or two of a search is to advertise in a paid placement listing. Major search engines such as Google AdWords and Microsoft's Bing invite you to bid on the terms you want to appear for, by way of a set sum per click.

Tracking traffic

A wealth of information is available on who visits your website: where they come from in terms of geography, search engine and search term used; where they enter your website (homepage, FAQs, product specifications, price list, order page) and how long they spend in various parts of your website. That information is aside from the basic information you automatically receive from orders placed, enquiries made or email contacts.

You can use visitor data to tweak your website and content to improve the user experience and so achieve your goals for the website. For example, you may find that lots of visitors are entering your website via a link found on a search engine that takes them to an inappropriate section of your site, say the price list, when you want them to start with the benefits of your product or success stories. By changing the key words on which your website is optimized, or by putting more visible links through the site, you can drive traffic along your chosen path.

A good way to measure the success of your website is to make use of the free Google Analytics package available from the Google website. Google Analytics tracks the traffic that comes to your website from all referrers, email marketing, search engines, pay-per-click downloads, display advertising and links from PDF documents. In doing so, Google Analytics gathers and reports data that shows how well your website is doing and enables you to make sense of all this information. The package also serves up statistics that provide details about the people who visit your website and allows you to track your landing page quality and to see the specific pages your visitors are viewing.

Google Analytics is aimed at marketers and business types, rather than webmasters and technologists and techie types, which makes it easy to use.

Managing email, forums, blogs and websites

Electronic mail (email) was the earliest online marketing tool, used for sending direct messages to one person or to many people. Messages that could be read by groups of people morphed into forums, known as Usenet newsgroups, and eventually became the current form of online web-based forums. Throughout these fast technological changes, the way people communicate has changed in major ways. Social networks and other multimedia and social media tools and platforms are incredibly popular, but the use of traditional online communications tools still has a lot of value.

Email

Email is still the most important online marketing tool now in use, and it can tie in with all kinds of initiatives more easily than ever. Doing business consists of reactions, interactions and actions and as such email clearly has a major role to play. When you send out an email, you and others can react, respond, interact and take actions such as these:

- Pass along the email to others.
- Download a file attached to an email.
- Click a link to visit a website.
- Play an embedded audio or video file.
- Fill out a form embedded into the body of the email.
- Take a poll or survey embedded in the email.
- Connect to someone's social networking accounts.
- Click a link to begin an online purchase.

Email is more than a message carrier. It's a conversation starter as well as a multimedia and multi-featured communications tool to engage others beyond simple back-and-forth communications.

Online forums (groups) and blogs

When you have people gathering online to discuss common topics, you have the seeds for building online community. Where you have online community, you have the potential for actions, reactions and interactions. Online forums and groups work well when several factors are present:

- *A focused topic area or theme.* Conversations in the best forums remain on topic.
- *Like-minded or interested people.* People join groups voluntarily based on their interests and needs.

- *Strong community leadership.* A good moderator keeps the discussion going with a light touch so that everyone feels welcome to the conversation.
- *Clear community rules.* Every group needs publicly posted guidelines that define proper behaviour and spell out bad behaviour.
- *Fair policing.* Many online communities police themselves, admonishing or removing individuals who post inappropriately, and others let moderators ban people.

You can find out more about the range of online communities and blogs that you can tap into at Blogpress.

Social media

The dictionary defines social media as 'websites and applications that enable users to create and share content or to participate in social networking'. Social media can be seen as a collection of online communications channels dedicated to community-based input, interaction, content sharing and collaboration. Social media may be still in its infancy, but it is prolific and influential. That using social media for business has become a mainstream activity is evident in the fact that the options are numerous and expanding fast. Aside from the usual suspects – Facebook, LinkedIn and Twitter – hundreds of sector-specific sites exist. Pinterest, for example, is a tool for collecting and organizing pictures of things that inspire you. YouTube provides a forum for people to inform billions of people around the world by distributing videos for free. eHarmony, Match.com and 6,000 other dating sites aim to help the lonely find love. Social bookmarking sites, including Digg, Delicious, Newsvine and Reddit, allow users to recommend online news stories, music and videos. Then you have word-of-mouth forums including blogs, company-sponsored discussion boards and chat rooms, and consumer product or service ratings websites and forums like Skytrax airlines rating, TripAdvisor and local-business review site Yelp.

Social media sites make up at least half of the top 20 websites in most regions of the world. Today even the smallest of businesses can incorporate social media into their promotional plan, and at Social Media Examiner you'll find tips on how to get started on Facebook, Twitter, Instagram, LinkedIn, Google+, Pinterest and YouTube, as well as how to get your first blog (a web page where people record and share opinions) and podcast (a digital file containing video or audio material that can be accessed online) off the ground.

CASE STUDY
Hotel Chocolat

Generating a buzz of interest using social media is one thing, but you can get a lot more than that from a social media drive; you can push the real sales curve up too. In a recent analysis of more than 60 Facebook marketing campaigns, 49 per cent reported a return on investment of more than five times, and 70 per cent had a return on investment greater than three times. Forums, online communities with an interest in your product, can be tapped into for more than ideas; they can be induced to part with upfront cash, given the right proposition.

Hotel Chocolat, winner of prestigious awards including Number 1 in the *Times* 'Fast Track 100', Retail Week 'Emerging Retailer of the Year' and one of the UK's prestigious 'Cool Brands', did just that. Angus Thirlwell, Hotel Chocolat's co-founder, launched a chocolate tasting club to develop recipes and ideas. To join the 'club' you have to place an initial order for £9.95's worth of chocolates, representing a 60 per cent saving on the retail price. For that you get a box of chocolates, tasting notes and a free gift from Munch & Nibble. From there you can then continue and become a tasting club member with all-new selections regularly sent to your door. Thirwell's social media strategy is a neater and more effective way of generating a customer's first order than by using a crude discount on its own. The tasting club's 100,000 members demonstrates the power of having a strong social media presence as part of an online marketing strategy.

WORKSHEET FOR ASSIGNMENT 12: COMPETING ONLINE

1 To gain visibility, run a competitive website analysis into the performance of your website or proposed website with those of your competitors. Use Alexa or any similar website comparison tool.

2 Brainstorm a list of key words that people could use when searching for your products or services online. Then see how those could be built in and repeated on your website.

3 Decide on your domain name, making sure first that you can use it. Test it out online to make sure it can be found easily, does not conflict with similar names that might 'steal' you web traffic and does not pull up your direct competitors.

4 Check out submission services to see if they could be useful.

5 Review social media activity in your market and see which channels – Instagram, Pinterest, Twitter, Facebook, LinkedIn etc are most used by current players.

6 Start using Google Analytics to track and analyse your website traffic.

Suggested further reading

Croxen-John, D and van Tonder, J (2017) *eCommerce Website Optimization*, Kogan Page, London

Gil, C (2019) *The End of Marketing: Humanizing your brand in the age of social media and AI*, Kogan Page, London

Kingsnorth, S (2019) *Digital marketing strategy: An integrated approach to online marketing*, Kogan Page, London

Rowles, D (2017) *Mobile Marketing*, Kogan Page, London

Ryan, D (2014) *Understanding Digital Marketing: Marketing strategies for engaging the digital generation*, Kogan Page, London

Van Dyck, F (2014) *Advertising Transformed: The new rules for the digital age*, Kogan Page, London

Operations

Introduction

Operations is the general name given to all the activities required to implement strategy. So, for example, once you have decided what to sell, to whom and at what price, you may still need to find someone to sell, make and distribute for your business.

Of necessity, the emphasis you put on each element of this assignment will depend entirely on the nature of your business. Your business plan need not show the complete detail of how every operational activity will be implemented. Clearly, you and your colleagues will need to know, but for the business plan it is sufficient to show that you have taken account of the principal matters that concern your venture, and have a workable solution in hand.

This section discusses some of the most important operational issues to be addressed in your business plan. Assignments 13–15 are intended to help you to bring your customers, competitors and the marketplace more sharply into focus, and to identify areas you have yet to research.

ASSIGNMENT 13

The selling methods plan

Anyone considering backing your plans will look long and hard at how you plan to sell. Unbelievably, it is an area often dismissed in a couple of lines in a business plan. That error alone is enough to turn off most investors. Just because customers know you are in the market is not in itself sufficient to make them buy from you. Even if you have a superior product at a competitive price they can escape your net.

Getting people to sign on the dotted line involves selling, and this is a process that anyone championing a new proposition will have to use in many situations other than in persuading customers to buy. They have to 'sell' to their bank manager the idea that lending them money is worthwhile, to a potential partner that he or she should team up with them; and eventually to employees that working for their company is a good career move.

How selling works

There is an erroneous view that salespeople, like artists and musicians, are born, not made. Selling can be learnt, improved and enhanced just like any other business activity. First, you need to understand selling's three elements.

- Selling is a *process* moving through certain stages if the best results are to be achieved. First, you need to listen to the customers to learn what they want to achieve from buying your product or service; then you should demonstrate how you can meet their needs. Often entrepreneurs launch into a pitch about their product from the outset without listening first. Often this results in a missed opportunity to stress particular relevant benefits, or worse still, alienates the potential customers as the impression is given that their needs are secondary. The next stage in the selling process is handling questions and objections; this is a good sign as it shows that the customer is sufficiently interested to engage. Finally comes 'closing the sale'. This is little more than asking for the order with a degree of subtlety. Once again many owner-managers feel too embarrassed to push for a conclusion. This stage is a bit like fishing; pull before the hook is in and you lose the fish. You need a bite, a buying signal, before you close.

- Selling requires *planning* in that you need to keep records and information on customers and potential customers so that you know when they might be ready to buy or reorder. This is particularly important if you have to travel any distance to visit them. You need to plan your territory so that your time is used efficiently and you don't end up criss-crossing the country wasting hours in travel time. Second, you need to plan each sales pitch, trying to anticipate needs and objections beforehand, so that you can have answers to hand and close the sale.

- Selling is a *skill* that can be learnt and enhanced by training and practice, as shown in the case study. The Free Index lists over 7,400 sales training providers searchable by location and specialization.

CASE STUDY
1E

When Sumir Karayi, with a B.Eng and an MSc (IT) from Warwick University, started up in business in the spare room of his flat in West Ealing, London, he wanted his business to be distinctive. He was a technical expert at Microsoft, and with two colleagues he set up 1E as a commune aiming to be the top technical experts in their field. The business name comes from the message that appears on your screen when your computer has crashed. Within a year of starting up the team had learnt two important lessons. Businesses need leaders, not communes, if they are to grow fast and prosper; and they need someone to sell.

On the recommendation of an adviser Karayi went on a selling course, and within months he had won the first of what became a string of blue chip clients. The company is now one of the 10 fastest-growing companies in the Thames Valley, with annual turnover approaching £25 million, profits of 30 per cent, and partners and reseller partners worldwide.

Today 1E is headquartered in London, with regional offices in New York, Dublin, and New Delhi. They have deployed more than 26 million licences worldwide, helping 1,700 organizations in 42 countries work more efficiently, productively and sustainably.

Using agents

If you are not going to be your business's main salesperson you need to brace yourself for costs of around £50,000 a year to keep a good salesperson on the road, taking salary, commission and expenses into account. The problems with employing your own salespeople is that initially they won't sell enough to cover their costs, and you may get the wrong person and so end up with just a big bill and no extra sales.

A less-risky sales route is to outsource your selling to freelance salespeople. Here you have two options.

- Employ a sales outsourcing company such as Pareto's Sales as a Service. Using Pareto you get a graduate sales team, fully assessed and trained in the fundamentals. They enter your business ready to hit the ground running, without adding to your fixed sales costs, but with the flexibility to take them on as permanent staff, or give notice to end the contract at any time. For an even more flexible and cost-effective route it is worth considering People per Hour, which can find and manage a salesperson for you on a short-term basis.

- Find an agent yourself, ideally with existing contacts in your field, who knows buyers personally and can get off to a flying start from day one. The Manufacturers Agents Association has a directory of commission agents selling in all fields of business. You have to pay £330 (incl. VAT) by credit card for an MAA Net Search allowing you to contact up to 20 agents in one search.

CASE STUDY
Howard Fabian

Howard Fabian's business was designing and selling greetings cards. His main market was London and the south-east of England, where there were 120 important shops to be sold to. He planned to sell to these accounts himself. This meant visiting all the outlets once at the outset. He could make four to five calls a day, so it would take between four and five weeks to cover the ground. After that he would visit the most important 30 every month, the next 30 every two months, and he would phone or visit the remainder from time to time, and send samples of new designs in the hope of encouraging them to order. While on an enterprise programme at Cranfield he took a professional selling skills course.

Outside London and the south-east, Howard proposed to appoint agents, based in the principal provincial cities. To recruit these he planned to use the trade press and the Manufacturers Agents Association. Each appointment would be made on a three-month trial basis, and he had an agency contract explaining this business relationship drawn up. He proposed to set each agent a performance target based on the population in this catchment area. Sales within 25 per cent of target would be acceptable; outside that figure he would review the agent's contract.

Initially he was looking for 10 agents, whom he would visit and go out with once a quarter. As selling time in a shop was short, it was important that he and his agents should have a minimum set agenda of points to cover, and a sales presenter to show the range quickly and easily from the standing position.

Getting paid

The sale process is not complete until, as one particularly cautious sales director put it: 'the customer has paid, used your product and not died as a consequence'. You do have responsibilities for the safety of everyone involved in your business, including customers, the legal aspects of which are dealt with at the end of this chapter. One of the top three reasons that new businesses fail is because a customer fails to pay up in full or on time. You can take some steps to make sure this doesn't happen to you by setting prudent terms of trade and making sure the customers are creditworthy before you sell to them.

Checking creditworthiness

There is a wealth of information on credit status for both individuals and businesses of varying complexity, at prices from £5 for basic information through to £200 for a very comprehensive picture of credit status. So there is no need to trade unknowingly with individuals or businesses that pose a credit risk.

The major agencies that compile and sell personal credit histories and small-business information are Experian, Dun & Bradstreet and Creditgate.com. Between them they offer a comprehensive range of credit reports instantly online, including advice on credit limit and CCJs (county court judgements).

Setting your terms of trade

You need to decide on your terms and conditions of sale, and ensure they are printed on your order acceptance stationery. Terms should include when and how you require to be paid, and under what conditions you will accept cancellations or offer refunds. The Law Donut website contains information on most aspects of trading relationships.

EXAMPLE

One unfortunate entrepreneur felt that his business, a management training consultancy, had got off to a good start when his first client, a major US computer company, booked him for three courses. Just three weeks prior to the first of these courses, and after he had carried out all the preparatory work and prepared relevant examples, handouts, etc, the client cancelled the order. The reason given was a change in 'policy' on training dictated by the overseas parent company.

If this entrepreneur had included in his standard terms and conditions a cancellation clause, then he would have received adequate compensation. In fact, he was operating on a 'wing and a prayer', had no terms of trade, and wasn't even aware there was an industrial 'norm'. Most of his competitors charged 100 per cent cancellation fee for cancellations within three weeks, 50 per cent within six weeks, 25 per cent within eight weeks, and for earlier cancellations no charge.

Cash or cheque

Cash has the attraction in that if you collect as you deliver your product or service you are sure of getting paid and you will have no administrative work in keeping tabs on what is owed you. However in many business transactions this is not a practical option, unless as in retailing for example, you are present when the customer buys. A cheque underwritten with a bank guarantee card is as secure as cash, assuming the guarantee is valid. But the cheque will take time to process. In practice you would be wise, until you have checked out the creditworthiness of the customer in question, to await clearance of the cheque before parting with the goods.

You need to be careful in interpreting banking terminology here. Your bank may state that the cheque is 'cleared' when in fact it is only in transit through the system. The only term in bank parlance that means your money is really there is 'given value'. If you have any concerns, ring your bank and ask specifically if you can withdraw funds safely on the cheque in question.

Credit cards

Getting paid by credit card makes it easier for customers to buy and makes it certain that you will get your money almost immediately. With a merchant account, as the process of accepting cards is known, as long as you follow the rules and get authorization the cash, less the card company's 1.5–3 per cent, gets to your bank account the day you charge.

You can get a merchant account without a trading history as a new venture, depending of course on your credit record. See Streamline, a division of Worldpay, who in turn are owned by venture capital firms Bain Capital and Advent International, Barclaycard and HSBC.

Dealing with delinquents

However prudent your terms of trade and rigorous your credit checks, you will end up with late payers and at worst nonpayers. There are ways to deal with them, but it must be said that experience shows that once something starts to go wrong it usually gets worse. There is an old investment saying, 'the first loss is the best loss', that applies here.

The most cost-effective and successful method of keeping late payers in line is to let them know you know. Nine out of 10 small businesses do not routinely send out reminder letters advising customers that they have missed the payment date. Send out a polite reminder to arrive the day after payment is due, addressed to the person responsible for payments, almost invariably someone in the accounts department if you are dealing with a big organization. Follow this up within five days with a phone call, keeping the pressure up steadily until you are paid.

If you are polite and professional, consistently reminding them of your terms of trade, there is no reason your relationship will be impaired. In any event the person you sell to may not be the person you chase for payment.

If you still have difficulty consider:

- Using a debt collection agency. You can find a directory of registered agents on the Credit Service Agency website.

- If your claim is for less than £100,000 and is for a fixed specific sum then you can use the UK government's Make a money claim online service. For small amounts, up to around £3,000, the fee is mostly less than £100. Over £10,000 and the fee is 5 per cent of the claim. The service has the merit of saving legal costs and the expense is a finite sum.

WORKSHEET FOR ASSIGNMENT 13: THE SELLING METHODS PLAN

Describe briefly the main operational aspects that are involved in ensuring that your strategy is successfully implemented. In particular, you should consider:

1 Who will conduct the selling for your business, and have they been professionally trained to sell?

2 What selling methods will they employ?

3 Will you use point-of-sale material – leaflets, brochures or videos, for example?

4 Who will manage, monitor and control your sales effort and how will they do so?

5 Describe the selling process, leading from an unaware prospect to a converted client, covering identification of decision makers, overcoming objections, gaining agreement, etc.

6 What procedures do you have for handling customer complaints?

7 What incentives are there for people to meet sales targets and how will you motivate them to do so?

8 Who will direct, monitor and control your sales effort and what experience/ skills do they have?

9 How long is the process from becoming aware of your product or service to making the buying decision, receiving the product or service and finally paying for it? This will have an important bearing on your cash flow and initial sales forecast.

10 What sales volume and activity targets, such as calls per day, etc, have you set for each salesperson or selling method?

11 What processes will you use to ensure you are paid on time?

Suggested further reading

Barnes, C, Blake, H and Howard, T (2107) *Selling Your Value Proposition*, Kogan Page, London

Denny, R (2013) *Selling to Win*, Kogan Page, London

Hazeldine, S (2013) *Neuro-sell: How neuroscience can power your sales success*, Kogan Page, London

Johnston, M W and Marshau, G W (2016) *Sales Force Management: Leadership, innovation, technology*, Routledge, London

Kolah, A (2013) *The Art of Influencing and Selling*, Kogan Page, London

Maes, P (2018) *Disruptive Selling: A new strategic approach to sales, marketing and customer service*, Kogan Page, London

ASSIGNMENT 14

Making, outsourcing and supplies

Organizations are usually, in fact almost invariably, in the business of adding value to bought-in resources. These may be as trivial as stationery for correspondence, packaging for software, or as complex as the many ingredients needed to make a computer or a motor vehicle.

Your business plan needs to show how you have addressed these crucial issues, as in the first place you must demonstrate that you have thought through how to turn what is in effect at this stage a concept into a 'concrete' product or service that can be brought to market. You also need to show an awareness that value added is itself determined by the careful management of costs.

Making and assembling

If you need specific machinery, the general rule is that you should buy as little as possible as inexpensively as possible, as there is one certain fact about a new venture – after a few weeks or months of trading it will resemble less and less the business you planned to start. That in turn means that your initial investment in equipment could be largely wasted when you find you need to re-equip. Look back to the section on 'Outsourcing' in Assignment 10, and consider whether there are any less risky or costly methods of getting your product ready for market.

For machinery and equipment you should use a trade magazine to search out suppliers. Alternatively Friday-Ad and Machinery Classified have second-hand machinery and tools of every description for sale.

If your business involves making or constructing products, then you should address the following issues in the business plan:

CASE STUDY
Production methods

One Cranfield graduate enterprise programme had these examples of different types of operation:

- Jenny Row designed her knitwear herself, but had it made up by out-workers. In this way she could expand or contract output quickly, paying only the extra cost of materials and production, for more orders. It also left her free to design new products to add to her existing range.

- Tim Brown sold computer systems tailor-made to carry out solicitors' conveyancing work. He commissioned software writers to prepare the programs, bought in computers from the manufacturer and selected a range of printers to suit individual customers' requirements. His end product was a total system, which he bought in 'kit' parts from his various subcontractors. Apart from IBM and a handful of giants, no one company could produce all these elements in-house.

- Graham Davy designed and manufactured his own range of furniture. He rented a Beehive workshop and bought in cutting, turning and polishing tools, and a finish spraying room. He bought in wood, and worked on it himself, producing batches of three or four of each design. The equipment needed for design and prototype work was also sufficient for small-batch production.

- Will you make the product yourself, or buy it in either ready to sell, or as components for assembly? You should also explain why you have chosen your manufacturing route.

- Describe the manufacturing process to be used, and if appropriate explain how your principal competitors go about their manufacturing.

- What plant and equipment will you need and what output limits will they have? (See Table 14.1.)

- Provide a rough sketch of the layout of your manufacturing unit, showing the overall size of facility needed, the positioning of equipment, etc, and the path of materials and finished goods.

- What engineering support, if any, will you need?

- How will you monitor and control quality?

TABLE 14.1 Example showing goods needed, their purpose and cost

Plant/ equipment	Process (what does it do?)	Maximum volume	Cost	Do you already own it?

There are a number of well-regarded quality standards that may help you monitor and control your quality. The BS/ISO 9000 series are perhaps the best-known standards. They can ensure that your operating procedure will deliver a consistent and acceptable standard of products or services. If you are supplying to large firms they may insist on your meeting one of these quality standards, or on 'auditing' your premises to satisfy themselves. The British Standards Institution can provide details of these standards.

A number of commercial organizations will provide user-friendly guidelines and systems to help you reach the necessary standard. Searching the web using key words such as 'quality standards' (or 'measurement') will bring you some useful sites.

Materials and sources of supply

Your business plan should also explain what bought-in materials you require, who you will buy them from, and how much they will cost. Finding suppliers is not too difficult; finding good ones is less easy. Business-to-business directories, such as Kelly Search, Kompass and Applegate, between them have global databases of over 2.4 million industrial and commercial companies in 190 countries, listing over 230,000 product categories. You can search by category, country and brand name. You should check the supplier's:

- terms of trade;
- level of service;
- customer list, getting feedback from other customers;

- guarantees and warranties on offer;
- price, making sure that they are competitive;
- compatibility, ie that you will enjoy doing business with them;
- What major items of bought-in materials or services will you require?
- Who could supply those and what are the terms and conditions of sale?
- Why have you chosen your supplier(s)?

Keep stock cards so that you can identify fast- and slow-moving stock.

Other buying options

Aside from searching out suppliers through directories and word of mouth, consider one or more of the following strategies.

BARTERING ONLINE

You can avoid using up your cash by bartering your products and services for those of other businesses. An organization that can help you get started with bartering is Bartercard.

BUY ONLINE

There are over 200 price comparison websites covering computer hardware and software, phones, travel, credit cards, bank accounts, loans, utilities, electrical goods, office products including inkjet and printer supplies, and a few thousand more items a business might purchase. Paler.com, a quirky website run by Petru Paler has a directory listing these sites, with brief explanations and a helpful comment page where users have inserted more sites and additional information.

Fitting out an office

You will need an 'office' to work from, but this should not be a costly affair at the outset. There are plenty of sources offering good-quality office furniture and equipment at a low cost. For new furniture supplied to most European countries and around the world, check out Amazon and IKEA, who both have Home Office categories. For second-hand office furniture search Wantdontwant.com and Reuse Network, a national network of reuse centres stocking, affordable office furniture, electrical appliances, IT equipment and more.

WORKSHEET FOR ASSIGNMENT 14: MAKING, OUTSOURCING
AND SUPPLIES

Describe briefly the main 'manufacturing' aspects that are involved in ensuring
that your strategy is successfully implemented. In particular, you should
consider:

1 How much of your product or service do you plan to produce in-house?

2 If you are making a product, describe the production process; also explain
how your principal competitors go about manufacturing.

3 What plant and equipment will you need, what can it do, how much will it
cost and where will you get it from?

4 What bought-in materials and/or services will you need, where will you buy
them from and how much will they cost?

5 How will you equip your office?

Suggested further reading

Lefteri, C (2012) *Making It: Manufacturing techniques for product design,*
Laurence King, London

Vagadia, B (2011) *Strategic Outsourcing: The alchemy to business transformation
in a globally converged world*, Springer, Germany

ASSIGNMENT 15

Legal and regulatory factors

The manner in which businesses and organizations operate, whether they are for profit, in the charity and not-for-profit sector or even a public service, is governed by regulations.

All of these regulations have a major impact on cash flow, the amount of start-up capital required and the profit margins that can be obtained. For example, electing to pay value added tax on a cash accounting basis can lower cash needs and speed up cash flow, attractive attributes for any venture. However, selling on credit, for which a licence is required, can increase funding needs and add to administrative costs. But if selling on credit is the norm in the business sector you plan to enter, or is a key ingredient of your competitive strategy, that burden has to be faced and prepared for.

These regulations can be loosely clustered under two headings: *customer facing*, those that deal with the rules concerning relationships with consumers; and *taxation*, those that deal with the various dues to the state that organizations have to either pay directly or to collect for onward transmission. Omitting the implications of these regulatory matters in your business plan will seriously weaken it and may even, when subsequently the financial implications are included, render a proposition unviable.

Other specific regulatory matters such as legal form, intellectual property, property consents and employment matters are covered in the relevant sections of this workbook.

Customer-facing regulations

From the claims being made by some businesses and the shoddy treatment handed out to customers you might be forgiven for believing that *caveat emptor* (let the buyer beware) was the rule of the marketing road. Far from it. In fact, organizations are heavily regulated in almost every sphere of their operations. What follows are the main customer-facing regulations that you will need to take account of in running any venture.

CASE STUDY
Google fights the law

Google China, founded in 2005, was headed by former Microsoft executive, Kai-Fu Lee until 4 September 2009. His appointment was just the first of a number of serious controversies that beset Google, with Microsoft initially suing both parties for breach of contract only to reach a confidential settlement within months. The Chinese government operated, and still does, a level of censorship on all communication media, alien to Western culture. To enter the Chinese market Google had to operate a form of self-imposed censorship known as the 'Golden Shield Project'. The effect of this was that whenever people in China searched for keywords on a list of blocked words maintained by the government, google.cn displayed the following at the bottom of the page (translated):

> 'In accordance with local laws, regulations and policies, part of the search result is not shown.'

Though this form of restriction appeared contrary to Google's culture, its management argued that it could be more useful to the cause of free speech by participating in China's IT industry even under such terms, rather than being excluded. In a company statement Google declared: 'While removing search results is inconsistent with Google's mission, providing no information (or a heavily degraded user experience that amounts to no information) is more inconsistent with our mission.' In short, Google chose what it saw as the lesser of two evils. Nevertheless, in deciding to launch the censored service, Google was attacked on all fronts by free-speech campaigners and accused of 'sickening collaboration' in a Congressional hearing.

By the start of 2010 Google had only a third of the search-engine market in China, a market dominated by local giant Baidu. Though its sales revenues continued to rise, it was finding business hard going. On 12 January 2010, Google and more than a score of other US companies recognized that they had been under cyber attack from an organization or organizations based in mainland China. During an investigation into these attacks evidence came to light to demonstrate that the Gmail accounts of key human rights activists connected with China were being routinely accessed by third parties. Also, attempts over the preceding year were made in China to further limit free speech on the web, including the persistent blocking of Facebook, Twitter, YouTube, Google Docs and Blogger.

On 12 January 2010 Google declared it was no longer willing to censor content on its Chinese site after discovering that hackers had obtained proprietary information and email data of some human-rights activists. Google is still reckoned to be popular with Chinese citizens, though they wisely take the precaution of accessing via a VPN (virtual private network) to hide their IP addresses.

Getting a licence or permit

Some businesses, such as those working with food or alcohol, employment agencies, mini-cabs and hairdressers, need a licence or permit before they can set up in business at all. Your local authority planning department can advise you what rules will apply to your business. You can also use the GOV.UK website to find out which permits, licences and registrations will apply and where to get more information.

Complying with advertising and descriptive standards

Any advertising or promotion you undertake concerning your business and its products and services, including descriptions on packaging, leaflets and instructions and those given verbally, has to comply with the relevant regulations. You can't just make any claims you believe to be appropriate for your business. Such claims must be decent, honest, truthful and take into account your wider responsibilities to consumers and anyone else likely to be affected. If you say anything that is misleading or fails to meet any of these tests, you could leave yourself open to being sued.

The four bodies concerned with setting the standards and enforcing the rules are:

- The Advertising Authority for printed matter, newspapers, magazines and so forth and the internet.
- Ofcom is responsible for ensuring advertisements on television and radio comply with rules on what can and cannot be advertised, including any special conditions such as the timing and content of material aimed at children.

- The Financial Conduct Authority has the responsibility to see that financial promotions are clear, fair and not misleading.
- The Trading Standards Institute covers anything such as quantity, size, composition, method of manufacture, strength, performance, place of manufacture, date, brand name, conformity with any recognized standard or history.

Dealing with returns and refunds

Customers buying products are entitled to expect that the goods are 'fit for purpose' in that they can do what they claim to. Also, if the customer has informed you of a particular need the products must be suitable for that purpose. The goods also have to be of 'satisfactory quality', ie durable and without defects that would affect performance or prevent their enjoyment. For services you must carry the work out with reasonable skill and care, and provide it within a reasonable amount of time. The word 'reasonable' is not defined, and is applied in relation to each type of service. So for example, repairing a shoe might reasonably be expected to take a week, while three months would be unreasonable.

If goods or services don't meet these conditions customers can claim a refund. If they have altered an item or waited an excessive amount of time before complaining, or have indicated in any other way that they have 'accepted' the goods, they may not be entitled to a refund, but may still be able to claim some money back for a period of up to six years.

Distance selling and online trading

Selling by mail order, via the internet, television, radio, telephone, fax or catalogue, requires that you comply with some additional rules over and above those concerning the sale of goods and services described above. In summary, you have to provide written information, an order confirmation, and the chance to cancel the contract. During the cooling-off period customers have the unconditional right to cancel within seven working days, provided they have informed you in writing by letter, fax or email.

There are, however, a wide range of exemptions to the right to cancel, including accommodation, transport, food, newspapers, audio or video recordings and goods made to a customer's specification. GOV.UK publishes a guide for business on distance selling on its website.

Protecting customer data

If you hold personal information on a computer on any living person, a customer or employee for example, then there is a good chance you need to register under the Data Protection Act. The rules state that the information held must have been obtained fairly, be accurate, held only for as long as necessary and held only for a lawful purpose.

You can check whether you are likely to need to register on the GOV.UK website.

Getting a consumer credit licence

If you plan to let your customers buy on credit, or hire out or lease products to private individuals or to businesses, then you will in all probability have to apply for a licence to provide credit. If you think you may need a licence, read the regulations on the website of the Financial Conduct Authority. Businesses must be authorized by the FCA, or have interim permission, to offer consumer credit.

Computing taxes

Any organization handling money is responsible for paying a number of taxes and other dues to the government of the day, both on its own behalf and for any employees it may have, as well as being an unpaid tax collector required to account for end-consumers' expenditure.

There are penalties for misdemeanours and late payments, and more serious penalties for anything that could be construed as tax evasion – a crime, as opposed to tax avoidance, the prudent arrangement of your affairs so as to minimize taxes due. You are required to keep your accounting records for six years, so at any point should tax authorities become suspicious they can dig into the past even after they have agreed your figures. In the case of suspected fraud there is no limit to how far back the digging can go.

Value added tax (VAT)

VAT, a tax common throughout Europe though charged at different rates, is a tax on consumer spending, collected by businesses. Basically it is a game of pass the parcel, with businesses that are registered for VAT (see below) charging each other VAT and deducting VAT charged. At the end of each accounting period the amount of VAT you have paid out is deducted from the amount you have charged and the balance is paid over to HM Revenue & Customs (HMRC).

In the United Kingdom the standard rate is 20 per cent, while some types of business charge lower rates and some are exempt altogether. The way VAT is handled on goods and services sold to and bought from other European countries is subject to another set of rules and procedures. HMRC provides full details on VAT.

PAYMENT METHODS

Normally VAT is paid each quarter but small businesses can take advantage of a number of schemes to simplify procedures or aid their cash flow. The annual accounting scheme lets you pay monthly or quarterly estimated figures, submitting a single annual return at the end of the year with any balancing payment. The cash accounting scheme allows you to delay paying over any VAT until you have actually collected it from your customers. The flat-rate scheme allows you to calculate your VAT as a flat percentage of your total sales, rather than having to record the VAT charged on individual purchases and sales.

Accounting for profit

You will pay tax on any profit made in your business. The rate at which you will pay depends on the legal structure chosen. If you are a sole trader or in a partnership you will pay tax at your personal marginal rate, either 20 per cent or 40 per cent; limited companies will pay at a rate of 20 per cent on profits. These tax rates are subject to change each year or so.

THE FINANCIAL YEAR AND PAYMENT DATES

The financial year for tax purpose is usually 6 April to 5 April, although some businesses use different dates such as the calendar year-end if it is more appropriate for their type of business. You need to get your tax return back to HMRC by 30 September if you want it to calculate the tax due, or by 31 January if you are happy for you or your accountant to do the sums. The tax itself is paid in two stages at the end of July and January. Companies have to calculate their own tax due and pay it nine months after their year-end. You will be fined and charged interest on any late tax payments.

FILING ACCOUNTS FOR A COMPANY

A company's financial affairs are in the public domain. As well as keeping HMRC informed, companies have to file their accounts with Companies House. Accounts should be filed within 10 months of the company's financial year-end. Small businesses (turnover below £5.6 million) can file abbreviated accounts which include only very limited balance sheet and profit and loss account information, and these do not need to be audited. You can be fined up to £1,500 for filing accounts late. You can find out how to file your companies accounts and complete a tax return online.

ESTIMATING TAX DUE

Tax is due on the profit of your business, which might not be the same amount as the figure arrived at in your profit and loss account. For example, you will include depreciation, entertainment and perhaps other expenses in your profit and loss account. Although it is important for you to know how much and on what they were incurred, these are not allowable expenses for tax purposes. Your accountant will be able to give you a good steer in this area. Bytestart. co.uk, the small business portal, has a useful overview of business expenses which goes someway to clarifying what are 'allowable' and 'non-allowable' expenses. This guide provides an overview of business expenses, with links to further resources which provide more in-depth information.

PAYE (PAY AS YOU EARN)

Employers are responsible for deducting income tax from employees' wages and making the relevant payment to HMRC. If you trade as a limited company, then as a director any salary you receive will be subject to PAYE. You will need to work out the tax due. HMRC has guidance on PAYE on its website, together with all the necessary forms. There are also a range of PAYE tools for employers to carry out all the tedious calculations.

Dealing with National Insurance (NI)

Almost everyone who works has to pay a separate tax – National Insurance (NI) – collected by HMRC, which in theory at least, goes towards the state pension and other benefits. NI is paid at different rates, and self-employed people pay Class 4 contributions calculated each year on the self-assessment tax form.

The amount of NI paid depends on a mass of different factors: married women, volunteer development workers, share fishermen, self-employed and small earnings are all factors that attract NI rates of between 1 per cent and 13.8 per cent. The UK government website, for example, provides all the information required to calculate and pay the appropriate National Insurance.

Help and advice with tax

HMRC has online guides for employers and business and corporations linked directly from its home page. Tax Café has a series of guides priced at around £25 each on such subjects as *Using a company to save tax* and *Salary vs dividends* as well as tax saving tactics.

WORKSHEET FOR ASSIGNMENT 15: LEGAL AND REGULATORY FACTORS

1   Does your venture require a licence to operate?

2   Will you be holding data on customers, suppliers and employees, and if so what are the implications of the Data Protection Act on your plans?

3   Does your proposed advertising, both print and website, comply with the various advertising regulations?

4   How will you handle refunds?

5   Will you have to register for VAT, or could it be to your advantage to do so?

6   If you have to register for VAT, which is the best scheme for you?

7   How much tax do you expect to have to pay?

8   Will you have to collect and pay tax for any employees?

9   How much NI will you be responsible for paying?

10   Have you incorporated the cost implications of these operating regulations in your financial forecasts?

Suggested further reading

Kolah, A (2014) *Essential Law for Marketers*, Kogan Page, London

Pink, A (2020) *Practical Tax Planning for Business*, Pink Proactive Publishing LLP, Tunbridge Wells, Kent

Reviewing financing requirements and options

Introduction

Once you have formulated a basic or new strategy for your business, you will have to make some forecast of the likely results of your endeavours. These projections are essential to show how much cash you will need and how much profit you could make, and to chart a safe financial strategy. This is the part of your business plan of greatest interest to potential backers and anyone else whose support is essential to your venture.

Your forecasts may well prove wrong, and initially at least, you may have little confidence in them being achieved. But the learning that comes from carrying out these projections will serve to increase the chances of ending up with a plan that you do believe in, and that has a good chance of achieving results that will ensure your venture survives.

The task in forecasting is to get your dart on the board, rather than to hit the bullseye first time. Once on the board you can correct your aim with subsequent throws. Remember these forecasts are being made before you commit resources, so in effect, you can have as many throws as you like at this stage, without the pain of the resultant consequences.

The final chapter in this section is Stress testing your business projections. This is a timely reminder, as shown during the recent pandemic, that events can take a radically unexpected turn.

Suggested further reading

Allen, F, Meijun Q and Xie J, Understanding informal financing, *Journal of Financial Intermediation*, 2019, 39, 19–33, 52.76.234.106/media/abfer-events-2013/annual-conference/corporate-finance/track2-understanding-informal-financing.pdf (archived at https://perma.cc/Y2G5-M59Q)

Arundale, K (2007) *Raising Venture Capital Finance in Europe: A practical guide for business owners, entrepreneurs and investors*, Kogan Page, London

Bloomfield, S (2008) *Venture Capital Funding: A practical guide to raising finance,* 2nd edn, Kogan Page, London

Cumming, D J and Johan, S (2013) *Venture Capital and Private Equity Contracting: An international perspective,* Academic Press, Massachusetts

Parsons, N (nd) Do You Need a Business Plan? Scientific Research Says Yes, *Bplans,* articles.bplans.com/do-you-need-a-business-plan-scientific-research-says-yes/ (archived at https://perma.cc/C4C9-44ZJ)

ASSIGNMENT 16

The sales forecast

The precision of numbers often bears no relation to the facts.
DENIS HEALEY, FORMER CHANCELLOR OF THE EXCHEQUER

The sales forecast is perhaps the most important set of numbers to come out of the business planning process. How much stock to hold, how many staff to employ, how much material to buy, are all decisions that hinge on the sales forecast. These sales figures are also used to predict the cash-flow forecast and hence the funding requirements of the business.

These projections are also the key to valuing the business, so they will determine whether or not bankers will lend and investors invest. Furthermore, they will give some guidance as to how much of an enterprise investors expect in exchange for funding.

Naturally enough, potential backers do not accept a sales forecast unchallenged as, in their experience, new ventures nearly always miss the target by a wide margin.

While forecasts may turn out to be wrong, it is important to demonstrate in your business plan that you have thought through the factors that will have impact on performance. You should also show how you can deliver satisfactory results even when many of these factors may be working against you. Backers will be measuring the downside risk to evaluate the worst scenario and its likely effects, as well as looking towards an ultimate exit route.

Here are some guidelines to help you make an initial sales forecast.

- *Check how others have fared*: your overall projections will have to be believable. Most lenders and investors will have an extensive experience of similar business proposals. Unlike yourself, they will have the benefit of hindsight, and are able to look back several years at other ventures they have backed to see how they fared in practice compared with the ventures' initial forecasts. You could gather some useful knowledge on similar businesses yourself by researching filed company accounts and trade magazines, or by talking with the founders of such ventures who will not be your direct competitors. Look back to Assignments 5 and 6 for guidance on how to research competitor performance.

CASE STUDY
Scoops

Edmund Bradley estimated that in its first year of trading, Scoops would generate £50,000 worth of sweet sales. The projection was based upon observation of the numbers of purchases made by a competitor's outlet in Bath (Confetti), over a one-week period. The number of customers per hour varied between 34 (during rainy weather) and 140 (when sunny), with an average expenditure per purchase of £1. Discussions with confectionery-shop owners revealed that the summer months of June, July and August, plus Christmas (December), accounted for half of the year's sales. In other months, purchases made on Saturdays accounted for half the weekly sales.

Based on a different town population (Taunton is half the size of Bath), Edmund estimated that Scoops would only attract half the customers of Confetti and would require an average of 25 customers per hour to reach his sales target. As well as working there himself, he planned to employ one full-time assistant, part-time help on Saturdays and student part-timers in the summer and Christmas vacations.

- *Work out market share*: how big is the market for your product or service? Is it growing or contracting? At what rate and percentage per annum? What is its economic and competitive position? These are all factors that can provide a market-share basis for your forecasts.

An entry market share of more than a few per cent would be most unusual. In spite of all the hype, after more than a decade of hard work the internet booksellers still account for less than 10 per cent of all books sold, and Amazon is just one of a score of major players. But beware of turning this argument on its head.

Many sales forecasts are made on the premise that 'If we capture just 1 per cent of the potential market, we'll be a great success.' This statement is made so that no time is wasted in doing basic market research – after all, the business only has to sell to this tiny percentage of possible buyers!

In fact, this type of thinking leads to more business failures than any other single factor. If the market is so huge as to make 1 per cent of it very profitable, then inevitably there are large and established competitors. For a small firm to try to compete head on in this situation is little short of suicidal. It can be done, but only if sound research has clearly identified a market niche. No investor will be impressed by unsubstantiated statements such as 'In a market of £/$/€1 billion per annum, we can easily capture 1 per cent – £/$/€1 million a year.'

• *Think about your customers*: how many customers and potential customers do you know who are likely to buy from you, and how much might they buy? You can use many types of data on which to base reasonable sales projections: you can interview a sample of prospective customers, issue a press release or advertisement to gauge response and exhibit at trade shows to obtain customer reactions.

CASE STUDY
Werner Herker

Having arranged UK suppliers and fixed teams to install Victorian conservatories in Germany, qualified engineer and Cranfield MBA Werner Herker formed a company and placed a tiny advertisement in the leading German television listings magazine. With over 15 replies, and knowing that an average fitted installation costs at least £25,000, Werner was able to accurately forecast his first year's sales and accordingly launched a successful company.

• *Be aware of order cycles and timescales*: if your product or service needs to be on an approved list before it can be bought, then your forecast should confirm you have that approval.

• *Look at seasonality*: you should consider seasonal factors that might cause sales to be high or low in certain periods of the year. For example, 80 per cent of toys are sold in just three months of the year, leaving nine very flat months. If you were selling toys, this would have a significant effect on cash-flow projections.

CASE STUDY
Using rules of thumb: Tim Brown

When Tim Brown founded his second restaurant, Alamo, in Los Angeles, with substantial backing from private investors, he used one such rule. In his experience, once a restaurant has served 25,000 clients it can expect sufficient repeat business to break even. In his first eight months of operation he had achieved 20,000.

- *Use rules of thumb where possible*: for some businesses, there are rules of thumb that can be used to estimate sales. This is particularly true in retailing, where location studies, traffic counts and population density are all known factors.

- *Work out your desired income*: forecasts will accommodate the realistic aims of the proprietor. You could even say that the whole purpose of strategy is to ensure that certain forecasts are achieved. This is more likely to be the case in a mature company with proven products and markets than with a start-up. Nevertheless, an element of 'how much do we need to earn?' must play a part in forecasting, if only to signal when a strategy is not worth pursuing.

- *Relate the sales forecast to activity*: however they are arrived at, sales figures will convince no one unless they are related back to the specific activities that will generate business. For example, if, in your business, salespeople have to make visits to generate orders, then knowing how many calls need to be made to get one order and what the average order size could be are essential pieces of information to include in your sales forecast.

- *How far ahead should you forecast?* Opinions are divided between three and five years ahead. However, financiers we have talked to, while often asking for a five-year view, only pay serious attention to the first three years.

    The arguments for looking this far ahead are twofold. First, most new ventures are at their greatest risk in the first few years, so investors and lenders want to see that the proprietors have a well-thought-out strategy to cover this period. Second, venture capitalists in particular want to look forward to the time when they can realize their investment and move on. Typically their exit route has to materialize between years 3 and 5 – they hope, during the earliest of the three.

    The first two years of the sales forecast should be made on a monthly basis, and the remaining three years on a quarterly basis.

The examples below provide a flavour of the range of possible outcomes for the first few years of a new venture's life.

CASE STUDY
Starbucks – forecasting is believing

Most people believe Howard Schultz to be the founder of Starbucks, but that accolade belongs to Jerry Baldwin, Zev Siegl and Gordon Bowker, three friends, who shared a passion for fresh coffee. They opened their first outlet in Seattle in 1971 and by the time Shultz, a plastics salesman for Hammarplast, saw the opportunity to roll the business out, it was 1981 and Starbucks was the largest coffee business in Washington with six retail outlets selling fresh coffee beans. The founders were forecasting a similar pace of growth for the next decade or so, but Shultz's vision was to create community gathering places like the great coffee houses of Italy and transplant them to the United States.

The idea didn't strike a chord with Baldwin, who had hired Shultz as his marketing manager, but he let him try out the concept of selling espresso by the cup in one of his stores. Baldwin remained unconvinced, so Shultz started out on his own, opening a coffee house he named Il Giornale, after Italy's then biggest-selling newspaper.

In 1987 the owners of Starbucks sold out to Schultz who convinced a group of local investors to stump up US$3.7 million (£2.22 million/€2.6 million) with the goal of opening 125 outlets over the following five years. Shultz abandoned the name Il Giornale in favour of Starbucks, and has gone on to open more than 15,000 retail locations in North America, Latin America, Europe, the Middle East and the Pacific Rim.

Forecasting sales once you have started trading

While your business plan will contain your sales objectives – that is, what you want to achieve over the coming three years or so – the base forecast is the most likely future outcome, given what has happened in the past. That forecast provides the momentum to underpin the sales figures that you put into your cash-flow and profit projections. Figure 16.1 shows an example sales history for years one to three, the trend of those sales over the coming three years, and the sales objectives for the next three years that will be used for the financials of the business plan. You can see that the objectives are moving well ahead of trend and it is the filling of this gap that your marketing strategy needs to justify.

FIGURE 16.1 Sales history, trend and future objectives

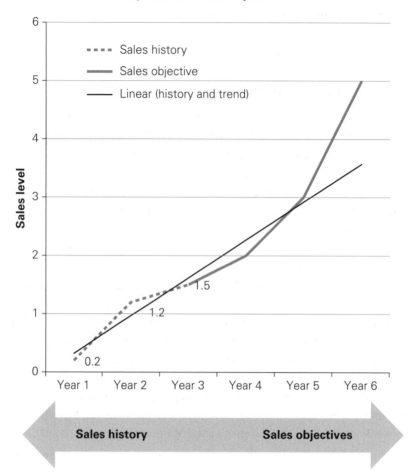

Forecasting tools

With a sales history there are a number of techniques that can make a fore-cast easier to make and more credible.

- *Moving average.* This method takes a series of data from, say, the last six months' sales, adds them up, divides by the number of months and uses that figure as being the most likely forecast of what will happen in month seven. This method works well in a static, mature marketplace where change happens slowly, if at all.

- *Weighted moving average.* This method gives the most recent data more significance than the earlier data since it gives a better representation of current business conditions. So before adding up the series of data each figure is weighted by multiplying it by an increasingly higher factor as you get closer to the most recent data.

There are a number of much more sophisticated forecasting techniques but for business planning purposes these will be sufficient to show you have applied some serious thought to your sales projections. Professor Hossein Arsham of the University of Baltimore provides a useful tool that allows you to enter your historical data and see how different forecasting techniques perform (Arsham, 1994–2015).

WORKSHEET FOR ASSIGNMENT 16: THE SALES FORECAST

1 Provide details of any firm orders on hand.

2 Provide details of all customers you expect to sell to over the forecast period, and how much you expect to sell to each.

3 Give market research data that support or verify these forecasts. This is particularly important for ventures in the retail field, for example, when names of customers are not necessarily known in advance.

4 Prepare a sales forecast by value and volume for each major product group (eg for a hotel: bedrooms, restaurant, off-licence) throughout the whole period of the business plan – eg up to five years (monthly for years one and two and quarterly thereafter).

5 Support your forecast with examples from other similar ventures started recently, and drawing from company accounts and other sources.

6 Give an estimate of the likely market share that these forecasts imply.

Suggested further reading

Berry, T (2010) *Sales and Market Forecasting for Entrepreneurs*, Business Experts Press, US

Leventhal, B (2018) *Predictive Analytics for Marketers: Using data mining for business advantage*, Kogan Page, London

Mason, R (2013) *Successful Budgeting and Forecasting in a Week (Teach Yourself)*, Hodder & Stoughton, London

Reference

Arsham, H (1994–2015) *Time-Critical Decision Making for Business Administration*, home.ubalt.edu/ntsbarsh/stat-data/Forecast.htm (archived at https://perma.cc/E22F-FPTA)

ASSIGNMENT 17

Cash-flow projections

Cash flow versus profit

It is a generally accepted principle that the purpose of business is to make a profit. There is, however a purpose that is even more important – survival. In the short term, a business can survive even if it is not making a profit as long as it has sufficient cash reserves, but it cannot survive without cash even though it may be making a profit. The purpose of the cash-flow projection is to calculate how much cash a business is likely to need to accomplish its objectives, and when it will need it in the business. These projections will form the basis of negotiations with any potential provider of capital.

Cash-flow assumptions

The future is impossible to predict with great accuracy, but it is possible to anticipate likely outcomes and be prepared to deal with events by building in a margin of safety. The starting point for making a projection is to make some assumptions about what you want to achieve and test them for reasonableness.

Take the situation of High Note, a new venture being established to sell sheet music, small instruments and CDs to schools and colleges, which will expect to be given trade credit, and members of the public, who will pay cash. The owners plan to invest £10,000 and to borrow £10,000 from a bank on a long-term basis. The business will be run initially out of a converted garage adjoining their home and will require £11,500 to install windows, heat, light, power, storage shelving and a desk and chairs. A further £1,000 will be needed for a computer, software and a printer. That should leave around £7,500 to meet immediate trading expenses such as buying in stock and spending £1,500 on initial advertising. They hope customers' payments will start to come in quickly to cover other expenses such as some wages for bookkeeping, administration and fulfilling orders. Sales in the first six months are expected to be £60,000 based on negotiations already in hand, plus some cash sales that always seem to turn up. The rule of thumb in the industry seems to be that stock is marked up by 100 per cent; so £30,000 of bought-in goods sell on for £60,000.

Forecasting cash needs

On the basis of the above assumptions it is possible to make the cash-flow forecast set out in Table 17.1. It has been simplified and some elements such as VAT and tax have been omitted for ease of understanding.

TABLE 17.1 High Note six-month cash-flow forecast

Month	April	May	June	July	Aug	Sept	Total
Receipts							
Sales	4,000	5,000	5,000	7,000	12,000	15,000	
Owners' cash	10,000						
Bank loan	10,000						
Total cash in	24,000	5,000	5,000	7,000	12,000	15,000	48,000
Payments							
Purchases	5,500	2,950	4,220	7,416	9,332	9,650	39,108
Rates, elec, heat, tel, internet, etc	1,000	1,000	1,000	1,000	1,000	1,000	
Wages	1,000	1,000	1,000	1,000	1,000	1,000	
Advertising	1,550	1,550	1,550	1,550	1,550	1,550	
Fixtures/ fittings	11,500						
Computer, etc	1,000						
Total cash out	21,550	6,500	7,770	10,966	12,882	13,240	
Monthly cash surplus/ deficit (−)	2,450	(1,500)	(2,770)	(3,966)	(882)	1,760	
Cumulative cash balance	2,450	950	(1,820)	(5,786)	(6,668)	(4,908)	

The maths in the table is straightforward; the cash receipts from various sources are totalled, as are the payments. Taking one from the other leaves a cash surplus or deficit for the month in question. The bottom row shows the cumulative position. So, for example, while the business had £2,450 cash left at the end of April, taking the cash deficit of £1,500 in May into account, by the end of May only £950 (£2,450 – £1,500) cash remains.

Based on these projections this business would require at least £6,668 of cash to meet the goals in its business plan. A margin of safety would be prudent, so the financing requirement for this venture would be somewhere between £8,000–10,000.

Avoiding overtrading

In the example above the business has insufficient cash, based on the assumptions made. An outsider, a banker perhaps, would look at the figures in August and see that the faster sales grew, the greater the cash-flow deficit would become. We know, using our crystal ball, that the position will improve from September and that if the owners can only hang on in there for a few more months they should eliminate their cash deficit and perhaps even have a surplus. Had they made the cash-flow projection at the outset and either raised more money (perhaps by way of an overdraft), spent less on refurbishing the garage, or set a more modest sales goal, which would have meant a need for less stock and advertising, they would have had a sound business. The figures indicate a business that is trading beyond its financial resources, a condition known as overtrading, which is anathema to bankers the world over.

Estimating start-up cash requirements

The example above takes the cash-flow projection out to six months. You should project your cash needs forward for between 12 and 18 months. Make a number of projections using differing assumptions (for example, seeing what will happen if you get fewer orders, people take longer to buy or adapting your office costs more). Finally when you arrive at a projection you have confidence in, and you believe you can justify the cash needed, build that figure into the financing needs section of your business plan.

If that projection calls for more money than you are prepared to invest or raise from outside, don't just steam ahead and hope for the best. The result could well mean that the bank pulls the plug on you when you are within sight of the winning post. There is a useful spreadsheet that will prompt you through the most common costs at MrSpreadsheet.

Pre-trading cash-flow forecast

Typically a new venture will take a few months to start generating income. Your cash-flow projections need to start from the moment you anticipate incurring costs or generating income. In other words day zero is the time expenses are incurred or a sale is made, even if such expenses or sales are made on a credit basis and are not due to be paid for a further month or more.

WORKSHEET FOR ASSIGNMENT 17: CASH-FLOW PROJECTIONS

Using the cash-flow spreadsheet given above:

1 Construct a cash-flow statement for the pre-trading period leading up to 'opening' day.

2 Construct a cash-flow statement for years 1, 2, 3, 4 and 5 assuming that you achieve the level of sales in your sales forecast.

Remember you should produce years 1 and 2 monthly and years 3, 4 and 5 quarterly. Do not forget to state the key assumptions that you have made in arriving at your figures.

Suggested further reading

Barrow, C (2011) *Practical Financial Management: A guide to budgets, balance sheets and business finance*, 8th edn, Kogan Page, London

Barrow, C (2017) *Understanding Business Accounting for Dummies*, 4th edn, Wiley, New York

ASSIGNMENT 18

The profit and loss account

You may by now be concerned about the financial situation at High Note as revealed in the preceding chapter. After all the business has sold £/$/€60,000 worth of goods that it only paid £/$/€30,000 for, so it has a substantial profit margin to play with. While £/$/€39,108 has been paid to suppliers only £/$/€30,000 of goods at cost have been sold, meaning that £/$/€9,108 worth of instruments, sheet music and CDs are still in stock. A similar situation exists with sales. High Note has billed for £/$/€60,000 but only been paid for £/$/€48,000; the balance is owed by debtors. The bald figure at the end of the cash-flow projection showing High Note to be in the red to the tune of £/$/€4,908 seems to be missing some important facts.

The profit and loss account, the subject of this assignment, and the balance sheet that follows in the next assignment, will complete our picture of this business's financial situation. In practical terms, the cash-flow projections and the profit and loss account projections are parallel tasks which are essentially prepared from the same data. They may be regarded almost as the 'heads' and 'tails' of the same coin – the profit and loss account showing the owner/manager the profit/loss based on the assumption that both sales income and the cost of making that sale are 'matched' together in the same month; and the cash-flow statement looking at the same transactions from the viewpoint that in reality the cost of the sale is incurred first (and paid for) and the income is received last, anywhere between one week and three months later.

Obviously, the implications for a non-cash business of this delay between making the sale and receiving the payment and using a service/buying goods and paying for them are crucial, especially in the first year of the business and when your business is growing quickly.

Some ground rules

The profit and loss account sets out to 'match' income and expenditure to the appropriate time period. It is only in this way that the profit for the period can be realistically calculated. Before we look at the structure of the profit and loss account, it might be helpful to look at the accounting concepts to help us to apply the matching principle.

The realization concept

A particularly prudent entrepreneur once said that an order was not an order until the customer's cheque had cleared, he or she had consumed the product, had not died as a result and, finally, had shown every indication of wanting to buy again.

Most of us know quite different people who can 'anticipate' the most unlikely volume of sales. In accounting, income is usually recognized as having been earned when the goods (or services) are dispatched and the invoice sent out. This has nothing to do with when an order is received, or how firm an order is, or how likely a customer is to pay up promptly.

It is also possible that some of the products dispatched may be returned at some later date – perhaps for quality reasons. This means that income, and consequently profit, can be brought into the business in one period and have to be removed later on. Obviously, if these returns can be estimated accurately, then an adjustment can be made to income at the time.

So the 'sales income' figure that is seen at the top of a profit and loss account is the value of the goods dispatched and invoiced to customers in the period in question.

The accrual concept

Suppose, for example, that you are calculating one month's profits when the quarterly telephone bill comes in. The picture might look like Table 18.1.

This is clearly wrong. In the first place, three months' telephone charges have been 'matched' against one month's sales. Equally wrong is charging anything other than January's telephone bill against January's income. Unfortunately, bills such as this are rarely to hand when you want the

TABLE 18.1 Example showing mismatched account

Profit and loss account for January 2020–21	
	£/$/€
Sales income for January	4,000
Less telephone bill (last quarter)	800
Profit	3,200

accounts, so in practice the telephone bill is 'accrued' for. A figure (which may even be absolutely correct if you have a meter) is put in as a provision to meet this liability when it becomes due.

The difference between profit and cash

Cash is immediate and takes account of nothing else. Profit, however, is a measurement of economic activity that considers other factors which can be assigned a value or cost. The accounting principle that governs profit is known as the 'matching principle', which means that income and expenditure are matched to the time period in which they occur. So for High Note the profit and loss account for the first six months is as shown in Table 18.2.

TABLE 18.2 Profit and loss account for High Note for the six months Apr–Sept

	£/$/€	£/$/€
Sales		60,000
Less cost of goods to be sold		30,000
Gross profit		30,000
Less expenses:		
Heat, electric, tel, internet, etc	6,000	
Wages	6,000	
Advertising	9,300	
Total expenses		21,300
Profit before tax, interest and depreciation charges		8,700

(See Assignment 19 for an explanation of depreciation.)

Structuring the profit and loss account

This account is normally set out in more detail for a business in order to make it more useful when it comes to understanding how the business is performing. For example, although the profit shown in our worked example is £8,700, in fact it would be rather lower. As money has been borrowed to finance cash flow there would be interest due, as there would be on the longer-term loan of £10,000.

In practice we have four levels of profit:

- *Gross profit* is the profit left after all costs related to making what you sell are deducted from income.

- *Operating profit* is what is left after you take away the operating expenses from the gross profit.

- *Profit before tax* is what is left after deducting any financing costs.

- *Profit after tax* is what is left for the owners to spend or reinvest in the business.

For High Note this could look much as set out in Table 18.3.

TABLE 18.3   High Note's extended profit and loss account

	£/$/€
Sales	60,000
Less the cost of goods to be sold	30,000
Gross profit	30,000
Less operating expenses	21,300
Operating profit	8,700
Less interest on bank loan and overdraft	600
Profit before tax	8,100
Less tax at 21%	1,827
Profit after tax	6,723

Making profit projections

You can make the above task a lot easier by using the online spreadsheet at the QuickBooks website, which offers a downloadable Excel spreadsheet that enables you to tailor a cash-flow statement to your own needs. You can find the spreadsheet by scrolling through the Resource Center until you reach the Free Cash Flow Statement Template, Example and Guide.

WORKSHEET FOR ASSIGNMENT 18: THE PROFIT AND LOSS
ACCOUNT

Using the spreadsheet given above:

1   Construct a profit and loss account for years 1, 2, 3, 4 and 5, assuming you
    achieve the level of sales in your sales forecast. Include a statement of key
    assumptions made.

2   Construct a four-line summary (sales, gross profit, operating profit and profit
    before tax) of your profit and loss accounts for the full five years (annually).

3   Carry out a sensitivity analysis, noting by how much each of the following
    must change seriously to affect the apparent viability of your business plan:

    (a) Sales lower by x per cent

    (b) Fixed costs higher by x per cent

    (c) Cost of goods sold higher by x per cent.

Suggested further reading

Barrow, C (2011) *Practical Financial Management: A guide to budget, balance
    sheets and business finance*, 8th edn, Kogan Page, London
Barrow, C (2017) *Understanding Business Accounting for Dummies*, 4th edn,
    Wiley, New York

ASSIGNMENT 19

The balance sheet

So far in our example the money spent on 'capital' items such as the £/$/€12,500 spent on a computer and on converting the garage to suit business purposes has been ignored, as has the £/$/€9,108 worth of sheet music etc remaining in stock waiting to be sold and the £/$/€12,000 of money owed by customers who have yet to pay up. An assumption has to be made about where the cash deficit will be made up, and the most logical short-term source is a bank overdraft. The balance sheet is the accounting report that shows at any moment of time the financial position taking all these longer-term factors into account.

For High Note, the example we have been using in the other finance chapters, at the end of September the balance sheet is set out in Table 19.1.

There are a number of other items not shown in this balance sheet that should appear, such as liability for tax and VAT that have not yet been paid and should appear as current liability. You will find a spreadsheet template to help you construct your own balance sheets at Business Accounting Basics.

The language of the balance sheet

The terms used in financial statements often seem familiar but they are often used in a very particular and potentially confusing way. For example look at the balance sheet below and you will see the terms 'assets' and 'liabilities'. You may think that the money put in by the owner and the profit retained from the years trading are anything but liabilities, but in accounting 'liability' is the term used to show where money has come from. Correspondingly 'asset' means, in the language of accounting, what has been done with that money.

You will also have noticed that the assets and liabilities have been jumbled together in the middle to net off the current assets and current liabilities and so end up with a figure for the working capital. 'Current' in accounting means within the trading cycle, usually taken to be one year. Stock will be used up and debtors will pay up within the year, and an overdraft, being repayable on demand, also appears as a short-term liability.

TABLE 19.1   High Note balance sheet at 30 September

	£/$/€	£/$/€
Assets		
Fixed Assets		
Garage conversion etc	11,500	
Computer	1,000	
Total Fixed Assets		12,500
Working Capital		
Current Assets (CA)		
Stock	9,108	
Debtors	12,000	
Cash	0	
	21,108	
Less Current Liabilities (CL)		
Overdraft	4,908	
Creditors	0	
	4,908	
Working Capital (CA − CL)		16,200
Total Assets		28,700
Liabilities		
Owners' capital introduced	10,000	
Long-term loan	10,000	
Profit retained (from P&L account)	8,700	
Total Liabilities		28,700

Assets

Assets are 'valuable resources owned by a business'. You can see that there are two key points in the definition:

- To be valuable the resource must be cash, or of some use in generating current or future profits. For example, a debtor (someone who owes a business money for goods or services provided) usually pays up. When he or she does, the debtor becomes cash and so meets this test. If there is no hope of getting payment, then you can hardly view the sum as an asset.

- Ownership, in its legal sense, can be seen as being different from possession or control. The accounting use of the word is similar but not identical. In a business, possession and control are not enough to make a resource an asset. For example, a leased machine may be possessed and controlled by a business but be owned by the leasing company. So it is not an asset, but a regular expense appearing on the profit and loss account.

Liabilities

These are the claims by people outside the business. In this example only creditors, overdraft and tax are shown, but they could include such items as accruals and deferred income. The 'financed by' section of our example balance sheet is also considered in part as liabilities.

Current

This is the term used with both assets and liabilities to show that they will be converted into cash, or have a short life (under one year).

Now let's go through the main elements of the balance sheet.

Net assets employed

This is the 'what have we done with the money?' section. A business can only do three things with funds:

- It can buy *fixed assets*, such as premises, machinery and motor cars. These are assets that the business intends to keep over the longer term. They will be used to help to make profits, but will not physically vanish in the short term (unless sold and replaced, like motor cars, for example).

- Money can be tied up in *working capital*, that is, 'things' immediately involved in the business's products (or services), that will vanish in the short term. Stocks get sold and are replaced; debtors pay up, and creditors are paid; and cash circulates. Working capital is calculated by subtracting the current liabilities from the current assets. This is the net sum of money that a business has to fund the working capital. In the balance sheet this is called the net current assets, but on most other occasions the term 'working capital' is used.

- Finally, a business can put money aside over the longer term, perhaps in local government bonds or as an investment in someone else's business venture. In the latter case this could be a prelude to a takeover. In the former it could be a cash reserve for future capital investment. The account category is called *investments*. It is not shown in this example as it is a fairly rare phenomenon in new or small businesses, which are usually cash hungry rather than rich.

Financed by

This section of the balance sheet shows where the money came from. It usually has at least two subheadings, although larger companies can have many more.

- *Share capital.* This is the general name given to the money put in by various people in return for a part share in the business. If the business is successful they may get paid a dividend each year, but their principal reward will come from the expected increase in the worth of the business and the consequent rise in value of their share.

  The profit or loss for each year is added to or subtracted from the shareholders' investment. Eventually, once the business is profitable, it will have some money left each year to plough back into reserves. This term conjures up pictures of sums of cash stored away for a rainy day. It is important to remember that this is not necessarily so. The only cash in a business is that shown under that heading in the current assets. The reserves, like all the other funds, are used to finance a business and are tied up in the fixed assets and working capital.

- The final source of money to finance a business are long- or medium-term loans from outside parties. These loans could be in the form of debentures, a mortgage, hire purchase agreements or long-term loans from a bank. The common features of all such loans are that businesses have to pay interest on the money and eventually repay the capital, whether or not the business is successful. Conversely, if the business is a spectacular success the lenders, unlike the shareholders, will not share in the extra profits.

Some ground rules

These ground rules are generally observed by accountants when preparing a balance sheet.

Money measurement

In accounting, a record is kept only of the facts that can be expressed in money terms. For example, the state of your health, or the fact that your main competitor is opening up right opposite in a more attractive outlet, are important business facts. No accounting record of them is made, however, and they do not show up on the balance sheet, simply because no objective monetary value can be assigned to these facts.

Expressing business facts in money terms has the great advantage of providing a common denominator. Just imagine trying to add laptops and motor cars, together with a 4,000 square foot workshop, and arrive at a total. You need a common term to be able to carry out the basic arithmetical functions, and to compare one set of accounts with another.

Business entity

The accounts are kept for the business itself, rather than for the owner(s), workers, or anyone else associated with the firm. If an owner puts a short-term cash injection into his or her business, it will appear as a loan under current liabilities in the business account. In his or her personal account it will appear as an asset – money he or she is owed by someone else. So depending on which point of view you take, the same sum of money can be an asset or a liability. And as in this example the owner and the business are substantially the same person, the possibilities of confusion are considerable.

This source of possible confusion must be cleared up and the business entity concept does just that. The concept states that assets and liabilities are always defined from the business's viewpoint.

Cost concept

Assets are usually entered into the accounts at cost. For a variety of reasons, the real 'worth' of an asset will probably change over time. The worth, or value, of an asset is a subjective estimate on which no two people are likely to agree. This is made even more complex and artificial because the assets themselves are usually not for sale. So, in the search for objectivity, the accountants have settled for cost as the figure to record. It means that a balance sheet does not show the current worth, or value, of a business.

Depreciation

Fixed assets are usually depreciated over their working life rather than taken as one hit on the profit and loss account. There are accounting rules on the appropriate period to depreciate different assets over, usually somewhere between 3 and 20 years. If we believe the computer has a useful life of four years and the rules allow it, we take £250 a year of cost, by way of depreciation, as an expense item in the profit and loss account for the year in question. Depreciation, though vital for your management accounts, is not an allowable expense for tax purposes. The tax authorities allow a 'writing down' allowance say of 25 per cent of the cost of an asset each year which can be set as an expense for tax purposes. There are periods when the government of the day wants to stimulate businesses to invest, say in computers, and it will boost the writing-down allowance accordingly. This figure will almost certainly not correspond to your estimate of depreciation, so you need a profit for tax purposes and a profit for management purposes. You can see the effect of deprecation on the accounts in Table 19.2. Fixed assets reduce by £/$/€125 of depreciation and there is a corresponding reduction in profit retained for the year, thus ensuring the balance sheet balances.

One of the books you will keep will be a Capital Register, keeping track of the cost and depreciation of all fixed assets. Another accounting rule, that of 'materiality', comes into force here. Technically a pocket calculator costing £/$/€5 is a fixed asset in that it has been bought to use rather than sell and it has a life of over one year. But it is treated as an expense as the sum involved is too small to be material. There are no clear rules on the point at which a cost becomes material. For a big organization it may be for items costing a few thousand pounds. For a small business £/$/€100 may be the appropriate level.

Other assets, such as freehold land and buildings, will be revalued from time to time, and stock will be entered at cost, or market value, whichever is the lower.

The QuickBooks website offers a downloadable Excel spreadsheet that enables you to tailor a balance sheet to your own needs, You can find the spreadsheet by scrolling through the Resource Center until you reach the Free Balance Sheet Template, Example and Guide.

TABLE 19.2   The changes to High Note's balance sheet to account for depreciation

Balance sheet	£/$/€
Asset changes	
Fixed assets at cost	12,500
Less depreciation for six months	125
Net book assets	12,375
Liability changes	
Profit from P&L account reduced by £/$/€125 to	8,575

Going concern

Accounting reports always assume that a business will continue trading indefinitely into the future, unless there is good evidence to the contrary. This means that the assets of the business are looked at simply as profit generators and not as being available for sale.

For example, a motor car might be recorded in the accounts at £3,000 having been depreciated down from its purchase cost. If we knew that the business was to close down in a few weeks, then we would be more interested in the car's resale value than its 'book' value; the car might fetch only £2,000, which is a quite different figure.

Once a business stops trading, we cannot realistically look at the assets in the same way. They are no longer being used in the business to help to generate sales and profits. The most objective figure is what they might realize in the marketplace. Anyone who has been to a sale of machinery will know the difference between book and market value!

Dual aspect

To keep a complete record of any business transaction we need to know both where money came from, and what has been done with it. It is not enough simply to say, for example, that someone has put £/$/€1,000 into their business. We have to show how that money has been used to buy fixtures, stock in trade, etc.

WORKSHEET FOR ASSIGNMENT 19: THE BALANCE SHEET

Using the template link provided at the start of this chapter:

1   Construct a balance sheet for your business as it might look on the day before you start trading. This should be done now.

2   List and explain the assumptions underpinning your financial forecasts.

3   Construct a balance sheet at the end of years 1, 2 and 3 assuming you achieve the level of sales in your sales forecast. These should be done after you have completed the pro forma profit and loss account (Assignment 18) and pro forma cash-flow forecast (Assignment 17).

Suggested further reading

Barrow, C (2011) *Practical Financial Management: A guide to budget, balance sheets and business finance*, 8th edn, Kogan Page, London

Barrow, C (2017) *Understanding Business Accounting for Dummies*, 4th edn, Wiley, New York

ASSIGNMENT 20

Break-even analysis

Calculating your break-even point

Let's take an elementary example: a business plans to sell only one product and has only one fixed cost, the rent.

In Figure 20.1 the vertical axis shows the value of sales and costs in thousands of pounds, and the horizontal axis the number of 'units' sold. The second horizontal line represents the fixed costs, those that do not change as volume increases. In this case it is the rent of £/$/€10,000. The angled line running from the top of the fixed costs line is the variable costs. In this example the business plans to buy in at £/$/€3 per unit, so every unit it sells adds that much to its fixed costs.

Only one element is needed to calculate the break-even point – the sales line. That is the line moving up at an angle from the bottom left-hand corner of the chart. The business plans to sell out at £/$/€5 per unit, so this line is calculated by multiplying the units sold by that price.

The break-even point is the stage at which a business starts to make a profit. That is when the sales revenue begins to exceed both the fixed and variable costs. Figure 20.1 shows the example's break-even point is 5,000 units.

A formula, deduced from the figure, will save time for your own calculations.

$$\text{Break-even point} = \frac{\text{Fixed costs}}{\text{Selling price} - \text{Unit variable cost}}$$

$$\frac{10,000}{£/\$/€5 - £/\$/€3} = 5,000 \text{ units}$$

FIGURE 20.1 Graph showing break-even point

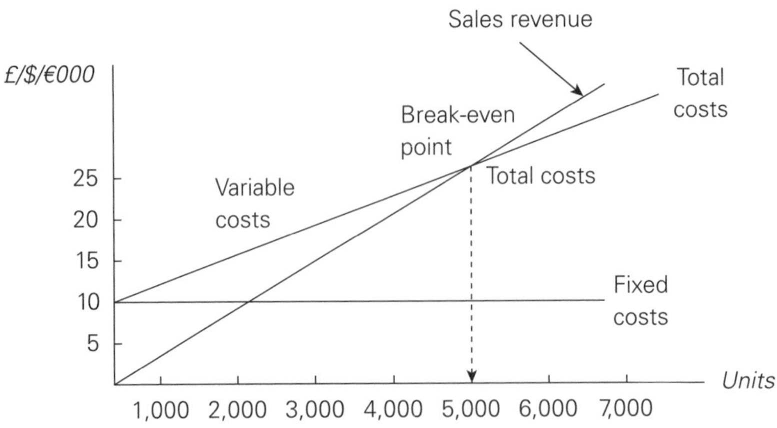

Profitable pricing

To complete the break-even picture we need to add one further dimension – profit. It is a mistake to think that profit is an accident of arithmetic calculated only at the end of the year. It is a specific and quantifiable target that you need at the outset.

Let's go back to our previous example. You plan to invest £/$/€10,000 in fixed assets in a business, and you will need to hold another £/$/€5,000 worth of stock too – in all say £/$/€15,000. You could get £/$/€1,500 profit just leaving that money in a bank or building society, so you will expect a return of say £/$/€4,000 (equal to 27 per cent) for taking the risks of setting up on your own. Now let's see when you will break even.

The new equation must include your 'desired' profit, so it will look like this:

$$\text{Break-even profit point (BEPP)} = \frac{\text{Fixed costs} + \text{Profit objective}}{\text{Selling price} - \text{Unit variable cost}}$$

$$= \frac{10,000 + 4,000}{£/\$/€5 - £/\$/€3} = 7,000$$

We know that to reach our target we must sell 7,000 units at £/$/€5 each and have no more than £/$/€10,000 tied up in fixed costs. The great strength of this equation is that each element can be changed in turn on an experimental basis to arrive at a satisfactory and achievable result. For instance, suppose you decide that it is unlikely that you can sell 7,000 units, but that 6,500 is achievable. What would your selling price have to be to make the same profit?

Using the BEPP equation you can calculate the answer:

$$\text{BEPP} = \frac{\text{Fixed costs} + \text{Profit objective}}{\text{Selling price} - \text{Unit variable cost}}$$

$$6,500 = \frac{10,000 + 4,000}{6,500} = £/\$/€2.15$$

$$£/\$/€x = £/\$/€2.15 + £/\$/€3 = £/\$/€5.15$$

If your market will bear a selling price of £/\$/€5.15 as opposed to £/\$/€5, all is well; if it won't, the ball is back in your court. You have to find ways of decreasing the fixed and/or variable costs, or of selling more, rather than just accepting that a lower profit is inevitable.

From the particular to the general

The example used to illustrate the break-even profit point model was of necessity simple. Few if any businesses sell only one or two products, so a more general equation may be more useful if your business sells hundreds of products, as, for example a real shop does.

In such a business, to calculate your break-even point you must first establish your gross profit. If you are already trading, this is calculated by deducting the money paid out to suppliers from the money received from customers. If you are not yet trading, then researching your competitors will give you some indication of the sort of margins you should aim for.

For example, if you are aiming for a 40 per cent gross profit, your fixed costs are £/\$/€10,000 and your overall profit objective is £/\$/€4,000, then the sum will be as follows:

$$\text{BEPP} = \frac{10,000 + 4,000}{0.4} = \frac{14,000}{0.4}$$

$$= £/\$/€35,000$$

So to reach your target you must achieve a £/\$/€35,000 turnover. (You can check this out for yourself: look back to the previous example where the

BEPP was 7,000 units, and the selling price was £/$/€5 each. Multiplying those figures out gives a turnover of £/$/€35,000. The gross profit in that example was 2/5, or 40 per cent, also.)

Getting help with break-even

BizPep has a useful piece of software, called Pricing Breakeven Analysis, that allows you to calculate your optimal selling price under a wide range of business conditions. A fully functioning download is available free for a seven-day trial. The outputs include break-even charts for current, increased, decreased and optimum pricing calculated for prices ranging from −50 to +50 per cent of your current actual or proposed price. You can carry out the same analysis yourself using the free software from the Harvard Business School (see the earlier section 'Pricing for profit'), but BizPep's templates do some of the grunt and groan for you.

WORKSHEET FOR ASSIGNMENT 20: BREAK-EVEN ANALYSIS

Using the format on the break-even analysis sheet (Table 20.1):

TABLE 20.1

1	Calculate your gross profit		
	Projected sales	£/$/€	
	− Direct costs:		
	Purchases (material costs)	£/$/€	
	Labour costs	£/$/€	
	= Gross profits	£/$/€	(A)
2	Calculate your gross profit margin		

$$\frac{\text{Gross profit (A)} \quad £/\$/€}{\text{Sales} \qquad £/\$/€} \times 100$$

= Gross profit margin   % (B)

Notes:

(continued)

TABLE 20.1 (Continued)

3   Calculate your overheads

Indirect costs:

Business salaries

(including your own drawings)   £ / $ / €

+ Rent   £ / $ / €

+ Rates   £ / $ / €

+ Light/heating   £ / $ / €

+ Telephone/postage   £ / $ / €

+ Insurance   £ / $ / €

+ Repairs   £ / $ / €

+ Advertising   £ / $ / €

+ Bank interest/HP   £ / $ / €

+ Other expenses

(eg depreciation of fixed assets)   £ / $ / €

                                     £ / $ / €

                                     £ / $ / €

                                     £ / $ / €

                                     £ / $ / €

= Overheads   £ / $ / €   (C)

4   Calculate your actual turnover required to break even

$$\frac{\text{Overheads (C)} \qquad £ / \$ / €}{\text{Gross profit margin (B)} \qquad \%} \times 100$$

= Break-even sales £ / $ / €   (D)

5   Calculate the monthly target to break even

$$\frac{\text{Break-even sales (D) £ / \$ / €}}{6}$$

= Monthly break-even sales £ / $ / €

(continued)

TABLE 20.1 (Continued)

---

6   Calculate your estimated profit

   Projected sales   £/$/€

   – Break-even sales (D)   £/$/€

   + Gross profit margin (B)   %

   = Profit (for 12 months)   £/$/€

---

1 Construct a break-even analysis for year 1 of your business from the figures calculated in the last three chapters.

2 Estimate the effect of the following events on your break-even point for each year:

(a) a 10 per cent rise/fall in sales volume;

(b) a 10 per cent rise/fall in unit selling price;

(c) a 10 per cent rise/fall in variable costs per unit of sale, eg a meal;

(d) a 10 per cent rise/fall in fixed costs;

(e) a requirement for achieving your profit objective by year 1 – now what 'volume' of product must you sell to break even?

3 Look back to Assignment 8 on Pricing, and review your proposed selling price in the light of work/research carried out during this assignment.

Suggested further reading

Barrow, C (2011) *Practical Financial Management: A guide to budget, balance sheets and business finance*, 8th edn, Kogan Page, London

Barrow, C (2012) *Business Accounting for Dummies*, 3rd edn, Wiley, New York

ASSIGNMENT 21

Estimating financing requirements

Your business plan may look very professional, showing that you have a very high probability of making exceptional returns, but it will fall at the first hurdle if your funding requirements have not been properly thought out and communicated to potential lenders and investors. It is not sufficient for you to look at your pro forma cash-flow statement and, taking the maximum overdraft position, say:

> The management require £150,000 to commence business, which may come either from bank loans or a share capital injection. The cash-flow projections show that if the funding was by way of a loan it would be repaid within three years. If the funding came from an issue of share capital an excellent return would be available by way of dividends.

Such a statement leaves many questions unanswered, such as:

- Why do you need the money?
- What type of money do you need?
- When will you need it?
- Who is the best source of money for your venture?

The more successful you are, the more money you will need to finance and store stock if you are selling products or to pay wages if you are in a service business. To remain competitive and visible your products and services will need to be kept up to date as will your website, all of which will call for some additional investment.

Santander has a neat tool that allows you to choose the trade you are interested in starting a business in – several hundred are shown, from acupuncture to windscreen services – and the cost calculator will provide a list of the items you may have to buy and their current cost. Scrolling through eight screens of cost prompts, you will arrive at the costs involved in starting that particular type of business.

Why do you need the money?

You probably have a very good idea of why you need the funds that you are asking for, but unless readers of your business plan have plenty of time to spare (which they have not) and can be bothered to work it out for themselves (which they can't), you must clearly state what you will use the funds received for. An example is:

A net investment of £/$/€150,000 is required, which will be used as follows:

	£/$/€
To purchase:	
Motor vehicle	5,000
Plant and equipment	100,000
To provide:	
Working capital for first 6 months	75,000
Total requirement	180,000
Less investment made by (you)	30,000
Net funding requirement	150,000

This statement clearly tells the reader how the funds will be used and gives clear pointers as to appropriate funding routes and timing of the funding requirements.

What type of money do you need?

There are many sources of funds available to independent businesses. However, not all of them are equally appropriate to all firms at all times. These different sources of finance carry very different obligations, responsibilities and opportunities for profitable business. The differences have to be understood to allow an informed choice.

Most new ventures confine their financial strategy to bank loans, either long term or short term, viewing the other financing methods as either too complex or too risky. In many respects the reverse is true. Almost every finance source other than banks will to a greater or lesser extent share some of the risks of doing business with the recipient of the funds.

The great attraction of bank borrowings lies in the speed with which facilities can usually be arranged. Most small businesses operate without a business plan, so most events that require additional funds, such as sudden expansion or contraction, come as a surprise, either welcome or unwelcome. It is to this weakness in financial strategy that banks are ultimately appealing, so it is hardly surprising that many difficulties arise.

Lenders and investors compared

At one end of the financing spectrum lie shareholders: either individual business angels, or corporates such as venture capital providers. These share all the risks and vagaries of the business alongside the founder, and expect a proportionate share in the rewards if things go well. They are not especially concerned with a stream of dividends, which is just as well, as few small companies ever pay them. Instead they hope for a radical increase in the value of their investment. They expect to realize this value from other investors who want to take their place for the next stage in the firm's growth cycle, rather than from any repayment by the founder.

Investors in new or small businesses do not look for the security of buildings or other assets to underpin their investment. Rather they look to the founder vision and the core management team's ability to deliver results.

At the other end of the financing spectrum are the banks, which try hard to take no risk, but expect some reward irrespective of performance. They want interest payments on money lent, usually from day one. While they too hope the management is competent, they are more interested in securing a charge against any assets the business or its managers may own. At the end of the day (and that day can be sooner than the borrower expects), a bank wants all its money back – no more and certainly no less. It would be more prudent to think of banks as people who will help you turn a proportion of an illiquid asset such as property into a more liquid asset such as cash at some discount.

Understanding the differences in expectation between lenders, who provide debt, and investors, who provide equity, or share capital, is central to determining who to approach for funding. In a nutshell, lenders are risk averse, want security cover for any loan, expect to receive interest and for it to be paid on time, and want their money back in a predetermined period of time. Investors, on the other hand, have an appetite for risk, do not expect any payment until the business has grown substantially or has been sold, and rely on the founder's vision and business plan for their confidence in the proposal.

In between the extremes of shareholders and the banks lie a myriad of other financing vehicles that have a mixture of lending and investing criteria. A business needs to keep its finances under constant review, choosing the most appropriate mix of funds for the risks it plans to take and the economic climate ahead. The more risky and volatile the road ahead, the more likely it is that taking a higher proportion of risk capital will be appropriate. In times of stability and low interest, higher borrowings may be more acceptable.

Sources of finance

There are five main sources of finance for new and established ventures:

- your own money;
- loans from banks and other institutions or from family and friends;
- taking investors whom you know something about onboard to share the risks and rewards alongside yourself;
- floating your business to the public at large on a stock market;
- 'free' money by way of grants or winning a competition.

Using your own resources

The first port of call when looking to finance your business should be your own resources. This is usually easier to arrange, cheaper, quicker and less time consuming than any other source of money. There is of course another important advantage in that if you don't tap into bank borrowing and the like you may get a better reception later on once your business is up and running.

Dipping into savings

If you have any savings put aside for a rainy day, you could also consider dipping into them now. You will need to discuss this with your financial adviser as there may be penalties associated with cashing in insurance policies early, for example. The Association of Investment and Financial Advisers can help you to find an adviser in the United Kingdom or abroad.

Remortgaging

If you bought your present home five years or more ago the chances are that you are sitting on a large amount of equity – the difference between the current market value of your house and the amount you still owe the mortgagor. You can dip into this equity by remortgaging for a higher sum and taking out some cash. You should be able to take out between 25 and 50 per cent of the equity, although this may mean paying between 0.5 per cent and 1 per cent more for the whole mortgage as well as an arrangement fee of anything from £500 to £1,500. If you need a relatively small amount of finance or only need the money for a short period to finance working capital, this is probably not the best option.

You will find a guide to the whole subject at Remortgage.com where you will also be able to set a mortgage quotation. The banks also offer advice on this subject.

Using credit cards

Why would anyone pay 18 per cent interest when they could get a bank overdraft at a third of that cost? The simple answer is that banks put their borrowers through a fairly stringent credit check (see below), while credit card providers have built a large volume of defaulting customers into their margins. In other words you are paying over the odds to get fairly easy money.

Use a credit card by all means for travel and the like. Keep one to hand as part of your contingency planning to handle financial emergencies. But this type of money should not become part of the core funding of any business. Money Supermarket.com has a comparison tool that lets you compare over 300 cards.

Earning sweat equity

If you work on your business for free the value put in is known as sweat equity. So if you build a prototype of your product, design a brochure or launch your website, the cost that would have been incurred had you paid for them can count as if you had put in the money yourself.

The attraction to this type of investment is that it is cost free to the business. Also it might act as a spur to encourage bankers or outside investors to match your notional investment with their cash, much as they would have done if you had actually put the money in yourself.

Obviously you can't live on air, so you will need to 'moonlight' while still in employment. As long as you perform well in your daytime job this should pose no difficulties, as employers usually only place restrictions on your having another paid job. It means you will have to work 80-hour weeks, but that will be useful preparation for when your business gets going.

Using a local exchange trading scheme

Local exchange trading schemes (LETS) allow anyone who joins a scheme to offer skills or services, such as plumbing, gardening or the use of a photocopier, to other members. A price is agreed in whatever notional currency has been adopted, but no money changes hands. The system is more ambitious than straight barter. The provider receives a credit on his or her account kept by a local organizer, and a debit is marked up against the user. The person in credit can then set this against other services.

The benefits of using LETS are that you can start trading and grow with virtually no start-up capital. All you need are time and saleable skills – once you have 'sold' your wares, payment is immediate by way of a LETS credit. Also, using LETS means that the wealth is kept in the local community, which means customers in your area may be able to spend more with you. One of the keys to success in using LETS is to have an enterprising organizer who can produce, maintain and circulate a wide-ranging directory of LETS services and outlets. Find out from Letslink UK more about the system and how to find your nearest organizer.

Borrowing money

Borrowing money is your main source of finance if you don't want to take in shareholders, or a partner (see Assignment 3 for information on types of partnership). Lenders for the most part will help you turn a proportion of an illiquid asset such as property, stock in trade or customers who have not yet paid up, into a more liquid asset such as cash, but of course at some discount. They rarely advance money without some form of collateral.

Using a bank

Banks are the principal, and frequently the only, source of finance for nine out of every 10 new and small businesses. Small firms around the world rely on banks for their funding.

Bankers, and indeed any other sources of debt capital, are looking for asset security to back their loan and provide a near-certainty of getting their money back. They will also charge an interest rate that reflects current market conditions and their view of the risk level of the proposal.

Bankers like to speak of the 'five Cs' of credit analysis, factors they look at when they evaluate a loan request. When applying to a bank for a loan, be prepared to address the following points:

- *Character.* Bankers lend money to borrowers who appear honest and who have a good credit history. Before you apply for a loan, it makes sense to obtain a copy of your credit report and clean up any problems.

- *Capacity.* This is a prediction of the borrower's ability to repay the loan. For a new business, bankers look at the business plan. For an existing business, bankers consider financial statements and industry trends.

- *Collateral.* Bankers generally want a borrower to pledge an asset that can be sold to pay off the loan if the borrower lacks funds.

- *Capital.* Bankers scrutinize a borrower's net worth, the amount by which assets exceed debts.

- *Conditions.* Whether bankers give a loan can be influenced by the current economic climate as well as by the amount required.

GIVING BANK GUARANTEES

Where the assets of a business are small, anyone lending it money may seek the added protection of requiring the owner to personally guarantee the loan. In the case of limited companies, this is in effect stripping away some of the protection that companies are supposed to afford the risk-taking owner-manager. You should resist giving guarantees if at all possible. If you have to do so, try to secure the guarantee against the specific asset concerned only, and set clear conditions for the guarantee to come to an end, for example when your overdraft or borrowings go down to a certain level.

Remember, everything in business finance is negotiable, and your relationship with a bank is no exception. Banks are in competition too, so if yours is being unreasonably hard, it may be time to move on. Obviously, to be able to move on, you need to have some advance notice of when the additional funds are needed. Rushing into a bank asking for extra finance from next week is hardly likely to inspire much confidence in your abilities as a strategic thinker. That is where your business plan will come into its own.

Overdrafts

The principal form of short-term bank funding is an overdraft, secured by a charge over the assets of the business. A little over a quarter of all bank finance for small firms is in the form of an overdraft. If you are starting out in a contract cleaning business, say, with a major contract, you need sufficient funds initially to buy the mop and bucket. Three months into the contract they will have been paid for, and so there is no point in getting a five-year bank loan to cover this, as within a year you will have cash in the bank and a loan with an early redemption penalty!

However, if your bank account does not get out of the red at any stage during the year, you will need to re-examine your financing. All too often companies utilize an overdraft to acquire long-term assets, and that overdraft never seems to disappear, eventually constraining the business.

The attraction of overdrafts is that they are very easy to arrange and take little time to set up. That is also their inherent weakness. The key words in the arrangement document are 'repayable on demand', which leaves the bank free to make and change the rules as it sees fit. (This term is under constant review, and some banks may remove it from the arrangement.) With other forms of borrowing, as long as you stick to the terms and conditions, the loan is yours for the duration. It is not so with overdrafts.

Term loans

Term loans, as long-term bank borrowings are generally known, are funds provided by a bank for a number of years. The interest can either be variable, changing with general interest rates, or fixed for a number of years ahead. The proportion of fixed-rate loans has increased from one-third of all term loans to around half. In some cases it may be possible to move between having a fixed interest rate and a variable one at certain intervals. It may even be possible to have a moratorium on interest payments for a short period, to give the business some breathing space. Provided the conditions of the loan are met in such matters as repayment, interest and security cover, the money is available for the period of the loan. Unlike in the case of an overdraft, the bank cannot pull the rug from under you if circumstances (or the local manager) change.

Just over one-third of all term loans are for periods greater than 10 years, and a quarter are for three years or less.

Government-supported funding

For decades, governments have played a role in helping finance new and small businesses. Start-up loans, equity for high tech, support for exporting and grants for attending exhibitions are typical of the areas where help is on offer. See the Index of key organizations and resources for business planning at the end of the book for more details.

Money through credit unions

If you don't like the terms on offer from the high street banks, as the major banks are often known, you could consider forming your own bank. This is not quite as crazy an idea as it sounds. Credit unions formed by groups of small businesspeople, both in business and aspiring to start up, have been around for decades in the United States, the United Kingdom and elsewhere. They have been an attractive option for people on low incomes, providing a cheap and convenient alternative to banks. Some self-employed people such as taxi drivers have also formed credit unions. They can then apply for loans to meet unexpected capital expenditure for repairs, refurbishments or technical upgrading.

Members have to save regularly to qualify for a loan, although there is no minimum deposit, and after 10 weeks, members with a good track record can borrow up to five times their savings, although they must continue to save while repaying the loan. There is no set interest rate, but dividends are distributed to members from any surplus, usually about 5 per cent a year. This too compares favourably with bank interest on deposit accounts. You can find more about credit unions and details of those operating in your area from the Association of British Credit Unions Limited.

Community Development Finance

Many communities, particularly those operating in rundown areas in need of regeneration, have a facility to lend or even invest in businesses that could bring employment to the area. Funding from these sources could be for anything from start-up, right through to expansion or in some cases even rescue finance to help prevent a business from folding, shedding a large number of jobs or relocating to a more benign business environment. Responsible Finance, formerly known as the Community Development Finance Association, maintains a directory of providers. In 2018, Responsible Finance providers lent a total of £254 million to 52,121 businesses.

CASE STUDY
Destination London

Rachel Lowe, a 29-year-old single mother with two children, came up with her winning business idea while working part time as a taxi driver in Portsmouth. She invented a game involving players throwing a dice to move taxi pieces around a board collecting fares to travel to famous destinations, while aiming to get back to the taxi rank before they ran out of fuel. Being able to run the business from home meant Rachel could spend more time with her children and still be a breadwinner.

But despite having a business plan written up when she entered a local business competition, she had serious hurdles to cross before she could get started. With a deal from Hamleys, the London toyshop, in the bag and a manufacturer and distributor lined up, all that was missing was a modest amount of additional funding to help with marketing and stock. She pitched her proposal to the BBC's *Dragons' Den* and was given a thorough roasting. To say the dragons weren't enthusiastic would be a serious understatement. They reckoned Monopoly would wipe the floor with her. Bowed but far from beaten, Rachel then turned to South Coast Money Line, a Community Development Finance Institution and part of the Portsmouth Area Regeneration Trust Group. With a loan from them she propelled her game Destination London into the top 10 best-selling games, even beating Monopoly! A deal with Debenhams to stock regional versions of the game and signing up to produce Harry Potter and Disney versions left her with a business worth £2 million, at a conservative estimate.

Leasing and hiring equipment

Physical assets such as cars, vans, computers, office equipment and the like can usually be financed by leasing them, rather as a house or flat may be rented. Alternatively, they can be bought on hire purchase. This leaves other funds free to cover the less tangible elements in your cash flow.

Leasing is a way of getting the use of vehicles, plant and equipment without paying the full cost all at once. Operating leases are taken out where you will use the equipment (for example a car, photocopier, vending machine or kitchen equipment) for less than its full economic life. The lessor takes the risk of the equipment becoming obsolete, and assumes responsibility for repairs, maintenance and insurance. As you, the lessee, are paying for this service, it is more expensive than a finance lease, where you lease the equipment for most of its economic life and maintain and insure it yourself. Leases can normally be extended, often for fairly nominal sums, in the latter years.

Hire purchase differs from leasing in that you have the option to eventually become the owner of the asset, after a series of payments.

FINDING A LEASING COMPANY

The Finance and Leasing Association gives details of all UK-based businesses offering this type of finance. The website also has general information on terms of trade and code of conduct.

Discounting and factoring

Customers often take time to pay up. In the meantime you have to pay those who work for you and your less patient suppliers. So the more you grow, the more funds you need. It is often possible to 'factor' your creditworthy customers' bills to a financial institution, receiving some of the funds as your goods leave the door, hence speeding up cash flow.

Factoring is generally only available to a business that invoices other business customers for its services, either in its home market or internationally. Factoring can be made available to new businesses, although its services are usually of most value during the early stages of growth. It is an arrangement that allows you to receive up to 80 per cent of the cash due from your customers more quickly than they would normally pay. The factoring company in effect buys your trade debts, and can also provide a debtor accounting and administration service. You will, of course, have to pay for factoring services. Having the cash before your customers pay will cost you a little more than normal overdraft rates. The factoring service will cost between 0.5 and 3.5 per cent of the turnover, depending on volume of work, the number of debtors, average invoice amount and other related factors. You can get up to 80 per cent of the value of your invoice in advance, with the remainder paid when your customer settles up, less the various charges just mentioned.

If you sell direct to the public, sell complex and expensive capital equipment, or expect progress payments on long-term projects, then factoring is not for you. If you are expanding more rapidly than other sources of finance will allow, this may be a useful service that is worth exploring.

Invoice discounting is a variation on the same theme, where you are responsible for collecting the money from debtors; this is not a service available to new or very small businesses.

Supplier credit

Once you have established creditworthiness, it may be possible to take advantage of trade credit extended by suppliers. This usually takes the form of allowing you anything from seven days to three months from receiving the goods, before you have to pay for them. Even if you are allowed time to pay for goods and services, you will have to weigh carefully the benefit of taking this credit against the cost of losing any cash discounts offered. For example, if you are offered a 2.5 per cent discount for cash settlement, then this is a saving of £25 for every £1,000 of purchases. If the alternative is to take six weeks' credit, the saving is the cost of borrowing that sum from, say, your bank on overdraft. So, if your bank interest rate is 8 per cent per annum, that is equivalent to 0.15 per cent per week. Six weeks would save you 0.92 per cent. On £1,000 of purchases you would save only £9.20 of bank interest. This means that the cash discount is more attractive.

CHECKING YOUR CREDITWORTHINESS

Your suppliers will probably run a credit check on you before extending payment terms. You should run a credit check on your own business from time to time, just to see how others see you. You can check out your own credit rating before trying to get credit from a supplier by using a credit reference agency such as Experian. Basic credit reports cost between £3 and £25 and may save you time and money if you have any reservations about a potential customer's ability to pay.

Family and friends

Those close to you might be willing to lend you money or invest in your business. This helps you avoid the problem of pleading your case to outsiders and enduring extra paperwork and bureaucratic delays. Help from friends, relatives and business associates can be especially valuable if you have been through bankruptcy or had other credit problems that would make borrowing from a commercial lender difficult or impossible. Their involvement brings a range of extra potential benefits, costs and risks that are not a feature of most other types of finance. You need to decide which of these are acceptable.

Some advantages of borrowing money from people you know well are that you may be charged a lower interest rate, may be able to delay paying back money until you are more established, and may be given more flexibility if you get into a jam. But once the loan terms are agreed, you have the same legal obligations as you would with a bank or any other source of finance.

In addition, borrowing money from relatives and friends can have a major disadvantage. If your business does poorly and those close to you end up losing money, you may well damage a good personal relationship. So, in dealing with friends, relatives and business associates, be extra careful not only to establish clearly the terms of the deal and put it in writing, but also to make an extra effort to explain the risks. In short, it is your job to make sure your helpful friend or relative will not suffer true hardship if you are unable to meet your financial commitments.

CASE STUDY
Hippychick

When new mother Julie Minchin discovered the Hipseat she knew she'd found a helpful product. Anything that makes carrying a baby around all day without ending up with excruciating backache has got to be a benefit. It was only later that she realized that selling the product for the German company that made the Hipseat could launch her into business. At first Julie acted as their UK distributor but later she wanted to make some major improvements to the product. That meant finding a manufacturer to make the product especially for her business. China was the logical place to find a company flexible enough to make small quantities as well as being able to help her keep the cost of the end product competitive.

Julie funded the business, Hippychick, with a small family loan, an overdraft facility and a variety of small grants. The company now has a turnover of £3 million a year, employs 24 people and sells 14 new and unique products aimed at the baby market. Hippychick supplies national chains such as Boots and Mothercare as well as independents. It also sells via a catalogue and website, and is in the process of building a network of distributors for the branded products. In 2013 it won the Best Distributor at the Nursery Industry Awards – probably the highest accolade in their industry. The company's latest accounts for 2019 showed they made close on £250,000 profit for their owners.

Getting an investor

If you are operating as a limited company or limited partnership you will have a potentially valuable opportunity to raise relatively risk-free money. It is risk-free to you – the business founder – that is, but risky, sometimes extremely so, to anyone advancing you money. Businesses such as these have shares that can be traded for money, so selling a share of your business is one way to raise capital to start up or grow your business. Shares also have the great additional attraction of having cost you nothing – nothing, that is, except blood, sweat, tears and inspiration.

Individual business angels, or corporates such as venture capital providers, share all the risks and vagaries of the business alongside you, the founder, and expect a proportionate share in the rewards if things go well. They are not especially concerned with a stream of dividends, which is just as well, as few small businesses ever pay them. Nor do they look for the security of buildings or other assets to underpin their investment. Instead they hope for a radical increase in the value of their investment. They expect to realize this value from other investors who want to take their place for the next stage in the firm's growth cycle, rather than from any repayment by the founder.

CASE STUDY
Moonpig

In March 2015 Nick Jenkins was appointed one of three new 'dragons' on the long-running BBC business programme, *Dragons' Den*. Jenkins graduated with a degree in Russian from Birmingham University, followed by a career in sugar trading, working in Moscow for Marc Rich, the Swiss-based commodity trading firm. By 1998, after eight years working in Russia, Nick decided to head back to the UK, prompted to some degree by finding a death threat from a former client nailed to his apartment door, but mainly motivated by the desire to start a business of his own. He started Moonpig, the greetings card business, in 1999 while completing an MBA at Cranfield School of Management.

His business idea back in 1999 was simple. He would take the bog-standard greetings card that has been around since Victorian times, and create a website where customers could personalize their own humorous cards. Nick calculated that he could create a profitable business where customers bought a single personalized card, with prices starting at £2.99 plus postage. The cards would be sent out the same day, either directly to the recipient or to the sender to pass on to someone else. Judging from the positive reaction he had had to his own rudimentary efforts, he was confident that the idea would catch on. Operating as an online business, he would also be collecting payments upfront, leading him to think that cash flow would be good.

Manufacturing and packing the cards looked like the biggest outlays, both were areas in which Nick had no expertise and neither was central to the value of his business proposition. He took the idea to Paperlink, a successful greetings card publishing company without an online presence, and offered them a small stake in the company if they would let the as-yet-unnamed company act as their outsource supplier of greeting cards. Miraculously they agreed and this was enough to convince Nick that the idea he had was worth pursuing, whilst also eliminating a major area of cost.

Nick ploughed £160,000 of his own money (from his share of a sugar trading management buy-out) into the business and raised a further £125,000 from three friends who were keen to invest in Moonpig. Immediately after registering the company in October 1999, Nick hired a website design agency to help him build and design the site, with the aim of going live by Christmas. In the business's first year of trading, it distributed around 40,000 cards, and made a loss of around £1 million on sales of £90,000. The losses were mostly incurred on overheads, such as staff, printing equipment, software development and marketing. By 2002 the economy was slowly starting to emerge from the shadows of the dotcom bust but things were still bleak. Nick had originally anticipated that the business would break even in year 3, but in fact, it took five years and six further rounds of fundraising from private investors for Moonpig to reach profitability.

By 2004 it seemed that all the hard work was finally paying off – sales were continuing to grow and the lines between loss and break-even were blurring. Sales had grown steadily from the beginning, based largely on word of mouth and referrals. As every product was unique and was branded with the Moonpig.com domain name, the more it sold the more customers it attracted. By 2005 the business was making a profit.

'Lean' and 'mean' were key watchwords and Nick even used the outsourcing concept with his office e-space. With capacity proving problematic in the early years

Moonpig's business flourished at peak seasons, such as Christmas and Easter – the business would typically sell up to 15,000 cards a day in the run-up to Christmas, for example. But it was a different story at other times of the year, when the business would only sell between 1,500 and 2,000 cards a day. It meant Nick had to be flexible and creative when it came to office space. At Moonpig's busiest times, when its office was near capacity with people stuffing envelopes, many other employees worked from home to free up desk space.

As well as offering personalized cards, Moonpig started creating cards that looked like spoof magazine covers, such as OK and Hello! In 2006, as well as expanding its product base, Moonpig made the decision to expand overseas, starting with Australia. Nick says it was the logical step towards growth as the country is culturally very similar to the UK when it comes to buying cards.

Moonpig now accounts for over 90 per cent of the online greetings card market and now sells more than 10 million cards a year which, if laid out end to end, would stretch from London to Moscow. In July 2011 the company was bought out by PhotoBox, a digital photo service provider, for £120 million.

Business angels

One likely first source of equity or risk capital will be a private individual with his or her own funds, and perhaps some knowledge of your type of business. In return for a share in the business, such investors will put in money at their own risk. They have been christened 'business angels', a term first coined to describe private wealthy individuals who back a play on Broadway or in London's West End.

Most angels are determined upon some involvement beyond merely signing a cheque and hope to play a part in your business in some way. They are hoping for big rewards – one angel who backed Sage with £10,000 in its first round of £250,000 financing saw his stake rise to £40 million.

These angels frequently operate through managed networks, usually on the internet. In the United Kingdom and the United States there are hundreds of networks, with tens of thousands of business angels prepared to put up several billion pounds each year into new or small business.

FINDING A BUSINESS ANGEL

UK Business Angels Association has an online directory of UK business angels. The European Business Angels Network (EBAN) has directories of national business angel associations both inside and outside Europe from which you can find individual business angels.

Venture capital/private equity

Venture capital (VC) providers are investing other people's money, often from pension funds. They have a different agenda from that of business angels, and are more likely to be interested in investing more money for a larger stake.

VCs go through a process known as 'due diligence' before investing. This process involves a thorough examination of both the business and its owners. Past financial performance, the directors' track record and the business plan are all subjected to detailed scrutiny, usually by accountants and lawyers. Directors are then required to 'warrant' that they have provided all relevant information, under pain of financial penalties. The cost of this process will have to be borne by the firm raising the money, but it will be paid out of the money raised, if that is any consolation.

In general, VCs expect their investment to have paid off within seven years, but they are hardened realists. Two in every 10 investments they make are total write-offs, and six perform averagely well at best. So the one star in every 10 investments they make has to cover a lot of duds. VCs have a target rate of return of 30 per cent plus to cover this poor hit rate.

Raising venture capital is not a cheap option, and deals are not quick to arrange either. Six months is not unusual, and over a year has been known. Every VC has a deal done in six weeks in its portfolio, but that truly is the exception.

CASE STUDY

The Internet Bookshop and why it was eclipsed by Amazon

UK entrepreneur Darryl Mattocks, a software engineer and computer enthusiast, entered the market in 1994, a year ahead of Amazon, but his approach was profoundly different. Mattock went into a bookshop in Oxford and picked up a book he had ordered a few days before. He paid for it, walked a few doors down to the Post Office and despatched it to the customer who had emailed his order the previous week. He was constrained initially to financing the business using credit cards, though later a friend introduced him to James Blackwell, a member of the family behind the Oxford booksellers, who put up £50,000 ($80,000/€59,000) for a 50 per cent stake in the venture.

Jeff Bezos, a former investment banker, raised $11 million (£6.9/€9.3 million) from Silicon Valley venture capitalists before starting up, and invested $8 million (£5/€6.8 million) of that in marketing. Mattock's Internet Bookshop had a database of 16,000 books, while Amazon was selling nearly $16 million (£10/€13.5 million) worth of books. In 1988, around the time it was buying Waterstone's, WH Smith bought out bookshop.co.uk, parent company of The Internet Bookshop, for £9.4 million ($15/€11 million). Amazon was then valued at $10.1 billion (£6.3/€8.6 billion).

FINDING A VENTURE CAPITAL PROVIDER

The British Venture Capital Association and Invest Europe both have online directories giving details of hundreds of venture capital providers.

You can see how those negotiating with or receiving venture capital rate the firm in question at The Funded website in terms of the deal offered, the firm's apparent competence and how good it is at managing the relationship. There is also a link to the VCs website. The Funded has 21,000 members.

CASE STUDY
Card Factory

Card Factory is the UK's leading manufacturer and retailer of greetings cards. It was founded in 1997 by husband and wife Dean and Janet Hoyle, with a single shop in Wakefield, Yorkshire. Today it operates around 700 stores throughout the UK, focusing on value for money cards and gifts. They employ 6,000 full-time staff and a similar number of part-timers to meet peak periods such as Christmas and Mother's Day when £164.4 million and £55.3 million respectively are spent on cards. The company is the leading specialist retailer in the large and competitive UK greetings card market; adults on average send 31 cards a year and spend some £1.37 billion on single cards. There are approximately 800 card publishers in the UK, most of which are small businesses with fewer than five employees. Approximately one third of the company's sales are from gift dressings, small gifts and party products, a market estimated to be worth £1–2 billion.

Private equity firm Charterhouse Capital Partners took a majority stake in the business in 2010. During the period of ownership, Charterhouse worked closely with management to grow the business, opening 250 further stores and in 2011 acquired gettingpersonal.co.uk, a growing online personalized gifts and cards provider.

With 16 years of unbroken revenue growth, sales turnover reached £327 million in year to 31 January 2014. Card Factory took that performance as an opportunity to launch on the London Stock Exchange. They listed on the 20 May 2014 selling £90 million worth of shares, representing about 13 per cent of the value of the business as a whole. In 2019, the company made nearly £80 million profit on £436 million of sales.

Corporate venturing

Venture capital firms often get their hands dirty taking a hand in the management of the businesses they invest in: another type of business also in the risk capital business, without it necessarily being their main line of business. These firms are known as corporate venturers, and they usually want an inside track to new developments in and around the edges of their own fields of interest.

McDonald's offloaded its Pret stake to Bridgepoint, a private equity firm. Bridgepoint in 2008 bought a majority stake, including McDonald's 33 per cent shareholding, for £345 million (US$542/€395 million). That would suggest that McDonald's at least quadrupled the value of its initial stake. Nokia Venture Partners (NVP), who makes significant minority investments in start-ups in the wireless internet space, had as its biggest success to date the Initial Public Offering of PayPal, in 2002. Corporate venturing entrepreneurs think big and are happy to cut others with cash in on the deal, if it will help make them rich. Independence for independence's sake is not a high priority.

The British Venture Capital Association has published a Guide to Corporate Venture Capital.

CASE STUDY
Meraki Corporate venture, multi-million dollar payday

Meraki (*may-rah-kee*), a Greek word that means doing something with passion and soul, could soon stand for how to make a billion in under a decade. Meraki was formed in 2006 by three PhD candidates from MIT, Sanjit Biswas, John Bicket and Hans Robertson, all currently on leave from their degree programme. Meraki, according to its website, 'brings the benefits of the cloud to edge and branch networks, delivering easy-to-manage wireless, switching and security solutions that enable customers to seize new business opportunities and reduce operational cost. Whether securing iPads in an enterprise or blanketing a campus with Wi-Fi, Meraki networks simply work.' With over 10,000 customers worldwide ranging from the English public school Wellington College to Burger King, Meraki was initially backed by Californian venture capital firm Sequoia Capital and Google, two early venture investors. Rajeev Motwani, the Stanford University professor who taught Google co-founders Larry Page and Sergey Brin, made the necessary introductions.

Payday came on 19 November 2012 when Cisco, who had been in exclusive talks since September with Meraki, bought the company for US$1.2 billion (£754 million).

The founders had been considering a flotation and at first rejected Cisco's overtures. Analysts think Cisco has overpaid, but with their greater market presence and cash resources the company is confident it will be able to expand.

Meraki's technology using their global networks, Cisco has included a retention package to keep Meraki's co-founders at Cisco to consummate the deal. Sujai Hujela, an executive at Cisco, also stated: 'We are making sure we want to preserve and pollinate the culture [at Meraki] into Cisco.'

Crowdfunding

Over the past few years, the business world has seen the birth and rapid growth of what appears to be a new way of raising funds, known as crowdfunding. *Crowdfunding* is an organized means for a large group of people to make mostly small individual donations to fund a business or an idea. It uses the power of the internet to bring the two sides together. Crowdfunding replicates some of the more traditional funding activities in an online format, such as pitching for a desired amount of finance. As finance for business goes, this new vehicle puts the entrepreneur in the driving seat, and empowers members of the public and the investor community – the *crowd* – to get a piece of the action as paying passengers in a number of companies.

Crowdfunding can raise funds in one of four ways or in any combination of all of them:

- *Equity.* Offers some share in the business for money invested, much as you would with a venture capital provider or business angel. By some accounts crowdfunding raises more money than VCs and business angels combined. Palo Alto-based smartwatch maker Pebble is one of the highest-funded campaigns in crowdfunding history, having raised over €20 million. It's also the fastest funded, raising $1 million in less than an hour.

- *Loans.* You can also pay interest treating the funds as a loan in the same way as with bank finance. The interest is likely to be higher than with comparable bank finance and the time horizon for paying the loan back will be shorter. Chilango, a London chain of fast-service Mexican restaurants founded by two ex-Skype executives, raised money through what they entertainingly called a Burrito Bond to help roll out more restaurants across London. They offered an interest rate of 8 per cent repayable over four years.

- *Reward-based.* This involves exchanging gifts or rewards based on the amount of giving. Smith & Sinclair completed a successful reward-based crowdfunding campaign to finance their Immersive Edible Alcohol Shop, creating inventive sweet treats for adults. The founders met their goal of £23,000 in only 49 days from 96 backers offering as rewards speciality alcohol-based jewellery. Chilango sweetened their deal by offering all investors two free burrito vouchers and those that put in more than £10,000 get free food for the entire duration of the bond.

- *Invoice financing platforms.* This works in much the same way as cash flow financing (see earlier in this chapter). Once approved, the business can sell an invoice (as small as £1,000 and as large as £1 million+) on the invoice trading platform. Once verified, the invoice is sold on the platform, where multiple investors buy slices of the invoice. The business receives funds in their account as an advance of up to 90 per cent of the invoice face value within 24–48 hours. When the invoice is settled in full the invoice trading platform makes the remaining balance available to the business, minus their fees. The advantages to the users of this service are speed – you can be up and funded in 24 hours; you only fund the invoices you want to, unlike conventional discounters who require to take on your whole debtors ledger; and there is no lengthy lock period – you just operate invoice by invoice.

Crowdfund providers

There are now literally hundreds of crowdfunding platforms around the world. And the last word in that sentence is the key to the competitive advantage of this type of funding. Unlike banks and private equity providers which tend to operate on a country or at best continent basis, crowdfunders can be anywhere.

You can find a complete list of crowdfunding sites in a directory that's produced by Nesta or the UK Crowdfunding Association website.

Here are a handful of operators just to get a flavour of the players.

CROWD CUBE

Crowd Cube was the first UK-based crowdfunding website, and the first crowdfunding website in the world to enable the public to invest in and receive shares in UK companies. They have 359,856 registered investors and have raised over £220 million of new capital for thousands of businesses.

The range of businesses that have used the site include:

- Darlington Football Club, who raised £291,450 from 722 investors over 14 days to help fend off closure after going into liquidation.

- Universal Fuels raised £100,000, making founder Oliver Morgan, at 20 the youngest entrepreneur to successfully raise investment through the process.

KICKSTARTER

Kickstarter is predominantly for creative projects, be they films, games, art, design or music. It has its roots in the United States. In 2012, a UK version was launched to encourage local giving for local projects, and nearly 10 million people have pledged nearly £2 billion. The site is a resounding success, demonstrating the power of people and the life-changing achievements that happen when people get behind each other.

In much the same way that other financially incentivized sites demand that projects reach full pledge subscription, Kickstarter is an *all-or-nothing site*, meaning that you get nothing unless your project is fully funded. You set the pledge amount and you set the deadline, but you must then go shake the trees and make the golden fruit drop into your funding crate. To some people this seems harsh, but it does mean that you need to mobilize the power of your crowd and get people doing something versus talking about doing something for your idea, so it's a great financial firecracker.

To date, an impressive 36 per cent of projects have reached their funding goals. Creators keep 100 per cent ownership of their work, but a 5 per cent success fee goes to Kickstarter.

INDIEGOGO

Founded in San Francisco in 2008, Indiegogo, one of the first crowdfunding sites, has a global audience. It covers the spectrum from creative ideas to start-up business ideas to charity projects.

The success rate is lower than Kickstarter's, at 34 per cent. Its success fee starts at 5 per cent on a fully funded pledge, and 5 per cent on a partially funded pledge (Kickstarter doesn't offer partial funding). Indiegogo also charges up to 9 per cent on credit card and PayPal pledges, so the fees can add up. On the plus side, it refunds 5 per cent if the campaign reaches its target.

In 2014, it launched Indiegogo Life (now called Generosity), enabling people to raise funds for life events, such as celebrations, and also for emergencies, medical expenses and so forth. Generosity is different from Indiegogo with regard to the fees it charges for the funds raised, allowing fundraisers to keep more of the money they raise.

Both loan- and equity-based crowdfunding platforms are regulated by the FCA (Financial Conduct Authority), which helps protect investors. Peer-to-peer (P2P) lenders have to adhere to strict guidelines around capital, money and disclosure requirements. Investment-based platforms, both debt and equity, also fall under this umbrella.

Incubators and accelerators

Tempting though it might be to believe that business accelerators are an internet phenomenon, incubators, science parks, innovation centres, technology parks and a whole variety of other names have been coined over the years to describe the task that accelerators and incubators perform.

The first serious attempt at incubation is credited to a near-derelict building near New York. The name came into common usage more by way of a joke than as a serious description of the task in hand. One of the incubators' first tenants was involved in incubating real chickens. Several waves of accelerators followed this inauspicious start and by the 1980s several hundred such facilities were scattered around the US, Canada, Europe and Australia. Later incubator progressions took in the developing economies and the internet variation, which came into being in the mid-1990s, swept across the US, Europe, India, China, Malaysia, Singapore, the Philippines and elsewhere, bringing the total to some 4,000 facilities worldwide

The terms *incubator* and *accelerator* are often used interchangeably, and although you can get funding from both, incubators are most useful in the idea or pre-start stage. An accelerator is helpful to speed up your growth using funding, education, learning, mentoring and showcasing.

An *accelerator* provides services to support your business, often in return for equity, as your business begins to scale and grow. *Incubators* focus on very early-stage, small companies that have an idea that needs developing into more of a business.

INCUBATORS

While there is no single model for business incubators, in most cases the concepts go beyond the simple provision of a shared office or workspace facility for small business clients. The hallmark of any effective business incubator programme should be its focus on the added value that it brings to small business 'tenants' in terms of strengthened business skills; access to business services; improved operating environment; and opportunities for business networking, etc, to nurture early-stage small businesses, increasing the prospects for business survival and growth compared with the situation outside the incubator.

ACCELERATORS

The McKinsey Accelerators was a response to the challenges of the first wave of internet businesses. Their service set out to turbocharge the launch and growth of new e-businesses worldwide. They aimed to offer access to their extensive network of 'best in class' third-party service providers and their Fortune 500 client and alumni database. McKinsey's Accelerators offered four main types of assistance, which is very much the model adopted as standard:

- *intensive business building* (six to 12 months). For ventures that need to move at maximum speed McKinsey offers a large team to provide day-to-day execution of the marketing plan, including product launch itself;

- *targeted projects* (one to six months). Accelerator teams provide in-depth analytical services to enable start-ups to pinpoint their market opportunities, position and vulnerabilities. They can also screen merger and acquisition projects;

- *burst services* (two days to two months). Based on the hypothesis that few start-ups have the resources for lengthy analysis and drawn-out marketing studies, McKinsey consultants can provide rapid-fire market data and other short-term targeted analysis needed for short-term decision making;

- *senior counselling* (as needed). Access to McKinsey partners for open, unbiased dialogues on any key business issues.

The National Business Incubation Association (NBIA) is the world's leading organization advancing business incubation and entrepreneurship. It has 1,900 members in 60 countries.

Free money

Depending on the industry sector, stage and location of your business, a *grant* or an *award* can be a terrific way to get some fairly free cash into your business, especially at the very early stages when cash is generally in short supply. You can also use such monies to widen your network, boost your company profile and potentially enable your business to do some good or make a positive difference to a deprived or marginalized area of society.

Given that some of the more traditional forms of finance may be beyond your current reach, a *research grant* to develop a new product or service, or a *proof of concept grant* to prove that your product or service is viable, for example, may seem like manna from heaven.

APPLING FOR AWARDS

Even though it can be a time-consuming process to hunt them down and fill in the forms, applying for and winning awards can be a great source of additional cash. Winning an award – or even being shortlisted for one – often carries other benefits as part of the prize, including business support, mentoring, free work space and, of course, potentially very useful publicity and networking.

Certain sectors, such as technology, biology and life sciences, green energy, long-term healthcare, education, socially minded businesses, manufacturing and certain regional businesses, have more grant funding available from both UK and EU organizations than other sectors. In fact, a number of *evergreen programmes* – awards that roll over each year – may be relevant to you and your business, even in its early stages.

Grant programmes are listed on the Innovate UK website. If you're serious about applying for grants and awards, visiting the site can pay dividends. Some of the awards you can find on Innovate UK cover:

- feasibility studies for cleaner, more efficient fuels;
- the agri-tech industry;
- supply chain integration for the construction industry;
- enhancing the user experience in retail.

A regular visit to the Innovate UK website is worthwhile to see what's current – and critically, when the deadlines are!

Most of these applications are complex and lengthy, so do *not* leave them until the night before. Be aware that they can put a strain on the twin resources of time and people, and plan accordingly. Set strict project management timelines and deadlines if you want to have half a chance of success.

CHECKING ON GRANTS

Nearly every country or region has an agenda and aims that it wants to promote and develop, and using grants to encourage businesses to help them achieve their objectives is very common now. That's great news, we hear you say, and it is. However, locating the application forms, understanding the criteria, taking the time to complete the forms, applying at the right time and understanding how to utilize the money for a commercial proposition can have you spending many precious hours working on something that may or may not give you a positive result. Be prepared to trawl through the mire of dozens of websites, racking up loads of hours and often taxing your brain to understand how you fit into the scheme, with the knowledge that you have a relatively slim chance of success. Although it's tempting to apply for free money, think long and hard before you start off down the grant road. It may well be a long and frustrating journey, with an uncertain destination.

Stay informed about current programmes:

- The business centre in the British Library Business and IP Centre in London has low-cost workshops, events, free access to databases on available funding and staff to help you research and identify appropriate grants for your business. They also partner with organizations that may be able to help you identify and apply for grants.

- The UK government site covers a variety of funding options, including grants, and has a handy search function on the site, as well as links to the grants it lists.

- The website F6S is another good source of information, and has some applications on its site as well. F6S is a leading portal for start-ups to find and discuss information on funding, start-up business support programmes, jobs and events. Some grant-awarding programmes use the F6S portal as an entry point to providing you with information and the initial stages of an application for funding.

Grants and awards come and go on a regular basis. If you're serious about trying to attract some of this money, register on sites such as F6S – and regularly check sites that aggregate grant data, so you can receive regular newsletters, updates, changes, notices and so on. You don't want to miss out on an opportunity because you didn't know the deadline had passed.

If you're successful in your grant applications, you won't have to chase anyone to get the cash, and as grants are different from debt, you don't have to repay them. They differ from equity as well in that you don't have to provide a return to the investor. In general, they're non-refundable chunks of money, doled out over a predetermined period of time – usually linked to achieving milestones – and are offered as an incentive to entrepreneurs and business people to develop something innovative or positive for the community at large. As such, a grant can provide a very welcome boost to your cash flow.

Grants aren't all good news, though, as they usually have very detailed terms and conditions that you must strictly adhere to, including regular financial updates, quarterly reporting on progress and updates on whether or not you are achieving your aims and objectives. They give with one hand and take with the other.

PAYING FOR APPLICATION HELP

A number of professional advisers specialize in grant applications. These people charge a fee, but they take a good deal of the pain away from making grant applications.

As with other advisers, it's essential that you check the person's track record and the integrity of the service before you sign on the dotted line. Use your network, rating sites, reviews and past clients to make sure the company is legitimate, relatively successful and good value for your money.

Beware anyone who guarantees success or refuses to explain his or her process. Grant funding is a highly competitive and complex arena, and no one can guarantee success.

CASE STUDY
Chilango – how the Burrito Bond was born

When former Skype employees Eric Partaker and Dan Houghton started Chilango they had in mind supplying mouth-watering Mexican food, something of a rarity when they launched seven years ago. Eric developed an appetite for tacos, burritos and the like in his native Chicago, but when he came to work in London was faced with a veritable Mexican cuisine desert. When Eric met Dan by coincidence also a Mexican food fanatic the pair made it their mission to plug what they saw as a gap in the market.

Eric Partaker, an American and Norwegian national, graduated from the University of Illinois at Urbana-Champaign with a Bachelor of Science degree in Finance, and is also an alumnus of Katholieke Universiteit Leuven, Belgium, where he studied History, Philosophy, and Literature. Dan is a Cambridge mathematics graduate, leaving with a First. They met up in 2005 when they were both on the new business ventures team reporting to the CEO of Skype Technologies.

By 2014, with seven London Mexican food outlets open, one opposite the Goldman Sachs headquarters, they had proved there was an appetite for their business model. But with each new restaurant costing around £500,000 to launch opening they discovered another gap – an urgent need for cash to achieve their goal to launch six new Chilango restaurants around London quickly.

In 2014 they hit the headlines for financial rather than culinary innovation. Using the Crowdfunding website they set out to raise £1 million in two months offering 8 per cent interest with the capital to be repaid in four years. With the minimum investment set at £500 those putting up £10,000 get free lunch once a week at one of their restaurants. Hence the name 'Burrito Bond' was born.

One day after books on the bond opened, investments had already been received from executives in the food and drinks business, including the chief executive officer and chief financial officer of café-chain Carluccio's, the former CEO of Domino's Pizza UK and the former CEO of Krispy Kreme UK, according to the prospectus website. By 3 July 2014, according to information on the Crowdfunding website the company had received £1,140,500 from 344 investors.

WORKSHEET FOR ASSIGNMENT 21: ESTIMATING FINANCING REQUIREMENTS

Based on your financial projections, state how much cash you need to raise to set up your business, and how and when you propose to repay it. Use the questions below as the format for your worksheet:

1   Based on the maximum figure in your cash-flow forecast, how much money do you need and what do you need it for?

2   How does this compare with the sum that you and your partners or shareholders are putting in (ie level of gearing)?

$$\text{Gearing} = \frac{\text{Total funds required for business}}{\text{Money put in by you + shareholders}}$$

For example, if you already have £/\$/€1,000 of assets and are looking for a loan of £/\$/€5,000, the funds required are £/\$/€6,000. If you have already invested £/\$/€500 and plan to put in a further £/\$/€2,500, then your gearing is:

$$\frac{6,000}{500 + 2,500} = \frac{6,000}{3,000} = 2{:}1$$

3 Where do you expect to raise the funds you need to finance your business?

4 Prepare a schedule showing when you need these funds.

5 How and when will any borrowing be repaid? Do a list like this:

Source of repayment   Amount £/$/€   Date
Total £/$/€

6 What percentage of your venture would you be prepared to sell to raise the required funds?

7 What exit route(s) could be open to potential investors?

8 What security, if any, is available as collateral for any loan?

Security   Value £/$/€
Total £/$/€

9 Will you be receiving any grants or loans to help to finance your business (other than from the organization to which you are now applying)?

Source   Date   Funds provided   Amount £/$/€
Total £/$/€

10 What further private cash, if any, is available to invest in the business?

Source   Date   Funds provided   Amount £/$/€
Total £/$/€

11 What are the key risks that could adversely affect your projections? (These could include technical, financial and marketing risks.)

Risk area   Financial impact on:
Sales   Profits

12 What contingency plans do you have to either manage or minimize the consequences of these risks?

Risk area   Plan   Effect

Suggested further reading

Barrow, C (2011) *Practical Financial Management: A guide to budgets, balance sheets and business finance*, 8th edn, Kogan Page, London

Barrow, C (2017) *Understanding Business Accounting for Dummies*, 4th edn, Wiley, New York

ASSIGNMENT 22

Stress testing your business projections

While you may have been realistic in preparing your forecasts of sales and related costs, it is highly probable that during year 1 especially, your actual performance will not be as expected. This could be for one or more reasons, such as resistance to innovation (if a new product), overestimate of market size, change in consumer demand, slow take-up of product – or worse still, you could hit a period when a pandemic or financial meltdown strikes. All these could mean that sales forecasts are significantly wrong. It is advisable to pre-empt any potential investor's question, such as 'What happens if your sales are reduced by 20, 30 or even 40 per cent?', by asking yourself the question first and quantifying the financial effects in your business plan. By way of example, Next, a British multinational clothing, footwear and home products retailer, has been wargaming for years. Until March 2020, the retailer's worst case scenario was a 25 per cent sales reduction. Since April 2020, they have drawn up a new set of stress tests in which the drop is as much as 40 per cent.

Building 'what ifs' into your cash flow projections

The questions at the front of you mind when making any kind of projection usually take the form of probing for risk factors: things that could work against you under certain circumstances. What if the economy turns sour; your patent takes longer to come through; you can't recruit staff as quickly as you had hoped; sales take longer to build up than you have forecasted; and a lot more similar 'what ifs'. The best framework for stress testing your business model is the cash-flow forecast checking the impact of your key business assumptions being disrupted.

Stress testing the revenue model

It is unlikely that anyone will take your sales revenue at face value. The norm in business is for something not to go to plan. Either you have fewer customers, the mix of customers changes, say, from cash to credit, less repeat business occurs, your prices don't hold as expected or you get more returns or defects. The list of reasons that could adversely hit your sales receipts is endless. Figure 22.1 shows the effect on cash flow for an example where sales revenue is 20 per cent adrift from the figures projected in the business plan. It is always prudent to leave payments broadly similar despite a drop in sales, although logic suggests that some costs would fall. Variable costs (see Chapter 20) such as materials should go down with sales volumes, but in practice you may buy in materials to meet the planned sales. In such cases, you will use fewer materials and carry them over in stock for a later period. Nevertheless, your cash position will be much as if you had actually used those materials.

Here you can see that under this 'what if' scenario funding requirements goes up from 25,000 to 45,000.

Stress testing the payments model

As with sales revenue, payments can take an unexpected turn for the worse. Inflationary pressures can push up wages and material costs. Utilities and

FIGURE 22.1 Testing the revenue model

Category	Initial projection	What if projection
Sales receipts		
Cash sales	50,000	40,000
Credit sales	50,000	40,000
Total cash in	100,000	80,000
		Sales -20%
Payments		
Salary and wages	25,000	25,000
Utilities	10,000	10,000
Rent and rates	15,000	15,000
Materials	35,000	35,000
Equipment	40,000	40,000
Total cash out	125,000	125,000
		Payments same
Net cash flow	–25,000	–45,000
		Funding needs +20,000
Funding needs	–25,000	–45,000

FIGURE 22.2 Testing the payments model

Category	Initial projection	What if	Revenue
Sales receipts			
Cash sales	50,000		50,000
Credit sales	50,000	Sales the same	50,000
Total cash in	100,000		100,000
Payments			
Salary and wages	25,000		35,000
Utilities	10,000		15,000
Rent and rates	15,000	Payments increase	12,000
Materials	35,000		40,000
Equipment	40,000		40,000
Total cash out	125,000		142,000
Net cash flow	−25,000	Funding needs +17,000	−42,000
Funding needs	−25,000		−42,000

motoring costs increased by nearly 40 per cent in the UK between 2008 and 2010. Figure 22.2 shows what would happen to cash flow if costs rise and sales revenue remains static. In this example, an additional £17,000 would be required to fund the venture, so the business plan would be looking to support a £42,000 investment, rather than just £25,000 before stress testing.

Testing to destruction

Calamitous accidents happen when two relatively unexpected events occur at the same time. On 5 November 2010, a cement lorry fell from Warren Lane Bridge at Oxshott on to the sixth and seventh coaches of an eight-car passenger service, derailing the train, seriously injuring the lorry driver and two passengers and causing days of major traffic disruption. Had the lorry fallen a couple of seconds later it would have missed the train completely.

From a business perspective it is more likely that a couple of things will go wrong over the planning horizon than with this type of railway disaster. Using the cash-flow model, check out a number of possible problem areas and see at what point these problems would cause you or your financial backers sleepless nights. For example, what would the effect be of a major

FIGURE 22.3 Testing to destruction

Category	Initial projection	What if	Revenue
Sales receipts			
Cash sales	50,000		40,000
Credit sales	50,000	Sales -20%	40,000
Total cash in	100,000		80,000
Payments			
Salary and wages	25,000		35,000
Utilities	10,000		15,000
Rent and rates	15,000	Payments	12,000
Materials	35,000	increase by 17,000	40,000
Equipment	40,000		40,000
Total cash out	125,000		142,000
Net cash flow	−25,000	Funding needs +37,000	−62,000
Funding needs	−25,000		−62,000

customer going bust, a supplier putting their prices up and a key employee leaving unexpectedly, all in the same quarter?

The funding needs projected in your business plan should accommodate a realistic amount of revenue shortfall and cost overrun. 'Realistic' is not an easy word to define, but the volatility of your business sector and the prevailing economic climate should be taken into account. Launching almost any new business in 2020 would have posed some challenges to cash flow that would not have been evident in the preceding decade.

WORKSHEET FOR ASSIGNMENT 22: STRESS TESTING YOUR BUSINESS PROJECTIONS

1 List the key assumptions that underpin the projections for your business.

2 List five factors that could adversely affect your sales projections.

3 List five factors that could adversely affect your costs and expense projections.

4 Under which of these circumstances would you plans be unviable?

5 What could be done to mitigate these risks?

Suggested further reading

Barrow, C (2011) *Practical Financial Management: A guide to budget, balance sheets and business finance*, 8th edn, Kogan Page, London

Barrow, C (2017) *Business Accounting for Dummies*, 4th edn, Wiley, New York

Holbeche, L (2018) *The Agile Organization: How to build an engaged, innovative and resilient business*, Kogan Page, London

Business controls

Introduction

No one is likely to take any business proposition seriously unless the founder(s) can demonstrate at the outset that they can monitor and control the venture. Just as your business plan should include a statement of objectives and strategy, it must also contain a brief description of how you will monitor results. Every business needs to monitor financial, sales and market performance. Manufacturing businesses or those involved in research, development and fashion may have to observe results on a much wider scale.

In these assignments you should address the issues of importance to your type of business. If you do not have first-hand experience of working in a similar business, either find someone who has or find a professional adviser, such as an auditor, with that experience. As a minimum, potential financiers will want to see that you have made arrangements to keep the books and analyse and interpret key business ratios.

ASSIGNMENT 23

Financial controls

To survive and prosper in business, you need to know how much cash you have and what your profit or loss on sales is. For a business to survive, let alone grow, these facts are needed on a monthly, weekly or occasionally even a daily basis depending on the nature of the business.

While bad luck plays a part in some business failures, a lack of reliable financial information plays a part in most. However, all the information needed to manage well is close at hand. The bills to be paid, invoices raised, petty-cash slips and bank statements between them are enough to give a true picture of performance. All that needs to be done is for the information on them to be recorded and organized so that the financial picture becomes clear. The way financial information is recorded is known as 'bookkeeping'.

The basic data derived from the bookkeeping process is turned into the historic profit and loss account and balance sheet. Then those accounts are in turn analysed using ratios, the subject of the second part of this chapter.

Keeping the books

There are no rules about the format to be used for a bookkeeping system. Records can be on paper, in ledgers or on a computer. You must, however, be able to account for where all your business income came from and who you have paid and for what services. If you are registered for VAT (see Assignment 15) you will also need to keep a record of the VAT element of each invoice and bill and produce a summary for each accounting period covered by your VAT returns.

Starting simple

If you are doing books by hand and don't have a lot of transactions, the single-entry method is the easiest acceptable way to go. This involves writing down each transaction in your records once, preferably on a ledger sheet. Receipts and payments should be kept and summarized daily, weekly or monthly, in accordance with the needs of the business. At the end of the year, the 12 monthly summaries are totalled up – you are ready for tax time.

This simple record system is known as a 'cash book' – an example is given in Table 23.1.

In the left-hand four columns, the month's expenses are entered as they occur, together with some basic details and the amount. At the head of the first column is the amount of cash brought forward from the preceding month.

On the right, expenses are listed in the same way. The total of receipts for the month is £/$/€1,480.15 and that for expenses is £/$/€672.01. The difference between these two figures is the amount of cash now in the business. As the business shown in Table 23.1 has brought in more cash than it has spent, the figure is higher than the amount brought forward at the beginning of the month. The figure of £/$/€808.14 is the amount that is 'brought down' to be 'brought forward' to the next month. The total of the month's payments and the amount 'carried down' are equal to the sum of all the receipts in the left-hand columns.

If there are a reasonably large number of transactions, it would be sensible to extend this simple cash book to include a basic analysis of the figures – this variation is called an 'analysed cash book'. An example of the payments side of an analysed cash book is shown in Table 23.2 (the receipts side is similar, but with different categories). You can see at a glance the receipts and payments, both in total and by main category. This breakdown lets you see, for example, how much is being spent on each major area of your business, or who your most important customers are. The payments are the same as in Table 23.1 but now you can see how much the business has spent on stock, vehicles and telephone expenses. The sums total both down the amount columns and across the analysis section to arrive at the same amount: £/$/€672.01. This is both a useful bit of management information and essential for your tax return.

If you are taking or giving credit, you will need to keep more information than the cash book, whether it is analysed or not. You will need to keep copies of paid and unpaid sales invoices and the same for purchases, as well as your bank statements. The bank statements should then be 'reconciled' to your cash book to tie everything together. For example, the bank statement for the example given in Table 23.1 should show £/$/€808.14 in the account at the end of June. Figure 23.1 outlines how this works.

TABLE 23.1 A simple cash-book system

	Receipts				Payments		
Date	Name	Details	Amount £/$/€	Date	Name	Details	Amount £/$/€
1 June	Balance	Brought forward	450.55	4 June	Gibbs	Stock purchase	310.00
4 June	Anderson	Sales	175.00	8 June	Gibbs	Stock purchase	130.00
6 June	Brown	Sales	45.00	12 June	ABC Telecoms	Telephone charges	55.23
14 June	Smith & Co	Refund on returned stock	137.34	18 June	Colt Rentals	Vehicle hire	87.26
17 June	Jenkins	Sales	190.25	22 June	VV Mobiles	Mobile phone	53.24
20 June	Hollis	Sales	425.12	27 June	Gibbs	Stock purchase	36.28
23 June	Jenkins	Sales	56.89				
							672.01
				30 June	Balance	Carried down	808.14
			1,480.15				1,480.15
1 July	Balance	Brought down	808.14				

Building a system

If you operate a partnership, trade as a company or plan to get larger, then you will need a double-entry bookkeeping system. This calls for a series of day books, ledgers, a journal, a petty-cash book and a wages book, as well as a number of files for copies of invoices and receipts.

The double-entry system requires two entries for each transaction – this provides built-in checks and balances to ensure accuracy. Each transaction requires an entry as a debit and as a credit. This may sound a little complicated, but you only need to get a general idea.

A double-entry system is more complicated and time-consuming if done by hand, since everything is recorded twice. If done manually, the method requires a formal set of books – journals and ledgers. All transactions would be first

TABLE 23.2 Example of an analysed cash book

Payments				Analysis			
Date	Name	Details	Amount £/$/€	Stocks	Vehicles	Telephone	Other
4 June	Gibbs	Stock purchase	310	310			
8 June	Gibbs	Stock purchase	130	130			
12 June	ABC Telecoms	Telephone charges	55.23			55.23	
18 June	Colt Rentals	Vehicle hire	87.26		87.26		
22 June	VV Mobiles	Mobile phone	53.24			53.24	
27 June	Gibbs	Stock purchase	36.28	36.28			
Totals			672.01	476.28	87.26	108.47	

entered into a journal and then 'posted' (written) on a ledger sheet – the same amount would be written down in two different places. Typical ledger accounts include those for titled income, expenses, assets and liabilities (debts).

To give an example, a payment of rent in a double-entry system might result in two separate journal entries – a debit for an expense of, say, £/$/€250 and a corresponding credit of £/$/€250 – a double entry (see Table 23.3). The debits in a double-entry system must always equal the credits. If they don't, you know there is an error somewhere. So, double entry allows you to balance your books, which you can't do with the single-entry method.

PAPER-BASED BOOKKEEPING SYSTEMS

If you expect to have fewer than 50 transactions each month, either buying or selling, then you can simply use analysis paper, either loose or in books that are available from any large stationers. These are sheets of paper A3 size, with a dozen or so lined columns already drawn so you can enter figures and extend your analysis as shown in Table 23.2. Alternatively you can buy a manual accounting system with a full set of ledgers and books for around £14.50 from Hingston Publishing Co or Collins Account Books available from most large stationers.

FIGURE 23.1 A simple system of business records

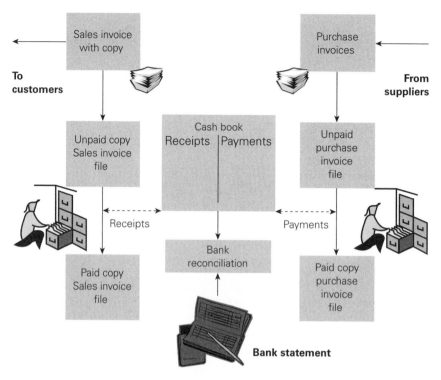

TABLE 23.3 An example of a double-entry ledger

General journal of Andrew's Bookshop			
Date	Description of entry	Debit	Credit
10 July	Rent expense Cash	£/$/€250	£/$/€250

Getting some help

You don't have to do the bookkeeping yourself, though if you do for the first year or so you will get a good insight into how your business works from a financial perspective. There are a number of ways in which you can reduce or even eliminate the more tedious aspects of the task.

1 Use an accounting software package. Brook City, a City-based accounting practice, provide a useful 'The Best Accounting Software for Small UK

Businesses' review each year. Xero, QuickBooks, Sage, Free Agent, Zoho, Clearbooks and Kashflow were their favourites in April 2020.

2 Employ the services of a bookkeeper. Professional associations such as the International Association of Bookkeepers (IAB) and the Institute of Certified Bookkeepers offer free matching services to help small businesses find a bookkeeper to suit their particular needs. Expect to pay upwards of £20 an hour for services that can be as basic as simply recording the transactions in your books, through to producing accounts, preparing the VAT return or doing the payroll. The big plus here is that professional bookkeepers have their own software.

3 If you plan to trade as a partnership or limited company (see Assignment 3) or look as though you will be growing fast from the outset, you may be ready to hire an accountant to look after your books. Personal recommendation from someone in your business network is the best starting point to finding an accountant. Meet the person and if you think you could work with him or her take up references, as you would with anyone you employ, and make sure he or she is a qualified member of one of the professional bodies, such as the Institute of Chartered Accountants.

Basic business ratios

Just keeping the books and accounts of a business is not of much use in itself if you can't analyse and interpret them. This involves measuring the relationship between various elements of performance to see whether you are getting better or worse. *Ratios* are the tools used here, and they are simply something expressed as a proportion of something else. So miles per gallon, for example, is a ratio showing a measure of the efficiency of fuel consumption.

Ratios are used to compare performance in one period, say last month or year, with another – this month or year. They can also be used to see how well your business is performing compared with another, say a competitor. You can also use ratios to compare how well you have done against your target or budget. In the financial field the opportunity for calculating ratios is great; for computing useful ratios, not quite so great. Here we shall concentrate on explaining the key ratios for a new venture.

Levels of profit

Look back to the profit and loss account and balance sheet for High Note, the example used in Assignments 18 and 19. These figures will be used in calculating the ratios that follow.

GROSS PROFIT

This is calculated by dividing the gross profit by sales and multiplying by 100. In this example the sum is 30,000/60,000 × 100 = 50 per cent. This is a measure of the value you are adding to the bought-in materials and services you need to 'make' your product or service; the higher the figure the better.

OPERATING PROFIT

This is calculated by dividing the operating profit by sales and multiplying by 100. In this example the sum is 8,700/60,000 × 100 = 14.5 per cent. This is a measure of how efficiently you are running the business, before taking account of financing costs and tax. These are excluded as interest and tax rates change periodically and are outside your direct control.

NET PROFIT BEFORE AND AFTER TAX

These are calculated by dividing the net profit before and after tax by the sales and multiplying by 100. In this example the sums are 8,100/60,000 × 100 = 13.5 per cent and 6,723/60,000 × 100 = 11.21 per cent. This is a measure of how efficiently you are running the business, after taking account of financing costs and tax. The last figure shows how successful you are at creating additional money to either invest back in the business or distribute to the owner(s) as either drawings or dividends. Once again the rule here is the higher the figure the better.

Working capital relationships

The money tied up in day-to-day activities is known as working capital, the sum of which is arrived at by subtracting the current liabilities from the current assets. In the case of High Note there is £/$/€21,108 in current assets and £/$/€4,908 in current liabilities, so the working capital is £/$/€16,200.

CURRENT RATIO

As a figure the working capital doesn't tell us much. It is rather as if you knew your car had used 20 gallons of petrol but had no idea how far you had travelled. It would be more helpful to know how much larger the current assets are than the current liabilities. That would give you some idea of whether the funds will be available to pay bills for stock, the tax liability and any other short-term liabilities that may arise. The current ratio, which is arrived at by dividing the current assets by the current liabilities, is the measure used. For High Note this is 21,108/4,908 = 4.30. The convention is to express this as 4.30:1, and the aim here is to have a ratio of between 1.5:1 and 2:1. Any lower and bills can't be met easily; much higher and money is being tied up unnecessarily.

AVERAGE COLLECTION PERIOD

We can see that High Note's current ratio is high, which is an indication that some elements of working capital are being used inefficiently. The business has £/$/€12,000 owed by customers on sales of £/$/€60,000 over a six-month period. The average period it takes High Note to collect money owed is calculated by dividing the sales made on credit by the money owed and multiplying it by the time period, in days; in this case the sum is as follows: 12,000/60,000 × 182.5 = 36.5 days.

If the credit terms are cash with order or seven days, then something is going seriously wrong. If it is net 30 days then it is probably about right. In this example it has been assumed that all the sales were made on credit.

DAYS STOCK HELD

High Note is carrying £/$/€9,108 stock of sheet music, CDs etc and over the period it sold £/$/€30,000 of stock at cost. (The cost of sales is £/$/€30,000 to support £/$/€60,000 of invoiced sales as the mark-up in this case is 100 per cent.) Using a similar sum as with average collection period we can calculate that the stock being held is sufficient to support 55.41 days' sales (9,108/10,000 × 182.5). If High Note's suppliers can make weekly deliveries, this is almost certainly too high a stock figure to hold. Cutting stock back from nearly eight weeks (55.41 days) to one week (seven days) would trim 48.41 days or £/$/€7,957.38 worth of stock out of working capital. This in turn would bring the current ratio down to 2.68:1.

Return on investment

The fundamental financial purpose in business is to make a satisfactory return on the funds invested. Return on investment is calculated as a percentage in the same way as the interest you would get on any money on deposit in a bank would be. In High Note £/$/€28,700 has been put into the business from various sources including the bank, to generate an operating profit of £/$/€8,700 – that is, profit before paying the bank interest on money owed or tax. The return is calculated as 8,700/28,700 × 100 = 30.31 per cent.

APPRECIATING GEARING

The return on investment ratio is arrived at taking into account all the sources of money used. However, High Note's owners only have £/$/€10,000 of their own money invested and the profit they make after paying bank interest of £/$/€600 is £/$/€8,100. So the return on the owner's investment is 8,100/10,000 × 100 = 81 per cent, which by any standards is acceptable.

If the owners had been able to get an overdraft of £/$/€15,000 rather than the £/$/€10,000 they secured and so only put in £/$/€5,000 of their own cash, the return on their investment would have been better still. Interest costs would increase to £/$/€900 so profit after interest would drop to £/$/€7,800, but the owners' investment being just £/$/€5,000 means that the return on their investment would rise to 156 per cent (7,800/5,000 × 100).

There is a limit to the amount of money banks will put up compared with the amount an owner puts in. Typically banks will look to no more than match the owners' funding, and in any event they will want to secure their loan against some tangible asset such as a property.

Ratio analysis spreadsheets

Bookkeeping and accounting software often have 'report generator' programs that crunch out ratios for you, sometimes with helpful suggestions on areas to be probed further. The Corporate Finance Institute has a large number of useful financial spreadsheet templates. (see these under Ratio analysis in the Index of key organizations and resources for business planning at the end of the book).

WORKSHEET FOR ASSIGNMENT 23: FINANCIAL CONTROLS

1 What bookkeeping and accounting system have you chosen and why?

2 What control information does it produce and with what frequency?

3 Who will keep the books and produce the accounts?

4 What will your basic business ratios be if you achieve your financial objectives?

5 How do those ratios compare with those of either a competitor or your current organization?

6 What would you consider changing as a result of carrying out your ratio analysis (for example, collect money in faster, carry less stock)?

Suggested further reading

Barrow, C (2011) *Financial Management for the Small Business*, 8th edn, Kogan Page, London

Barrow, C (2017) *Understanding Business Accounting for Dummies*, 4th edn, Wiley, New York

ASSIGNMENT 24

Sales and marketing controls

In the early weeks and months of any new venture, large amounts of both effort and money will be expended without any visible signs of sales revenue, let alone profits. Even once the business has been trading for some time, the most reliable predictor of likely future results will be the sales and marketing efforts for the immediate past. Your business plan should explain how you intend to monitor and control this activity.

CASE STUDY
The Supreme Garden Furniture Company

Gordon Smith set up his business, the Supreme Garden Furniture Company, shortly after being made redundant. Using 800 square feet on the ground floor of an old Lancashire textile mill, he planned to produce a range of one- to four-seat garden benches in an authentic Victorian design, together with matching tables. Each item in the range was manufactured to a very high standard using top-quality materials, such as kiln-dried African Iroko hardwood.

With professional advice he drew up a business plan incorporating cash and profit forecasts, an assessment of the market and his likely competitors, the plant and machinery required and the start-up capital he would need.

His main customers would be garden centres, and he planned to spend a couple of days a week out on the road selling, initially in Lancashire, Yorkshire and Cheshire. He also produced a leaflet and price list which he intended to send to potential customers further afield. These he would follow up later.

Once Smith had gained a number of customers, he found that future sales to existing customers were much easier than constantly seeking new customers. So, he kept records of existing customers, to monitor their purchases and plan follow-up visits.

From an analysis of his customer records Smith was subsequently able to discover that garden centres in the South East placed average orders of £2,000 a time, while in his home area a £500 order was exceptional. In his business plan for his future trading he would be able to incorporate this information and alter his selling strategy accordingly (see Table 24.1).

TABLE 24.1 Sales and marketing controls

Sales and marketing report for July				
Control	Objective	Result	Variance	Action
Sales volume	10	8	(2)	Step up sales activity
Sales value	£5000	£4500	(£500)	Emphasize higher-priced products
New customers	6	5	(1)	Make more calls
Repeat customer purchase – numbers	3	2	(1)	Incentivize existing customers
Average order size – North	£1000	£300	(£700)	Shift emphasis to visiting fewer but bigger accounts
Average order size – South East	£1000	£2000	£1000	Reduce sales activity in the North and do more in the South East
Number of sales visits	20	15	(5)	Plan territory and calls better to fit in more sales visits

Controlling your promotional costs and judging their cost-effectiveness is also an early, vital marketing control task.

CASE STUDY
Richer Sounds

Julian Richer opened his first Richer Sounds shop at London Bridge when he was 19. Today he has 53 outlets, and together with his online business generates sales of over £144 million a year. Richer was worth an estimated £115 million in 2014. Performance measurement and control is based on a wide range of financial measures, such as profit, sales, and stock turn, enhanced by measures of customer satisfaction, employee involvement and employee satisfaction. In addition stores are assessed by 'mystery shoppers'. Employees are given performance information through weekly reports and a monthly video from the chairman relaying facts about company performance on sales, margins, customer satisfaction and proposed changes.

Richer's plan by 2014 was to 'stick to the knitting' by doing more of what they do now – keeping everyone informed.

In May 2017 *Which?* awarded Richer Sounds the accolade of Retailer of the Year 2017 alongside Apple and John Lewis. In May 2019 Richer transferred 60 per cent of the companies shares over to his staff to be held for their benefit in an employee ownership trust.

Equally, advertising costs per sales lead generated and converted should be recorded, while tear-off coupons, discounts on production or special offer leaflets all help to measure the cost-effectiveness of your promotions.

Customer relationship management (CRM) and sales force management systems

CRM is the business strategy concerned with identifying, understanding and improving relationships with your customers to improve customer satisfaction and maximize profits. The myriad of facts and figures that need to be assembled have made the subject ideal for software applications.

For example, businesses can maintain a database of which customers buy and what type of product, and when, how often they make that purchase, what type of options they choose with their typical purchase, their colour preferences and whether the purchase needed financing. This information will advise the sales team on what products services or messages are likely to be the most effective and when would be a good time to target each customer.

While CRM systems put customers at the centre of the data flow, sales force management systems capture, track and manage sales enquiries in a central database that track leads throughout the sales cycle from lead generation to closed sale. Tech Radar, who provide insights for business users in this area produce a regular 'Best CRM software' review. (**www.techradar.com/uk/best/best-crm-software**)

WORKSHEET FOR ASSIGNMENT 24: SALES AND MARKETING
CONTROLS

1 Describe your records for monitoring sales activities.

2 Draw up a customer record card for your business, or show your existing one.

3 What other marketing records do you plan to keep, eg for advertising costs
   and results?

4 Explain the relationship between any sales activity and the results expected.
   For example: 'We expect to open one new account for every ten we
   cold-call; or for every 10,000 cold emails sent out.'

Suggested further reading

Barnes, C, Blake, H and Howard T (2017) *Selling Your Value Proposition*, Kogan
    Page, London

Cook, S (2011) *Customer Care Excellence: How to create an effective customer
    focus*, Kogan Page, London

Jobber, D and Lancaster, G (2012) *Selling and Sales Management*, Pearson
    Education, London

McClay, R (2014) *The Art of Modern Sales Management: Driving performance in
    a connected world*, American Society for Training and Development,
    Alexandria, VA

ASSIGNMENT 25

Other business controls

Depending on the nature of your venture, your business plan will have to show how you plan to control other aspects of the firm's performance. These could include:

- manufacturing and production;
- personnel records/accident reports;
- quality and complaints;
- new product development/design.

Stock cards for the different stages of your production process (raw materials, work-in-progress, finished goods) are particularly important to help you identify fast- and slow-moving items and to help you identify correct safety stock levels. Equally, to permit customers to complain (better than them voting with their feet, without telling you) you will need to provide customer suggestion boxes or explanations as to how to contact key managers, eg by giving a name and contact address on a restaurant menu.

WORKSHEET FOR ASSIGNMENT 25: OTHER BUSINESS CONTROLS

1 What other business controls do you plan to introduce into your business at the outset?

2 Why do you consider them important?

Suggested further reading

Eckerson, W E (2010) *Performance Dashboards: Measuring, monitoring and managing your business*, John Wiley and Son, Canada

Marr, B (2012) *Key Performance Indicators (KPI): The 75 measures every manager needs to know*, Pearson, London

Marshall, C (2013) *Monitoring and Control 52 Success Secrets: 52 most asked questions on monitoring and control – what you need to know*, Emereo Publishing, Brisbane

Milton, N and Lambe, P (2016) *The Knowledge Manager's Handbook*, Kogan Page, London

Pullan, P and Archer, J (2013) *Business Analysis and Leadership*, Kogan Page, London

Sultan, S (2017) *Financial Ratio: Quick Guide*, Expert of Course Publishing

Writing up and presenting your business plan

Introduction

This section is in effect the culmination of your work to date. Inevitably everything you have been preparing should be seen as 'work in progress'. At each stage you may well have had to go back and review an earlier one. For example your mission may change in the light of market research uncovering different needs or unexpected competitors. Your marketing strategy or sales projections may in turn be modified as a result of concerns about the amount and type of money that you could realistically raise.

Now, however, all strands need to be pulled together into a coherent whole, perhaps using one of the many free business plan writer templates now available.

ASSIGNMENT 26

Writing up and presenting your business plan

Up to now, the workbook assignments have focused on gathering data needed to validate a business idea, to confirm the business team's capability to implement their chosen strategy and to quantify the resources needed in terms of 'men, machinery, money and management'. Now this information has to be assembled, collated and orchestrated into a coherent and complete written business plan aimed at a specific audience.

In this assignment we shall examine the six activities that can make this happen:

- dividing up the task;
- packaging;
- layout and content;
- writing and editing;
- who to send it to;
- the oral presentation.

Dividing up the task

The preceding chapters, as well as having a practical logic to their sequence, will provide you with manageable 'chunks' of material to write up either yourself, or better still to delegate to partners and professional advisers. The niceties of grammar and style can be resolved later.

While it is useful to make use of as much help as you can get in preparing the groundwork, you should orchestrate the information and write up the business plan yourself. After all, it is your future that is at stake – and every prospective financier will be backing you and your ability to put this plan into action, not your scriptwriter.

Different people in your team will have been responsible for carrying out the work involved in answering the questions posed in the chapter checklists and in writing up different section(s) of the business plan. This information should be circulated to ensure that:

- Everyone is still heading in the same direction. Inevitably, thinking will change as result of discussions and debate. For example, the cash-flow stress tests may cause significant alterations to an original strategy.

- Nothing important has been missed out. Two or more sets of eyes are always better at spotting any gaps. Also, as the business plan's originator and champion you will be close to the subject and as such are in danger of taking for granted how much an outside reader really knows and understands.

- A timetable is established for when each section of the business plan should be ready in draft form, showing who is responsible for each task and when it should be ready.

Using a group writing tool such as the Track Changes facility in Microsoft Word will help to ensure that everyone involved can see who said or changed what and when changes were made.

If any of your team need a tutorial on business writing, there is one in the Index of key organizations and resources for business planning under Business writing guide.

Packaging

Every product is enhanced by appropriate packaging, and a business plan is no exception. The panellists at Cranfield's enterprise programmes prefer a simple spiral binding with a plastic cover on the front and back. This makes it easy for the reader to move from section to section, and it ensures the plan will survive frequent handling. Stapled copies and leather-bound tomes are viewed as undesirable extremes.

A near-letter-quality (NLQ) printer will produce a satisfactory type finish, which, together with wide margins and double spacing, will result in a pleasing and easy-to-read document.

Layout and content

There is no such thing as a 'universal' business plan format. That being said, experience at Cranfield has taught us that certain layouts and contents have gone down better than others. These are our guidelines to producing an attractive business plan, from the investor's point of view. Not every subheading will be relevant to every type of business, but the general format should be followed, with emphasis laid as appropriate.

First, the cover should show the name of the company, its address and phone number and the date on which this version of the plan was prepared. It should confirm that this is the company's latest view on its position and financing needs. Remember that your business plan should be targeted at specific sources of finance. It's highly likely, therefore, that you will need to assemble slightly different business plans, highlighting areas of concern to lenders as opposed to investors, for example.

Second, the title page, immediately behind the front cover, should repeat the above information and also give the founder's name, address and phone number. He or she is likely to be the first point of contact and anyone reading the business plan may want to talk over some aspects of the proposal before arranging a meeting.

The cover sheet

The cover sheet includes your venture's full legal name, address, phone and fax numbers, web address and name and title of the person to contact and their email and phone contact information. Also state who the business plan is going to. While you may well be sending your plan out to several organizations and those copies of the plan may be identical, it is always helpful to make readers feel that the plan is addressed personally to them. Ideally, place each piece of information on a separate line and centre it in the middle of your cover page using large font. Include your logo, strap line or an image that you use to convey what you do.

Lower down the page put the date of the business plan and its version number; this is important as people receiving your plan could be working from an earlier version if the approval process is drawn out, as is virtually inevitable if you are raising venture capital. Include some information showing that the information is provided in confidence, whether or not you require a confidentiality agreement. It will at least put people on their guard before passing on or discussing any aspect of your business plan.

Protecting your plan

Before you show or discuss your business plan with anyone outside your organization you should consider getting them to sign an NDA (non-disclosure agreement). NDAs are confidentiality agreements that bind recipients to maintain your 'secrets' and not to take any action that could damage the value of any 'secret'. This means that they can't share the information with anyone else or act on the idea themselves, for a period of time at least. NDAs are a helpful way of getting advice and help while protecting you from someone using your information to compete against you. The UK Government produces a guide to NDAs (see under Non-disclosure agreements in the Index of key organizations and resources for business planning at the end of the book), which gives information and guidance about what you need to consider when disclosing an invention, including example NDA templates.

The executive summary

Ideally one but certainly no longer than two pages, this should follow immediately behind the title page. Writing up the executive summary is not easy but it is the most important single part of the business plan; it will probably do more to influence whether or not the plan is reviewed in its entirety than anything else you do. It can also make the reader favourably disposed towards a venture at the outset – which is no bad thing.

These two pages must explain:

- the current state of the company with respect to product/service readiness for market, trading position and past successes if already running, and key staff on board;
- the products or services to be sold and to whom they will be sold, including details on competitive advantage;
- the reasons customers need this product or service, together with some indication of market size and growth;

- the company's aims and objectives in both the short and the longer term, and an indication of the strategies to be employed in getting there;
- a summary of forecasts, sales, profits and cash flow;
- how much money is needed, and how and when the investor or lender will benefit from providing the funds.

Obviously, the executive summary can only be written after the business plan itself has been completed.

The table of contents

After the executive summary follows a table of contents. This is the map that will guide the new reader through your business proposal and on to the 'inevitable' conclusion that they should put up the funds. If a map is obscure, muddled or even missing, then the chances are you will end up with lost or irritated readers unable to find their way around your proposal.

Each of the main sections of the business plan should be listed and the pages within that section indicated. There are two valid schools of thought on page numbering. One favours a straightforward sequential numbering of each page, 1, 2, 3 ... 9, 10 for example. This seems to us to be perfectly adequate for short, simple plans, dealing with uncomplicated issues and seeking modest levels of finance.

Most proposals should be numbered by section. In the example that follows, the section headed 'The Business and Its Management' is Section 1, and the pages that follow are listed from 1.1 to 1.7 in the table of contents, so identifying each page as belonging within that specific section. This numbering method also allows you to insert new material without upsetting the entire pagination during preparation. Tables and figures should also be similarly numbered.

Individual paragraph numbering, much in favour with government and civil service departments, is considered something of an overkill in a business plan and is to be discouraged, except perhaps if you are looking for a large amount of government grant.

The table of contents in Table 26.1 shows both the layout and the content that in our experience are most in favour with financial institutions. Unsurprisingly, the terminology is similar to that used throughout this workbook. For a comprehensive explanation of what should be included under each heading, look back to the appropriate assignments throughout this book.

Appendices

While a business plan is not a work of literature it should read well. Anything essential that could impede a smooth flow should be consigned to an appendix and either summarized or referenced in the main body of the business plan.

TABLE 26.1   Sample table of contents

Section		Page
Executive Summary		i, ii
1	The Business and Its Management	
	History and Position to Date	1.1
	Current or New Mission	1.2
	Objectives, Near Term	1.3
	Objectives, Long Term	1.4
	The Management Team	1.5
	Legal Structure	1.6
	Professional Advisers	1.7
2	The Products or Services	
	Descriptions	2.1
	Readiness for Market	2.2
	Applications	2.3
	Proprietary Position	2.4
	Comparison with Competition, Performance and Economics	2.5
	Guarantees and Warranties	2.6
	Future Potential/Product Development	2.7
	Sources of Supply (if not a maufacturing/assembling business)	2.8
3	Market and Competitors	
	Description of Customers	3.1
	Customer Needs and Benefits	3.2
	Market Segments	3.3
	Customer Decision Criteria	3.4
	Market and Segment Size and Growth	3.5
	Market Projections	3.6
	Competition	3.7

(continued)

TABLE 26.1 (Continued)

Section		Page
4	Competitive Business Strategy	
	Pricing Policy	4.1
	Promotional Plans	4.2
	Choice of Location and Premises	4.3
	Distribution Channels	4.4
	Anticipated Mark-up	4.5
	Competitor Response	4.6
	Market Share Projection	4.7
	Economic, Political, Social, Legal Factors that Affect Strategy	4.8
5	Selling	
	Current Selling Method(s)	5.1
	Proposed Selling Method(s)	5.2
	Sales Team	5.3
	In-house support	5.4
6	Manufacturing	
	Make or Buy Considerations	6.1
	The Manufacturing Process	6.2
	Facilities Needed	6.3
	Equipment and Machinery Needed	6.4
	Output Limitation, if any, and Scale-Up Possibilities	6.5
	Engineering and Design Support	6.6
	Quality Control Plans	6.7
	Staffing Requirements	6.8
	Sources of Supply of Key Materials	6.9
7	Forecasts and Financial Data	
	Summary of Performance Ratios, ROI, etc	7.1
	Sales Forecasts	7.2
	Assumptions Underpinning Financial Forecasts	7.3
	Profit and Loss Accounts	7.4
	Cash-flow Forecasts	7.5
	Balance Sheets	7.6
	Break-even Analysis	7.7
	Sensitivity Analysis	7.8

(continued)

TABLE 26.1 (Continued)

Section		Page
8	Financing Requirements	
	Summary of Operations Prior to Financing	8.1
	Current Shareholders, Loans Outstanding, etc	8.2
	Funds Required and Timing	8.3
	Use of Proceeds	8.4
	The Deal on Offer	8.5
	Anticipated Gearing and Interest Cover	8.6
	Exit Routes for Investor	8.7
9	Business Controls	
	Financial	9.1
	Sales and Marketing	9.2
	Manufacturing	9.3
	Other Controls	9.4

Items best included in an appendix include:

- CVs of key staff;
- detailed market research studies, surveys, questionnaires and findings;
- competitors' literature, accounts and related information;
- full financial projections – balance sheets, profit and loss accounts, cash-flow projections, 'what if' analysis, break-even calculations and detailed ratio analysis;
- patent and other IP currently owned or being applied for;
- website screenshots;
- literature, brochures, product specifications and designs.

Writing and editing

A 'prospectus', such as a business plan seeking finance from investors, can have a legal status, turning any claims you may make for sales and profits (for example) into a 'contract'. Your accountant and legal adviser will be able to help you with the appropriate language that can convey your projections without giving them contractual status.

This would also be a good time to talk over the proposal with a 'friendly' banker or venture capital provider. They can give an insider's view as to the strengths and weaknesses of your proposal.

When your first draft has been revised, then comes the task of editing. Here the grammar, spelling and language must be carefully checked to ensure that your business plan is crisp, correct, clear and complete – and not too long. If writing is not your trade, once again this is an area in which to seek help. Your local college or librarian will know of someone who can produce 'attention-capturing' prose, if you yourself don't.

However much help you get with writing up your business plan, it is still just that – your plan. So, the responsibility for the final proofreading before it goes out must rest with you. Spelling mistakes and typing errors can have a disproportionate influence on the way your business plan is received.

The other purpose of editing is to reduce the business plan to between 20 and 40 pages. However complex or sizeable the venture, outsiders won't have time to read it if it is longer – and insiders will only succeed in displaying their muddled thinking to full effect. If your plan includes volumes of data, tables, graphs, etc, refer to them in the text, but confine them to an appendix.

Getting the layout right

Your business plan should be visually appealing. Dense text, poor layout and clutter all serve to put your reader off. Create a favourable impression from the outset and you will have them on side. These are the most important guidelines to make your written business plan stand out from the crowd.

- *Layout.* The reasoning behind good layout is to entice the reader to read your words and take the action you want – back your proposition. Give your text room to breathe by leaving plenty of white space around it. You can achieve this by having wide margins. Use headlines to break up the text and different font sizes and styles to differentiate between sections of your business plan.

- *Font.* Don't be tempted to use a fancy font in the body of the business plan. Stick to serif fonts, those with slight 'tails' on the letters that lead the eye from letter to letter. Times New Roman, Book Antiqua and Century are good examples of texts that cause less eye strain. Sans-serif fonts – Arial, Calibri and Helvetica, for example – can cause eye fatigue when used in text so are best used in headlines, bullets or short paragraphs outside the main body of your text. Never use a font smaller than 10-point, unless your readership is mostly under 30. For over 70s the recommended size to cause the least pain is 14-point; however, most business plan writers settle on 12-point as the preferred size.

- *Pictures*. Images, charts, tables, graphs and pictures are powerful ways to convey large amounts of information quickly and efficiently. A picture, so the saying goes, is worth a thousand words. Which is excellent as they usually only need the space of 200. This is also a great way to break up the text and retain reader attention.

Who to send it to

Now you are ready to send out your business plan to a few carefully selected financial institutions that you know are interested in proposals such as yours.

This will involve some research into the particular interests, foibles and idiosyncrasies of the institutions themselves. If you are only interested in raising debt capital, the field is narrowed to the clearing banks for the main part. If you are looking for someone to share the risk with you, then you must review the much wider field of venture capital. Here, some institutions will only look at proposals over a certain capital sum, such as £250,000, or will only invest in certain technologies.

It is a good idea to carry out this research before the final editing of your business plan, as you should incorporate something of this knowledge into the way your business plan is presented. You may find that slightly different versions of Section 8.5, 'The deal on offer', have to be made for each different source of finance to which you send your business plan.

Do not be disheartened if the first batch of financiers you contact don't sign you up. One Cranfield enterprise programme participant had to approach 26 lending institutions, 10 of them different branches of the same organization, before getting the funds she wanted. One important piece of information she brought back from every interview was the reason for the refusal. This eventually led to a refined proposal that won through.

It is as well to remember that financial institutions are far from infallible, so you may have to widen your audience to other contacts.

Finally, how long will it all take? This also depends on whether you are raising debt or equity, the institution you approach and the complexity of the deal on offer. A secured bank loan, for example, can take from a few days to a few weeks to arrange.

Investment from a venture capital house will rarely take less than three months to arrange, and will more usually take six or even up to nine months. Although the deal itself may be struck early on, the lawyers will pore over the detail for weeks. Every exchange of letters can add a fortnight to the wait. The 'due diligence' process in which every detail of your business plan is checked out will also take time – so this will have to be allowed for in your projections.

The oral presentation

If getting someone interested in your business plan is half the battle in raising funds, the other half is the oral presentation. Any organization financing a venture will insist on seeing the team involved presenting and defending their plans – in person. They know that they are backing people every bit as much as the idea. You can be sure that any financiers you are presenting to will be well prepared. Remember that they see hundreds of proposals every year, and either have or know of investments in many different sectors of the economy. If this is not your first business venture, they may even have taken the trouble to find out something of your past financial history.

Keep these points in mind when preparing for the presentation of your business plan:

- Find out how much time you have, then rehearse your presentation beforehand. Allow at least as much time for questions as for your talk.

- Use visual aids and if possible bring and demonstrate your product or service. A video or computer-generated model is better than nothing.

- Explain your strategy in a businesslike manner, demonstrating your grasp of the competitive market forces at work. Listen to comments and criticisms carefully, avoiding a defensive attitude when you respond.

- Make your replies to questions brief and to the point. If members of the audience want more information, they can ask. This approach allows time for the many different questions that must be asked, either now or later, before an investment can proceed.

- Your goal is to create empathy between yourself and your listeners. While you may not be able to change your personality, you could take a few tips on presentation skills. Eye contact, tone of speech, enthusiasm and body language all have a part to play in making a presentation successful.

- Wearing a suit is never likely to upset anyone. Shorts and sandals could just set the wrong tone! Serious money calls for serious people.
- Be prepared. You need to have every aspect of your business plan in your head and know your way around the plan forwards, backwards and sideways! You never know when the chance to present may occur. It's as well to have a 5-, 10- and 20- minute presentation ready to run at a moment's notice.

The elevator pitch

Often the person you are pitching your proposal to is short of time. As a rough rule of thumb, the closer you get to an individual with the power to make decisions, the less time you will get to make your pitch. So you need to have a short presentation to hand that can be made in any circumstance – in a plane, at an airport or between floors in a lift, hence the name 'elevator pitch'.

CASE STUDY
Lara Morgan

Lara Morgan, founder of Pacific Direct, the hotel toiletries supplier, had come a long way from the garage in Bedford, England, where she started up her business, when she had the opportunity to pitch for a strategic alliance with one of the most influential players in her market. The scene was set for her to make a relaxed pitch over coffee at the Dorchester Hotel in Park Lane, when at a moment's notice the situation changed dramatically. Lara was told that due to a diary change she had 15 minutes in a chauffeur-driven limousine en route to Harrods to make her proposition.

She was prepared, made her presentation and secured a deal that was instrumental in creating Pacific's unique 5* hotel strategy. Pacific now has Penhaligons, Elemis, Ermenegildo Zegna, Nina Campbell, Floris, The White Company and Natural Products in its world-class product portfolio.

Taking professional advice

There is a tendency towards secrecy amongst innovators, and those starting new ventures are no exception to this rule. However with an NDA in place there is no reason not to take outside advice, and indeed every reason to do so. Anyone reading your business plan will draw comfort from the fact that they are not the first, and that your ideas have been honed on the wisdom and experience of others.

In fact the more qualified, experienced and prestigious your advisers, the more their input will enhance your business plan, in the eyes of the reader. After all, rather than being the untested ideas of one or two people, they have been validated by professionals. If an accountant has looked over the figures, a lawyer the intellectual property rights, an engineer your prototype design and a software consultant your website plans, then real value will have been added to your proposition.

If you know or have access to people with a successful track record in your area of business who have time on their hands, you can invite them to help.

Using business planning software

There are a number of software packages, some free, that will help you through the process of writing your business plan. The ones listed below include some useful resources, spreadsheets and tips that may speed up the process, but are not substitutes for finding out the basic facts about your market, customers and competitors.

Business.org, an online business magazine, produces a regular review of the best small business planning software. In 2020, their recommendations were:

- LivePlan: Best overall
- BizPlanBuilder: Most user-friendly
- GoSmallBiz.com: Best for non-profits
- Business Plan Pro: Best for customer support
- BizPlan: Honourable mention
- PlanGuru: Honourable mention

Dealing with rejection

Don't be either surprised or disheartened if your business plan doesn't get the reception you hope for. Anita Roddick's Body Shop proposition was turned down flat. It was only when a local garage owner, Ian McGlinn, advanced her £4,000 in return for 25 per cent of her company that she got the money to open a second shop; a deal that netted him a couple of hundred million pounds and her considerably more. Tim Waterstone's business plan was turned down by bank after bank, for being too ambitious. They wanted him to open a book-shop, while he had set his sights on a chain. Eventually he got backing and went on to build his chain, change the shape of book retailing in the UK and sell his business to his former employers, WH Smith, for £47 million.

There are hundreds of reasons why business plans are turned down. According to venture capitalists, who turn down 95 propositions for every 100 they receive, they are just not convinced by the proposition. That is, convinced that the plan has been well thought through, properly researched and that the person or team are up to the task.

These measures will help you to refine your business plan and minimize the chances of ultimate rejection.

- Listen carefully to criticisms when you are presenting your business plan. If it is clear at the time that you are going to be turned down ask two questions: why; and what can you do to improve your proposition?

- Go back over your business plan and see if there is anything you can change to make the financial proposition look less risky. High burn rate, that is cash pouring out in the early weeks and months on staff, offices and PR without any significant sales revenue coming in, is a big turn-off for financiers.

- If your credibility is questioned it may be time to consider strengthening your team, taking in a non-executive director or building a strategic alliance with an organization that can plug the gap in question.

- Consider whether you are pitching your proposition to the right audience. Risky technology-based ventures are more likely to appeal to VCs and corporate venture firms. Bankers are more interested in putting up cash for tangible assets such as property and elements of working capital including stock in trade and financing quality customers taking credit.

- If your business proposition is challenged, get out and secure some initial business. If that is impossible get some customers to agree to try out your product, perhaps agreeing to be a trial or demonstration site in return for a reduced price. You can then build in their acceptance as proof that your ideas have potential.

- See if there are elements of cost that can be eliminated, reduced or postponed. For example, a state-of-the-art website may be desirable, but a more basic site at a much reduced cost may be enough for the first few weeks and months.

- Is there a radically different approach to delivering your product that could work as a bridge between where you are and where you want to be? For example, one entrepreneur who wanted to open a bagel shop started out with a stall in a street market. Once that was a proven success he went on to launch his shops.

- Government guide to non-disclosure agreements can be found at: (www.gov.uk/government/publications/non-disclosure-agreements).

WORKSHEET FOR ASSIGNMENT 26: WRITING UP AND PRESENTING YOUR BUSINESS PLAN

1   Who do you propose to send your business plan to first, and why have you chosen them?

2   Write a first draft of your business plan along the lines recommended.

3   Who can help you to edit and rewrite the final version of your plan?

4   Prepare and rehearse a presentation of your business plan.

5   Who aside from your team can you enlist to advise on your business plan?

Suggested further reading

Barker, A (2016) *Improve Your Communication Skills*, 4th edn, Kogan Page, London

Forsyth, P (2016) *How to Write Reports and Proposals*, 4th edn, Kogan Page, London

Harvard Business School Press (2007) *Giving Presentations*, Harvard Business School, Boston, MA

Harvard Business School Press (2007) *Writing for Business*, Harvard Business School, Boston, MA

Moon, J (2008) *How to Make an Impact: Influence, inform and impress with your reports, presentations and business documents*, Pearson Education, London

Talbot, F (2016) *Better Business English: How to write effective business English*, 2nd edn, Kogan Page, London

INDEX OF KEY ORGANIZATIONS AND RESOURCES FOR BUSINESS PLANNING

These are the principal sources of help and advice for anyone writing a business plan. This index also contains a collation of all the resources mentioned throughout the book.

United Kingdom

ACCA (**www.accaglobal.com** (archived at https://perma.cc/XQ37-GV24)) provides access to over 2,400 Technical articles, on every aspect of starting a business including recruiting, advertising, grants, setting up an office, researching your market and effective selling. Just type 'starting a business' into the search pane.

The British Chambers of Commerce (**www.britishchambers.org.uk/** (archived at https://perma.cc/8RCD-A3LA)) helps British businesses to build relationships on every level. Across their network, they can connect your business locally, nationally and internationally, with other businesses, decision-makers and opportunities.

The British Library Business Information Service (**www.bl.uk/business-and-ip-centre** (archived at https://perma.cc/FV2H-NY68)) holds one of the most comprehensive collections of business information in the UK. Business information sources published in the UK are collected as comprehensively as possible; sources published elsewhere are taken selectively. It aims to cover the manufacturing, wholesale trading, retailing and distribution aspects of major industries and the following service sectors: financial services, energy, environment, transport, and food and drink.

British Services Trade Associations (**www.britishservices.co.uk/associations.htm#listings** (archived at https://perma.cc/FV3P-WSRU)) list pressure groups, unions, institutes, societies and more, which are profiled, representing every interest area from the Adhesive Tape Manufacturers Association to the Zinc Development Association.

BSI (**www.bsigroup.com/en-GB/small-business/** (archived at https://perma.cc/J7CB-PEF6)) provide information and resources to help small business introduce quality standards such as ISO 9000.

A Business Writing Guide (**libguides.tamusa.edu/businesswriting** (archived at https://perma.cc/UR3Z-E8JP)) is provided by Texas A&M University-San Antonio (A&M-SA).

The Central Intelligence Agency (CIA) World Factbook. (**www.cia.gov/ library/publications/the-world-factbook/** (archived at https://perma.cc/DR6Z-6HFH)). This link will take you straight to the latest edition of the Factbook. The CIA keeps the Factbook up to date on a regular basis throughout the year, so you can be reasonably confident of having the most current information to hand. From the Factbook you are offered a pull-down bar in the top right of the screen, which allows you to select any one of the 233 countries or regions. For each country there are around half a dozen A4 pages of basic economic, political and demographic information on each country, as well as information on political disputes that may cause problems in the future.

Cobweb (**www.cobwebinfo.com** (archived at https://perma.cc/2CKB-Q2ZQ)) is a specialist provider of information services for businesses, their advisers and other professional intermediaries. Its content is of particular benefit to new-start and small/medium enterprises. The production team continually researches, creates, updates and publishes a practical and authoritative range of business titles, subjects and products.

The knowledge base provides a blend of when, how, where and why content subjects covering thousands of business topics and types, market sectors, regulations, sources of business funding, advice, expertise, contacts and much more.

Companies House (**www.companieshouse.gov.uk** (archived at https:// perma.cc/AH92-LA9F)) is the official repository of all company information in the UK. Their WebCheck service offers a free-of-charge searchable Company Names and Address Index which covers 2 million companies, either by name or unique company registration number.

Department for International Trade (**www.gov.uk/government/organisations/ department-for-international-trade** (archived at https://perma.cc/T8Z9-X6FR)) is the government agency charged with helping UK-based businesses succeed in 'an increasingly global world'. It provides information on doing business with every country and every business sector from aerospace to water.

Enterprise Nation (**www.enterprisenation.com** (archived at https:// perma.cc/YU4V-LUHP)), founded in 2006, is aimed primarily at homework ventures: the site has dozens of podcasts and links to help would-be business starters get underway.

Entrepreneur Quiz (**www.humanmetrics.com/entrepreneur** (archived at https://perma.cc/F758-2KT7)) is a quiz to assesses your entrepreneur type based on your personality traits.

Everywoman (**www.everywoman.com/home-working-hub** (archived at https://perma.cc/PB45-CX4G); tel: 020 7981 2574) is a free service, registration required, giving access to over 30,000 like-minded women who are serious about business. The site has plenty of advice, tips, factsheets and online tools to help business starters.

The Federation of Small Businesses (**www.fsb.org.uk** (archived at https://perma.cc/T7UU-PN3A); tel: 0808 20 20 888) offers legal, environmental, fire and premises tips, as well as many other issues that the small businessperson may have to address as he/she grows. The Federation has the resources to take major test cases of importance to small businesses through the expensive legal process, and has been particularly effective in dealing with taxation and employment matters. Amongst the benefits on offer are access to in-house solicitors, barristers and tax experts and providing legal and taxation advice lines, including litigation and representation services. Membership is on a sliding scale dependent on number of employees, starting at c.£150.

Finance and support for your business. On the GOV.UK (**www.gov.uk/business-finance-support** (archived at https://perma.cc/7B5U-2B86)) you will find the full range of financial support on offer to businesses. The recent pandemic provided a flavour of the myriad ways governments can provide support, from funding furloughed staff through to low-interest loans, delaying tax payments, changing VAT rates and even subsiding meals out.

The Forum of Private Business (**www.fpb.org** (archived at https://perma.cc/M6MX-LW5M); tel: 01565 626001) is a membership organization costing c.£150. Joining gives you information on tap and management tools to help your business stay within the law, covering areas such as employment, health and safety, bank finance and credit control.

The UK Government website (**www.gov.uk/browse/business** (archived at https://perma.cc/X8LB-DKG2)) has an extensive A-Z of articles, tools and other resources for business starters.

Homeworking.com (archived at https://perma.cc/HVV6-QQGJ) (**www.homeworking.com** (archived at https://perma.cc/CPK4-E9YK)), started in 1999, is a resource rather than a job directory, and is full of useful tips and helpful warnings about the thousands of scam businesses on offer to would be homeworkers.

The Institute of Directors (**www.iod.com** (archived at https://perma.cc/Y2YL-FZTL); tel: 020 7766 8888) is the club for directors, membership of which costs £35 a month. For that you get access to a prestigious central London office and other offices around the United Kingdom and on the

Continent, business information and research provided for you by the IoD's expert researchers and bespoke business advice on tax and law. It is also considered one of the best networking associations for entrepreneurs.

Lexis-Nexis (**bis.lexisnexis.co.uk/research-and-insights/nexis** (archived at https://perma.cc/KA7J-9ADP)) strategically curates the most robust global collection of trusted premium and web news, company profiles, legal content and industry information, indexed so you can easily uncover the most relevant data on competitors and markets. You can try it for free.

LibrarySpot (**www.libraryspot.com** (archived at https://perma.cc/ZSG5-X3HA)) is a free virtual library resource centre for just about anyone exploring the web for valuable research information. Forbes.com (archived at https://perma.cc/LE2A-7RTE) selected it as the Best Reference Site on the web and *USA Today* described it as 'an awesome online library'.

The Market Research Society (**www.mrs.org.uk** (archived at https://perma.cc/A35Y-BSAT)) is the world's largest professional body for individuals employed in market research or with an interest in it. Founded in 1946, it has over 8,000 members working in most organizations currently undertaking market research in the UK and overseas.

National Federation of Enterprise Agencies (**www.nfea.com** (archived at https://perma.cc/6JHN-YPGW); tel: 01908 592033) membership includes traditional enterprise agencies: those that provide independent and impartial advice, training and mentoring to new and emerging businesses. Also represented are Chambers of Commerce, local authorities, other specialist enterprise providers, universities and corporate organizations.

The National Statistics (**www.statistics.gov.uk** (archived at https://perma.cc/K4NQ-PE8S)) website contains a vast range of official UK statistics and information about statistics, which can be accessed and downloaded for free. So whether you are looking to access the very latest statistics on the UK economy, or research and survey information released by the government, or want to study popular trends and facts, click on one of these themes and explore!

NewsDirectory (**www.newsd.com** (archived at https://perma.cc/U6ZK-UH5F)) is a guide to all online English-language media. This free directory of newspapers, magazines, television stations, colleges, visitor bureaux, governmental agencies and more can help you get to where you want to go, or find sites you didn't know about. It is a simple and fast site that can be used to access all the news and information that you can handle.

Non-disclosure agreements. A non-disclosure agreement (NDA) is the way to protect your invention when sharing information with others. You can find examples and some further information on the subject on the GOV.UK website (**www.gov.uk/government/publications/non-disclosure-agreements** (archived at https://perma.cc/7QY9-2MNB)).

The Princes Trust (**www.princes-trust.org.uk**; tel: 0800 842 842) runs business programmes and provides low interest loans for people aged 18–30 who want to start a business.

Ratio analysis. This refers to the analysis of various pieces of financial information in the financial statements of a business. You can see an explanation of these at the Corporate Finance Institute website (**corporatefinanceinstitute. com/resources/knowledge/finance/ratio-analysis/** (archived at https://perma. cc/F92Z-LRQL)).

Statistics. The Free Book Center (**www.freebookcentre.net/SpecialCat/ Free-Statistics-Books-Download.html** (archived at https://perma.cc/8CDC-8SV7)) has free ebooks and guides on Statistics, some of which can be downloaded.

The Telework Association (**www.tca.org.uk** (archived at https://perma.cc/ H8U4-TKY5)) costs from £34 a year to join its 7,000 other members who either work or are running a business from home. You get a bi-monthly magazine, a teleworking handbook with ideas for telebusinesses, and access to its help line covering all aspects of working from home.

Overseas agencies

Australia: Invest Australia (**www.investaustralia.gov.au** (archived at https:// perma.cc/MM5K-VDV6)) is the central information source for foreign investors. At the site you can find information, advice and contact points for all aspects of thinking about starting, starting, or setting up a business.

Canada: Canadian Federation of Independent Business (**www.cfib.ca** (archived at https://perma.cc/KF6M-E3PS)) represents the interests of over 105,000 owner-managers across the whole of Canada. There is a section on tools and resources at **www.cfib-fcei.ca/en/tools-resources/starting-a-business** (archived at https://perma.cc/73W8-4T58).

China: Invest in China (**www.fdi.gov.cn** (archived at https://perma. cc/3PAW-Z3YL)) is an interesting subsite on this government website giving you the opportunity to state your interests and also to see who else is currently planning to come into China.

Cyprus: Cyprus Profile (**www.cyprusprofile.com/en/doing-business/** (archived at https://perma.cc/KWZ8-XKPK)) has all the information on starting, running and accessing finance for a new or small business.

Developing Countries: the International Finance Corporation (**www.ifc.org** (archived at https://perma.cc/JBZ9-G2RL)), a member of the World Bank Group, provides advice, loans and equity to help foster entrepreneurship in developing countries.

Europe: European Commission Portal for SMEs (**europa.eu/youreurope/ business/running-business/start-ups/starting-business/index_en.htm** (archived at https://perma.cc/YGX6-HCY8)) is the entry point to access all the European Union's schemes to help small businesses and to a range of business tools and advice. There are direct links to a network of over 300 Euro Info Centres, 236 Innovation Relay Centres, 160 Business Incubation Centres and Your Europe – Business, a site with practical information on doing business in another country within the European Union.

France: Agence Pour la Création d'Entreprise (**www.apce.com** (archived at https://perma.cc/ZMP6-DN7S)) is the French small business service. The website is in English with advice and pointers on every aspect of starting and running a business.

Hong Kong: Hong Kong Trade Development Council (**smesupport. hktdc.com/** (archived at https://perma.cc/K9TM-PAFY)) is a comprehensive resource for information, tips, seminars, events and online forums aimed at the small business community. Its customized business matching service offers a suite of integrated matching services dedicated to helping global customers identify and screen potential Hong Kong business partners.

India: Indian Government National Portal (**www.startupindia.gov.in/ content/sih/en/ams-application/application-listing.html** (archived at https:// perma.cc/S8QA-2N8T)) covers all the regulatory issues about getting a business off the ground, hiring staff and raising money.

Ireland: Irish Small and Medium Enterprise Association (**www.isme.ie** (archived at https://perma.cc/G7TN-PZ9V)) offers a comprehensive range of advisory services and training and development for new and small businesses.

Italy: the Italian Trade Agency (**www.ice.it/en/** (archived at https://perma. cc/H2YX-JD6Z)) is the government agency that advises on information about the market, and gives help and advice with starting a business in Italy; you can also search for a compatible Italian business partner.

Malta: Malta Enterprise (**www.maltaenterprise.com** (archived at https://perma.cc/8GW9-DRFV)) is a government site with information on inward investment, enterprise support and innovation and enterprise.

New Zealand: Ministry of Business Innovation and Employment (**www.mbie.govt.nz/business-and-employment/business/** (archived at https://perma.cc/UHD8-Z824)) is the agency responsible for ensuring that New Zealand is one of the best places in the world to do business in.

Portugal: Agência Nacional de Inovação (**www.ani.pt/en** (archived at https://perma.cc/83FJ-8CL2)) is the agency that supports innovative businesses in Portugal. The 'Useful Links' section connects to other useful organizations including 'Invest in Portugal' and 'Portugal in Business'.

South Africa: the Small Enterprise Development Agency (**www.seda.org.za** (archived at https://perma.cc/7PHR-3BB9)) is the South African Department of Trade and Industry's agency for supporting small business. The site has all the information needed to start a business, find partners and access local regional support agencies throughout South Africa.

Spain: Invest in Spain (**www.investinspain.org/invest/en/index.html** (archived at https://perma.cc/G3A4-PC8B)), created only in 2005 as part of the State Department for Tourism and Trade in the Ministry of Industry, Tourism and Trade, is the point of contact for all state, regional and local institutions helping businesses set up or expand into Spain.

Turkey: the Turkish British Chamber of Commerce and Industry (**tbcci.org/starting-your-business-in-turkey/** (archived at https://perma.cc/WYV6-C346)) has all the information on starting a business in Turkey. Use the 'Business Partner Search' link in the 'Trade Services' box where you can state the type of business and relationship you are looking for and so find a partner in Turkey.

United States: Small Business Administration (**www.sba.gov** (archived at https://perma.cc/65XG-SA98); tel: 800 827 5722) provides financial, technical and management assistance to help Americans start, run and grow their businesses. The website has a large quantity of information and business tools of value to businesses starters anywhere.

World: the World Intellectual Property Organization (**www.wipo.int/directory/en/** (archived at https://perma.cc/24RT-2959)) provides country profiles giving quick access to a wide range of information data and economic intelligence for each of its 193 member countries using multiple WIPO databases.

Overseas government statistics

Most countries have their own government sites for national statistics data. Below are listed some of the main sites, which in turn have links to other sources of general statistical data.

stats.bls.gov/ (archived at https://perma.cc/8TVP-58SA). Site of the US Bureau of Labor Statistics, this contains lots of statistical material on the US economy and labour force.

www.insee.fr/fr/accueil (archived at https://perma.cc/PVY2-85J6). French National Statistics Organization.

www.destatis.de/EN/Homepage.html (archived at https://perma.cc/WX3T-VNF6). German National Statistics Organization.

www.istat.it/en/ (archived at https://perma.cc/S2CY-9VHP). Italian National Statistics Organization.

ec.europa.eu/eurostat/web/main/home (archived at https://perma.cc/EPW2-ZRGN). Site of Eurostat, which is the statistical organization of the European Communities.

www.un.org/en/sections/issues-depth/population/index.html (archived at https://perma.cc/L27B-MJG7). United Nations world population figures.

The US Bureau of Labor Statistics maintains the directory of Statistical Sites on the World Wide Web (**www.bls.gov/bls/other.htm** (archived at https://perma.cc/Q87T-NN63)).

INDEX